Identity and Intercultural Exchange in Travel and Tourism

D1555265

TOURISM AND CULTURAL CHANGE

Series Editors: Professor Mike Robinson, *Ironbridge International Institute for Cultural Heritage, University of Birmingham, UK* and Dr Alison Phipps, *University of Glasgow, Scotland, UK*

TCC is a series of books that explores the complex and ever-changing relationship between tourism and culture(s). The series focuses on the ways that places, peoples, pasts and ways of life are increasingly shaped/transformed/created/packaged for touristic purposes. The series examines the ways tourism utilises/makes and re-makes cultural capital in its various guises (visual and performing arts, crafts, festivals, built heritage, cuisine etc.) and the multifarious political, economic, social and ethical issues that are raised as a consequence.

Understanding tourism's relationships with culture(s) and vice versa is of ever-increasing significance in a globalising world. This series will critically examine the dynamic inter-relationships between tourism and culture(s). Theoretical explorations, research-informed analyses and detailed historical reviews from a variety of disciplinary perspectives are invited to consider such relationships.

Full details of all the books in this series and of all our other publications can be found on http://www.channelviewpublications.com, or by writing to Channel View Publications, St Nicholas House, 31–34 High Street, Bristol BS1 2AW, UK.

TOURISM AND CULTURAL CHANGE: 42

Identity and Intercultural Exchange in Travel and Tourism

Edited by
Anthony David Barker

CHANNEL VIEW PUBLICATIONS
Bristol • Buffalo • Toronto

Library of Congress Cataloging in Publication Data
A catalog record for this book is available from the Library of Congress.
Identity and Intercultural Exchange in Travel and Tourism/
Edited by Anthony David Barker.
Tourism and Cultural Change: 42
Includes bibliographical references.
1. Tourism–Psychological aspects. 2. Tourists–Psychology. 3. Identity (Psychology)
4. Cultural relations. I. Barker, A. D. (Anthony David) editor of compilation.
G155.A1I444 2015
910'.019–dc23 2014018929

British Library Cataloguing in Publication Data
A catalogue entry for this book is available from the British Library.

ISBN-13: 978-1-84541-463-4 (hbk)
ISBN-13: 978-1-84541-462-7 (pbk)

Channel View Publications
UK: St Nicholas House, 31-34 High Street, Bristol BS1 2AW, UK.
USA: UTP, 2250 Military Road, Tonawanda, NY 14150, USA.
Canada: UTP, 5201 Dufferin Street, North York, Ontario M3H 5T8, Canada.

Website: http://www.channelviewpublications.com
Twitter: Channel_View
Facebook: https://www.facebook.com/channelviewpublications
Blog: http://www.channelviewpublications.wordpress.com

The policy of Multilingual Matters/Channel View Publications is to use papers that are natural, renewable and recyclable products, made from wood grown in sustainable forests. In the manufacturing process of our books, and to further support our policy, preference is given to printers that have FSC and PEFC Chain of Custody certification. The FSC and/or PEFC logos will appear on those books where full certification has been granted to the printer concerned.

Typeset by R. J. Footring Ltd, Derby, UK
Printed and bound in Great Britain by Short Run Press Ltd

Contents

Contributors

Petra M. Bagley (MA Alberta, PhD Stirling) is Senior Lecturer in German in the School of Language, Literature and International Studies at the University of Central Lancashire, Preston, UK. Her research focuses on modern women's writing from German-speaking countries, in particular autobiographical fiction since 1968. She is the author of *Somebody's Daughter: The Portrayal of Daughter–Parent Relationships by Contemporary Women Writers from German-Speaking Countries* (Akademischer Verlag, 1996). Other publications include papers on the Catholic upbringing of women writers, daughter–father relationships, confessional literature, immigrant writing and the depiction of anorexia in recent Austrian women's literature.

Maria Manuel Baptista has been a teacher and researcher in cultural studies at the Departamento de Línguas e Culturas of the University of Aveiro since 1993. She is Director of the Cultural Studies Joint Doctoral Programme – Universities of Aveiro and Minho. She studied philosophy, social psychology and culture at the Universities of Porto, Coimbra and Aveiro. She defended her PhD thesis on the most important Portuguese contemporary essayist on Europe, Eduardo Lourenço. Her main scientific areas of research are the philosophy and psychology of culture, Portuguese and Lusophone cultures, and Iberian and Latin-America cultural studies.

Noémia Bárbara has a BA honours degree in modern languages and literature, a MA in Anglo-American studies and a PhD in education. She is Associate Professor at the Escola Superior Agrária, Polytechnic Institute of Coimbra, Portugal, and since 2000 has mainly been teaching English for specific purposes on engineering and, in particular, ecotourism courses. She has recently become responsible for the course units 'Introduction to Tourism for the BSc in Ecotourism' and 'Leisure and Recreation' for the MSc in ecotourism and is a coach and supervisor in tourism. Her research fields include creative tourism, ecotourism, tourism recreation, eco-lodging and dark tourism.

Anthony David Barker is Associate Professor and teaches film, drama, literature and research methodology at the Department of Languages and Cultures of Aveiro University. A former President of the Portuguese Association of Anglo-American Studies, his interests include the history of cinema, film narrative and genre, English literature since the 18th century and British and American drama. He has edited collections of essays on *Europe: Fact and Fiction* (Universidade de Aveiro, 2001), *The Power and Persistence of Stereotyping* (Universidade de Aveiro, 2003), *Television, Aesthetics and Reality* (Cambridge Scholars, 2006) and *Giving and Taking Offence* (Universidade de Aveiro, 2008) and published on Henry James on film, 1970s cinema, television comedy and cinema's attitudes to television.

Jenny Campos is a PhD candidate in cultural studies at the Universities of Aveiro and Minho and holds a degree in cultural heritage management from the School of Education of Porto. Her research project 'Trás-os-Montes and the Mythical Moors: Policies and Cultural Tourism' is financed by FCT (Foundation for Science and Technology) in the field of Political Sciences (SFRH/BD/80289/2011). She has worked for several years on projects that aim to protect local memories and identities. She is a researcher at the Communication and Society Research Centre (University of Minho). During the 2011/12 academic year she taught the courses Culture and Heritage, Cultural Management II, Theory and Design of the Cultural Project II and Natural and Cultural Heritage.

Marius-Mircea Crişan (PhD 2008 University of Turin, Italy) is Senior Lecturer at the West University of Timişoara, Romania. He is the author of the volumes *The Birth of the Dracula Myth: Bram Stoker's Transylvania* and *The Impact of a Myth: Dracula and the Fictional Representation of the Romanian Space* (Pro Universitaria, 2013), of several articles on imagology, reception theories and didactics, and co-author of *An Imagological Dictionary of the Cities in Romania Represented in British Travel Literature* (Mentor, 2012). For more information see the website http://www.themythoftransylvania.ro/home_en.htm, which also provides access to some of his articles.

Fernanda Luísa Feneja holds a PhD in American literature (2007), a master's degree in American studies (2000) and a degree in modern languages and literatures, English and German studies (1986). She is a teacher of English and German in Portuguese secondary education and has also lectured in English for tourism in higher education. She is a researcher at the University of Lisbon Centre for English Studies (ULICES – RG 3 – American Studies) and a member of the Portuguese Association for Anglo-American Studies. Her research interests focus on 20th-century American literature (narrative fiction, science fiction and fantasy narrative), American culture, literary theory, and literature and tourism. She has presented papers and published essays in these areas.

Silvio Lima Figueiredo has a BA in tourism from the Federal University of Pará (1993), a BA in business from the University of the Amazon (1990), an MA in sociology from the Federal University of Pará (1998) and a PhD in communication from the University of São Paulo (2005). He held a post-doctoral internship in sociology at the University Rene Descartes–Paris V, Sorbonne, France (2009–11). He has experience in urban and regional planning. He is Professor and Researcher at the Federal University of Pará's Centre for Advanced Amazonian Studies. His research interests are in travel and tourism theory, cultural and heritage tourism, epistemology and leisure.

Danuta Gabryś-Barker is Professor of English at the University of Silesia, Poland, where she lectures and supervises theses in applied linguistics, psycholinguistics and second language acquisition. Her areas of interest are multilingualism and applied psycholinguistics. A teacher trainer, she lectures on research methods in SLA and TEFL projects. She has published over 100 articles nationally and internationally and the books *Aspects of Multilingual Storage, Processing and Retrieval* (University of Silesia Press, 2005) and *Reflectivity in Pre-service Teacher Education* (University of Silesia Press, 2012). She has edited nine volumes, for Multilingual Matters, Springer, the University of Silesia Press and others. She is co-editor of the *International Journal of Multilingualism* (Taylor & Francis).

Susan Howcroft has a PhD in linguistics and is Assistant Professor at the University of Aveiro, Portugal. She has taught in Brazil, New Zealand, Italy and Portugal and her research interests are corpus linguistics, translation and English for specific purposes. She has published a number of articles in these areas as well as conference proceedings. She was also involved in the revision of the secondary school curriculum for English in Portugal and, together with two colleagues, published a grammar for secondary school pupils.

Monika Kowalczyk-Piaseczna is Senior Lecturer at the Institute of English Cultures and Literatures at the University of Silesia. She teaches creative and academic writing, interpretation of contemporary literature and literary translation. In 2013 she defended her PhD dissertation entitled 'Middle Easts: The rhetoric of somatics, otherness and sublimity in selected Polish and British travel reportages of the 20th and 21st century'. Her academic interests include postcolonial literature of Indian and African diaspora, magic realist discourse in Latin American fiction, as well as concepts of corporeality and identity in the contemporary travel writing.

Marzena Kubisz is Senior Lecturer in Cultural Studies at the University of Silesia, Poland, where she teaches British cultural studies and modern British literature. Her research interests include cultural history, the culture of speed, resistance studies and the contemporary British novel. She has written on mythologies of mass culture, transformations of the body and contemporary British literature. She is currently completing her book about deceleration in contemporary culture.

Larissa Latif graduated in social communication from Universidade Federal do Pará, Brazil, in 1994, has a master's degree in economics from the same university (1998) and a doctorate in performing arts from Universidade Federal da Bahia (2005). Her main interests are now in the field of cultural studies.

Gillian Moreira holds a PhD in culture from the University of Aveiro, Portugal, where she teaches in the areas of English studies and (inter)cultural studies at the Department of Languages and Cultures. She is a member of the Centre for Languages and Cultures of the same university and her research interests focus on intercultural relations, interculturality and inter-cultural competence in diverse social and professional contexts, particularly language education and business relations.

Ana Luísa Pires is Associate Professor at the Polytechnic Institute of Leiria, Portugal. She holds a PhD in Literature from the University of Aveiro, Portugal, with a dissertation entitled 'Present, imagination and memory in Zakes Mda and Mia Couto'. She is a member of GITUR (Tourism Research Unit of the Polytechnic Institute of Leiria) and Coordinator Editor of *EJTHR* (*European Journal of Tourism, Hospitality and Recreation*). She also collaborates with the Centro de Línguas e Culturas (Languages and Cultures Research Centre) of the University of Aveiro. Her research interests include post-colonial literature, tourism, cultural studies and cinema.

María del Pino Santana Quintana is Associate Professor of 19th- and 20th-century English literature and English language at the Faculty of English Studies at the Universidad de Las Palmas de Gran Canaria, Spain. Her publications focus on contemporary travel writing in English, a subject she has been researching for the last decade. Together with travel writing, she has teaching and research interests in English literature, mainly Shakespeare, identity studies and cosmopolitanism and transatlantic connections in Anglophone literature. Her essays and articles refer to figures such as Henry James, Edith Wharton, Nabokov and contemporary travel writers like Paul Theroux and Bill Bryson.

Joana Ferraz Ribeiro is a teacher of English at the Senior Academy of the Inatel Foundation, Porto, Portugal, and works as a tour guide in the tourist circuits associated with port wine. She holds a degree in modern languages and literatures at the Faculty of Arts of the University of Porto and a postgraduate degree in English studies from the University of Aveiro. She is currently taking a PhD in cultural studies at the Universities of Aveiro and Minho. Her research interests and publications focus on two fields: representations of women and intercultural encounters in tourism.

Introduction

Pennant seems to have seen a great deal which we did not see:
When we travel again let us look better about us.
Boswell's *Life of Johnson* (1791), vol. iii, p. 128

Samuel Johnson made this humble but somewhat mortified observation on reading Thomas Pennant's *Tour in Scotland*, of 1769. Pennant had made an earlier but similar journey to Johnson's own, recorded in *Journey to the Western Islands of Scotland*, published in 1775. Pennant had been the more perspicacious traveller and been rewarded with more interesting matter for the account of his travels. Johnson may have been wrong about the relative importance and longevity of their respective books but he expresses a legitimate piece of self-criticism about the type of travel writing he wished to produce: that of earnest sociological enquiry. For Johnson, one travels to accumulate information and to square that information against what is generally thought or believed. But gathering interesting or useful information begs many questions about what people find either useful or interesting. Neither Johnson nor Pennant took that process to its first principles, and instead asked only those questions that they presumed to be of interest to polite society in respect of the remote, wild and sadly declining cultures of the islands and Highlands of Scotland. Twenty-five years later, Alexander von Humboldt set out on his voyage to South America and over the next four and a half years posed questions that have proved to be absolutely foundational in biological and geographical sciences. The questions he asked made the difference between a historic expedition leading to the writing of *Le voyage aux regions equinoxiales du Nouveau Continent, fait en 1799–1804* for a worldwide scientific community and what, for all their literary merit, can fairly only be described as Pennant's and Johnson's journals of their tours, intended for their social peers who would not or could not make the tours themselves.

Along with Johnson was his companion and fellow writer James Boswell. Boswell belongs to a wholly different tradition of travel writing, one not so much concerned with what is 'about us' as with what is going on within us. He reports the nitty-gritty of travelling, the inconveniences and hardships, the minutiae which Johnson feels are unworthy of his attention. Boswell's *Journal of a Tour to the Hebrides with Samuel Johnson LL.D.* (1786) provides us with a unique opportunity to see the two styles of observation at work in parallel. Johnson sees only Scotland, whereas Boswell sees Johnson and himself in Scotland. He records the numerous conversations on many topics which took place during their journeys and the moments of rest in their lodgings. These extra elements give texture and warmth to the experience and are both valuable and illuminating. Boswell's text has immediacy, whereas Johnson's does not. Here Boswell is, self-referentially, on the trip itself, in an entry dated 'Tuesday, 5th October':

> I rose, and wrote my *Journal* till about nine; and then went to Dr Johnson, who sat up in bed and talked and laughed. I said, it was curious to look back ten years, to the time when we first thought of visiting the Hebrides. How distant and improbable the scheme then appeared! Yet here we were actually among them. – 'Sir,' (said he,) 'people may come to do anything almost, by talking of it. I really believe, I could talk myself into building a house upon island Isa, though I should probably never come back again to see it. (Birkbeck-Hill & Powell, 1964: 286)

Thus, the injunction to 'look better about us' is one we can all benefit from but it hardly helps us in the formulation of those questions that travel and all its related experiences might seek to answer. Those artefacts which most orient us in the formulation of travel objectives and itineraries are guidebooks and webpages. Without knowing anything about us as individuals, they seek to aggregate our preferences and tell us what is interesting and worthy of our time, energy and money. All too often, generally for reasons of brevity, they deny us the contexts which would make sense of their many judgements about what constitutes the interesting. They place us in a position of passivity before the world's multitudinousness, and create hierarchies of importance which are very much open to challenge.

There is a case to be made that it has never been easier, cheaper and more illuminating to travel than it is at the moment. Cut-throat competition in the aviation industry has kept prices stable even though fuel costs have soared, and the fortunate employed in the developed world have more leisure than ever to take holidays. We may be able to reach every part of the world but the example of the countries of the Middle East, the North West Frontier of the Indian sub-continent and the Horn of Africa, just to mention some obvious current trouble-spots, show that we are very far from understanding them and often seem powerless to prevent them from descending into conflict. Tourists, misunderstanding their status as perceived privileged visitors and emissaries of their country of origin, not infrequently become embroiled in these flare-ups. This thing called 'globalisation', so often and so glibly talked and written about, stands in need of sceptical investigation at a time when regional specificities can make viable or impossible, pleasurable or disastrous, our contact with those places.

To a less problematic degree, countries dependent on the income from tourism need to understand how they are perceived by visitors and to adjust their industries of hospitality accordingly. They also need to calculate the impact, economic, environmental and social, of the policy decisions they make. In governmental thinking, whether it be the carbon footprint of international travel or the provision of infrastructure, the economic aspects of travel and tourism always seem to predominate. We certainly consider these, but in this volume we are equally interested in the subjective and personal aspects of travel, its contribution to people's sense of themselves and their psychic health. This side of the subject is well expressed by the writer Michael Crichton when he reflects on why he travels:

> Often I feel I go to some distant region of the world to be reminded of who I really am. There is no mystery about why this should be so. Stripped of your ordinary surroundings, your friends, your daily routines, your refrigerator full of food, your closet full of your clothes – with all this taken away, you are forced into direct experience. Such direct experience inevitably makes you aware of who it is having the experience. That's not always comfortable, but it is always invigorating.
>
> I eventually realized that direct experience is the most valuable experience I can have. Western man is so surrounded by ideas, so bombarded with opinions, concepts, and information structures of all sorts, that it becomes difficult to experience anything without the intervening filter of these structures. And the natural world – our traditional source of direct insights – is rapidly disappearing. Modern city-dwellers cannot even see the stars at night. This humbling reminder of man's place in the greater scheme of things, which human beings formerly saw once every twenty-four hours, is denied them. It's no wonder that people lose their bearings, that they lose track of who they really are, and what their lives are really about. (Crichton, 2002: xii)

Inevitably, much of what will be discussed in this volume will be those 'information structures' Crichton reprehends. They are precisely what most people are exposed to and they have, as he suggests, an excessive influence on how we think about the world and how we experience it.

Another writer, Alain de Botton, in *The Art of Travel* (2004), deals directly with some of the most influential mediators of perceptions of place; among many, he cites Van Gogh and the district of Provence, Wordsworth and the Lake District, Edward Hopper and those liminal sites of travel, the motorway service station, the airport and the railway platform. Although he largely confirms Crichton's point in elegant detail, de Botton also problematises Crichton's panacea, 'direct experience', which itself is filtered through prior knowledge and expectation. Van Gogh and Wordsworth taught a sceptical public to see a landscape in the rich colours of their paintings and words, and before long it became difficult to regard them in any other terms. These artistic invocations make statements about human engagement with a landscape, which personal experience either does or does not respond to. In that sense, art sets a particular agenda for experience, but cannot wholly circumscribe it. This is in no way to deny that these artists have had palpable effects on people's behaviour. They began to flood to these places, with both negative and positive consequences. Hopper, on the other hand, does justice to other aspects of travel – the waiting, the boredom, *the suspension*, but also the rich possibilities for personal change stirring into life. The seasoned traveller will also appreciate the getting there as much as the being there. As de Botton writes:

> Journeys are the midwives to thought. Few places are more conducive to internal conversations than moving planes, ships or trains. There is an almost quaint correlation between what is before our eyes and the thoughts we are able to have in our heads: large thoughts at times requiring large views, and new thoughts, new places. Introspective reflections that might otherwise be liable to stall are helped along by the flow of the landscape. (de Botton, 2004: 54)

Of course, not everyone is a cultivated and appreciative traveller. Mark Twain's most successful book during his lifetime was *The Innocents Abroad*, his 1869 account of the 1867 voyage of wealthy Christian Americans around southern Europe and on to the Holy Land. Twain lampoons the pretensions of his travelling companions to understanding and empathy, and in particular notes the comic shifts of identity which can suddenly occur in inexperienced travellers:

We wish to learn all the curious, outlandish ways of all the different countries, so that we can 'show off' and astonish people when we get home. We wish to excite the envy of our untraveled friends with our strange foreign fashions which we cannot shake off.… The gentle reader will never, never know what a consummate ass he can become, until he goes abroad. (Twain, 2002: 166)

Twain particularly disdains people who affectedly forget to pronounce their own names correctly and to write their own language. The impressionable and pretentious tourist is perhaps the caricatural counterpart of a more positive figure, the sensitive traveller who finds his/her already unstable personal identity undergoing a radical but healthy self-questioning process in confrontation with foreignness.

Post-modern theory has come to regard the old, fixed, national or gender affirmations of identity as deeply misleading, the consequence of seeing ethnicities and even cultures as reified categories, which then become obstacles to an understanding of social processes. Travel literature suggests that identities are multiple and prone to fragmentation.

Twain's innocents abroad find their modern avatar in the boorish incurious tourists who can see nothing except through the prism of their own narrow culture. Karl Pilkington impersonates such a tourist to comic effect in the Sky TV show *An Idiot Abroad* (2010–13). Pilkington's pose is to be impressed by nothing and to be constantly finding analogies from the back streets of Manchester for all the marvels that he sees. This is Pilkington in Rio:

Christ the Redeemer isn't as big as I'd thought it would be, but being there on our own quite early in the day felt quite special. It's so high up you can look down through the clouds over the whole of Rio. The bloke who delivered my washer/dryer from Comet moaned about getting up to my flat on the third floor. I suppose that's why it could be a Wonder of the World.

I think the other reason that makes Christ the Redeemer one of the Wonders is the setting. I'm pretty sure if it was plonked down on a roundabout in Stretford, next to the Arndale Centre, it wouldn't get a look-in. (Pilkington, 2011: 41)

We are not just where we go and what we see; we are also who and what we take with us and what we bring home. Twain's travellers had their *Baedekers* and their moneyed sense of superiority; Pilkington has his prejudices and his Twix bars to help him to avoid the foreign food. But even in these works, with their calculated comic postures, there are moments of revelation. The authors find themselves impressed against their will and, perhaps less than we could wish but more than they would expect, are changed by their experiences.

The unimaginative Pilkington-type traveller is drawn to famous tourist venues and on-the-beaten-track experiences, but the face of holidaying is changing, even for the masses. Niche types of holidays are emerging and there are entrepreneurs ready to accommodate special interests. This process began modestly with a partial rejection of the overcrowded seaside holiday. As Hill writes about the late 1960s:

> [The inland beauty-spot] heralded the arrival of the more autonomous 'postmodern' tourist who, though still part of a mass movement of people, was beginning to reject the communal culture offered up by the urban resorts with their boarding houses, concentrated mechanical attractions, and increasingly polluted beaches. (Hill, 2002: 83)

This process gathered pace over the next 30 years. Routes constructed around old pilgrimages, like the Santiago de Compostella way in northern Spain, or in association with specific types of wine production, have been growing in popularity since the 1980s, along with river and canal holidays. There are also holidays targeted at specific age and income groups and geared for particular seasons: adventure holidays for the young and fit, more leisurely tours for the elderly, often out of high season.

The business of this book is to look at some of the interfaces of business and leisure insofar as they affect national and local identities in transition. The processes of European integration, along with the coming down of the Iron Curtain, have opened up a loosely frontiered Europe to ever more curious and mobile populations, to say nothing of the economic migrations and relocations that have seen Europeans born in one country working in another and perhaps retiring to a third. Who would have imagined the interest that Russians had in the island of Cyprus before the recent economic crisis in that country brought it to light? In a similar vein, the figure of the *retornado* is well known in Portugal, someone who emigrated, usually for economic reasons to Brazil or to France, but who in later life returned to their native country, often to the same village, and who implanted there many of the styles and fashions of their immigrant experience. They can bring back with them foreign spouses and their progeny but these latter, having become acculturated to their countries of adoption, can resist or resent these repatriations. There is a rich literature, and much statistical evidence, testifying to the prevalence of these practices.

This collection of essays is divided into three parts. The first, 'Exchanging Places', deals with general issues relating to innovative travel and tourist activities. These initiatives might be said to have come into being in reaction to the mass aggregation of tourist experience and unimaginative tourism management. Various niche activities have therefore emerged and these chapters look at the ways business has attempted to catch up with and cater for these trends. Chapter 1 surveys recent creative ideas in the provision and marketing of new holiday experiences. For the discerning traveller, the virtues of slow travel are discussed and recommended in Chapter 2. The special relationship which has developed between the German nation and the island of Mallorca is the subject of Chapter 3, which asks whether this phenomenon transcends traditional categorisation and opens up a whole new field of research in contemporary settler experience and narrative. In Chapter 4, I offer a brief pre-history of the symbiosis of the travel and film industries, leading to the current situation where movies actively promote holiday venues and, reciprocally, exotic places help to sell movies. The last chapter in Part 1 offers an anthropological overview of the human urge to travel, asking whether it is largely culturally driven or whether it is an innate propensity in all people.

Part 2, 'Narratives of Travel and Identity', addresses literary treatments of travel experience. Chapter 6 reviews some of the ways that major contemporary travel writers in English (Theroux, Raban, Iver, Bryson and Chatwin) have accounted for the impact of immersive travel experience and how it has changed them. Chapter 7 notices the more open and favourable responses of British women writers to rural Romania, in contrast to the more fastidious, denigratory accounts of male writers who have visited the country since it opened up again to the West. The chapter also remarks on the persistence of mythical associations deriving from the international success of Bram Stoker's *Dracula* (1897). Attention then switches to Italy and E.M. Forster's canonical work *A Room with a View* (1908), one of the most charming literary explorations of the expansive effect of holiday experience on personality. Forster also notably produced throughout his career one of the most sustained contrastive analyses of the ways of being of the peoples of Great Britain and Italy (and later India). The next chapter looks at the extraordinary particularity of the city of Venice, its attraction for visitors, and the no less extraordinary association of the city with death. This association is investigated by focusing on four accomplished 20th-century texts and their subsequent adaptation for the cinema. The chapter looks at how literature and film necessarily render a place differently. Chapter 10 considers the role of the objects we take with us when we travel, most notably the camera and the diary or journal. What we put in our suitcase binds us to the place we have come from and to some extent limits our openness to the places and people we encounter. Monika Kowalczyk-Piaseczna shows this operating in respect of two Farsi-speaking specialists in Middle Eastern travel reportage, the 1930s British gentleman scholar Robert Byron and his successor (and our contemporary), Jason Elliot. Part 2 concludes with a chapter making the case for postcolonial theory to be deployed in reconceptualising relations when gearing up ex-colonial countries to receive tourist visitors, many of whom may come from countries that were former occupiers. The appeal is made that old mistakes and injustices should not be repeated and that a sustainable, equal relationship can be established between countries with troubled but intimate past relations.

Part 3, 'The Case of Portugal', offers a quartet of studies of issues around tourism in Portugal, a country largely dependent in these difficult times on the income derived from visitors. Chapter 12 considers the phenomenon of 'intangible tourism' in the district of Valpaços. How can you interest visitors in ancient legends and myths when the physical remains are sketchy? The authors propose an itinerary of sites that bring alive the history of northern Portugal's vanished Moorish past through narratives of magical events. This proposal also envisages tied-in benefits for the more tangible crafts and foodstuff industries of the region. Chapter 13 then looks at the city of Oporto and its long association with one product, port wine. A highly sophisticated and modern tourist industry has grown up around the sights, sounds and tastes of this wine growing, making, bottling and shipping industry. It is argued that wine-related tourism has not only brought regeneration and vibrant economic activity to degraded parts of the inner city; it has also caused local communities to think more creatively about and participate more fully in the preservation of their heritage. Chapter 14 asks what sort of contribution proxemics could make to the organisation of tourist experience, since a people's expectations and comfort are clearly geared to their culture's sense of space. What objectively is a too-small hotel room? The figures suggest that Australians, Americans and Canadians are accustomed to over 70 square metres of space per person in their homes, whereas Russians and Chinese, on average, are used to less than 25 square metres each (Apartment Therapy, undated; Wilson, 2011). A Dane has twice as much living space as a Briton or an Italian. Evidence is produced in respect of two distant European peoples, the Portuguese and the Polish, to suggest that it is risky to dismiss this kind of thinking from tourist planning. Lastly, we return to issues of food and drink, as our final author looks at translation practices in printed texts and websites designed for visitors. Good translators know how to make local comestibles appetising and local products appealing. The figure of the translator is reviewed as an important cultural mediator, whose job is not merely linguistic; it is mostly shortcomings in cultural knowledge that account for breakdowns in communication between host and guest cultures, and teachers of translators would therefore be well advised to school their pupils in the target clients' social expectations. Part 3 therefore offers a particular perspective on issues of tourism, commerce and the preservation of local and national identities, one which brings together many of the disparate concerns of Parts 1 and 2.

References

Apartment Therapy (undated) Average home sizes around the world, at http://www.apartmenttherapy.com/average-home-sizes-around-the-151738 (accessed 29 October 2013).

Birkbeck-Hill, G. and Powell, L.F. (eds) (1964) *Boswell's Life of Johnson, Volume 5*. Oxford: Clarendon Press.

Crichton, M. (2002) *Travels*. New York: Perennial.

de Botton, A. (2004) *The Art of Travel*. New York: Vintage International.

Hill, J. (2002) *Sport, Leisure and Culture in Twentieth-Century Britain*. Basingstoke: Palgrave Macmillan.

Pilkington, K. (2011) *An Idiot Abroad: The Travel Diaries of Karl Pilkington*. Edinburgh: Canongate

Twain, M. (2002) *The Innocents Abroad*. London: Penguin Books.

Wilson, L. (2011) How big is a house? Average house size by country, at http://shrinkthatfootprint.com/how-big-is-a-house (accessed 29 October 2013).

Part 1
Exchanging Places

1 The Business of Creative Tourism and Creativity in the Tourism Business

Noémia Bárbara

You cannot use up creativity. The more you use the more you have.
Maya Angelou

The Industry of Tourism

Tourism is nowadays a multidisciplinary field of academic study, teeming with typologies and emerging activities, providing a vibrant untapped body of knowledge. Tourism is not only the largest of industries, it is also one of the most fascinating to study. Time and again, the tourism industry has shown its strength in the face of crises (Brunnermeier, 2009; Hall, 2010; Hall *et al.*, 2003). Despite the impacts of shocks, such as concerns about international security following the attacks of September 11, 2001 in the USA, and the SARS outbreak in Asia in 2003, the 2009 flu pandemic, or the current financial crisis in some parts of the globe, the apparently volatile tourism industry has managed to show its resilience, as is clear when recent data on its market growth were made known. According to the World Tourism Organization (WTO), even in a continuing uncertain economic climate, international tourist arrivals grew by 4% between January and August 2012 compared with the same period in 2011. Moreover, in 2011 international tourist arrivals reached 990 million and with the growth of 4% in 2012 (except for the Eurozone, with only 3%) this figure was forecast to reach one billion for the first time by December 2012 (WTO, 2012a). Thus, the date of 13 December was declared to symbolically mark the arrival of the one-billionth tourist, a landmark in the history of tourism, all the more so given the context of great economic upheaval in both tourist-receiving and tourist-sending countries in Europe and North America.

In the tourism business, receipts grew significantly during the first six to nine months of 2012. Among the five largest international tourism earners,

Hong Kong leads (more than 17% of GDP), followed by the USA (more than 8%), Germany (more than 7%), France (more than 5%) and the UK (more than 4%). Considering the top five international markets by expenditure on travel abroad, Russia leads (over 15%), followed by the USA (over 9%), Canada (over 6%) and Germany (over 5%) (WTO, 2012b).

In order to keep this large industry working, tourism marketers need to keep abreast of transformations occurring in related fields; tuned in to the latest trends, they introduce their products into the marketplace. As these products are intangible goods[1] they pose particular difficulties for their prospective purchasers for, as Holloway (1998) points out, they cannot be inspected as can a washing machine, a hi-fi or other consumer durables. The purchase of holidays is a speculative investment, involving a high degree of trust on the part of the purchaser, who, as has often been said, is not only buying holidays but also dreams (Holloway, 1998: 4). For instance, when tourists buy a package tour abroad they are buying more than a simple collection of services; they are buying the joy of the planning and anticipation of the experience, the actual experience and extensions of the experience through its recall by seeing videos, photographs and so on. Usually, the tourist has great expectations when embarking on these complex ventures, which involve both a psychological as well as a physical experience. The challenge for the marketer of tourism is to turn the dream into a reality.

This chapter explores and discusses the ingenuity that has taken root in the tourism business. In order to be competitive, tourism professionals have had to be creative, resourceful and inventive, and use all their imagination and initiative to keep up with this changeable market, where supply and demand can fluctuate wildly and thwart market expectations, and where the dream is always in the making. In the next section, the focus is on alternatives in creative tourism; in the subsequent section, multifarious creative business ideas are analysed.

The Business of Creative Tourism

Creative tourism – towards a definition

Cultural tourism is one of the fastest-growing segments of global tourism (Richards & Wilson, 2006; WTO, 2012a). The discussion of creative tourism within the context of alternative tourism cannot be divorced from the wider context of mass tourism. As was pointed out by Weaver (2001), mass tourism depends on the high volume of package tours, with a clear distinction between high and low seasons in a few dominant markets. Accommodation is usually high density, in selected tourist areas, employing an international architecture and owned by non-local, large corporations. In these contexts, tourism tends to dominate the local economy, with a view to short-term economic growth. On the other hand, alternative tourism rarely depends on market arrangements but rather on individual planning, seeking out a specific area, and is little commercialised; 'authentic' experiences are provided both for tourists and locals. It relies on small-scale accommodation, dispersed throughout the area and owned by local small businesses, thus tending to complement already existing commercial activity. It is normally regulated by the native population to minimise negative local impacts, and the aim is for economic growth in the long term, so that profits will bring holistic and integrated well-being and stability to the community (Weaver, 2001: 78).

Within this alternative tourism, several niches and micro-niches have emerged, where small numbers of tourists and travellers[2] with special interests, keen on culture and/or activity-based tourism in authentic settings, demand specialist holidays to meet their specific desires (Robinson & Novelli, 2005: 9). One of these recent niches, creative tourism, was first mentioned by Pearce and Butler in 1993 (see Richards, 2011). Moreover, the term was used to define a phenomenon growing not only in the cities but also in rural areas.[3] The development of crafts tourism was to be defined only some years later, by Richards and Raymond (2000: 18), as:

Tourism which offers visitors the opportunity to develop their creative potential through active participation in courses and learning experiences which are characteristic of the holiday destination where they are undertaken.

In 2005 Susan Briggs, the person responsible for the publication *Cultural Tourism. How You Can Benefit. A VisitBritain Advisory Guide*, provided a more detailed and comprehensive definition to clarify the concept for the general public:

Tourism motivated wholly, or in part, by interest in the historical, artistic or lifestyle/heritage offerings of a tourism destination emerged to meet the demand from visitors looking for more than 'sun, sea and sand' mass market experiences. It encourages arts and tourism sectors to work more closely together and it encompasses visits to enjoy visual and performing arts, museums, galleries, heritage attractions, artists' open studios, art fairs, auctions, public art and architecture, films, festivals and other cultural events. (Briggs, 2005: 5)

The prevalence of these practices increased in a fairly short period and they were taken up by the United Nations Educational Scientific and Cultural Organization (UNESCO), namely in the form of the Creative Cities Network, which developed the following definition:

> Creative tourism is travel directed toward an engaged and authentic experience with participative learning in the arts, heritage, or special character of a place, and it provides a connection with those who reside in this place and create this living culture. (UNESCO Creative Cities Network, 2006: 3)

Richards has written a great deal on this concept from its inception (Richards, 2001, 2010, 2011; Richards & Raymond, 2000; Richards & Wilson, 2006, 2007a), opening the field for other research on this kind of niche tourism, perceived both as an 'adjunct and as an antidote to mass forms of cultural tourism and the serial reproduction of culture' (Richards & Wilson, 2006: 1219).

Great criticism quickly followed on from the concept of cultural exploration, on the grounds that it had pushed urban and regional bodies to adopt questionable tourism strategies – the so-called phenomenon of *McGuggenheimisation*, that is, the proliferation of Guggenheim museums throughout the world to replicate the success of the *unique* popular experience of Bilbao (Bradburne, 2002a, 2002b; Thakara, 2002; Richards & Wilson, 2006). As culture has become a crucial commodity for generating profit in post-industrial economies, it is increasingly used as a resource in cities and regions across the European Union, as a means of preserving their cultural identity and fostering development. The European Capital of Culture programme, for example, has become a symbol of this striving both for development and for the reproduction and exploitation of cultural brands and 'commodities'.

In New Zealand the practical experience of developing creative tourism has led to the government initiative Creative Tourism New Zealand (CTNZ), greatly inspired by Raymond's works seeking to redefine this concept. In the light of its experience, CTNZ defines its creative tourism initiatives as:

> A more sustainable form of tourism that provides an authentic feel for a local culture through informal, hands-on workshops and creative experiences. Workshops take place in small groups at tutors' homes and places of work; they allow visitors to explore their creativity while getting closer to local people. (See Raymond, 2007: 145)

According to Richards (2011), recent research has identified this creative tourism as an escape route[4] from the reproduction of mass cultural tourism, since it offers more flexible and authentic experiences, which can be co-created between host and tourist. Although authentic experiences also buttress other niche tourism trends, such as ecotourism (Weaver, 2001), creative tourism has a different particularity in terms of its appeal to tourists. Instead of trying to find activities that provide an escape from everyday life, these are grounded in the very everyday life that many in the past seemed to want to escape from, in the migration from country to town and the movement from agricultural and artisanal work to urban and factory labour. In contrast, sensation-seekers engage in adventure tourism, motivated quite often not just by risk but also by 'rush', pursuing activities habitually described as 'ineffable' or 'indescribable' (Buckley, 2012), whereas creative tourists do not want to discard their everyday personas to satisfy a taste for adrenalin. They want to find the roots of their identity by developing new relationships with the community of their destination and these people's everyday lives (Raymond, 2007). Furthermore, they want to tap into and explore their own creative skills with a class of creative people from whom they can find new ways to learn and grow. In order to clarify this study and probe what is generally understood by creativity, some basic definitions and arguments should be briefly explored.

What is creativity?

There is no one accepted definition of creativity, but psychologists tend to perceive it as alternative visions or ideas useful in solving problems, and to highlight the originality of those alternatives or ideas (Franken, 2007: 394). Those who study creativity distinguish it from the myth of genius, for it is present in many people and requires hard work. Another feature of creativity is that, besides the novelty that accompanies it, it has to be useful, to have value and to be appropriate to the cognitive demands of the situation (Weiseberg, 1993: 4). Csikszentmihalyi (1996), who has analysed the characteristics of creative individuals, asserts that they are people who express unusual thoughts, who are interesting and stimulating, who appear unusually bright and who experience the world in novel and original ways; they are people whose perceptions are fresh and whose judgements are insightful. Csikszentmihalyi points out that these (anonymous) individuals may make important discoveries that only they know about, but when they are public figures they may change our culture in some important ways because their achievements are by definition public, and thus it is easier to write about them, as is the case with, for example, Leonardo, Edison, Picasso and Einstein (Csikszentmihalyi, 1996: 25–26).

Nowadays the popular expressions *thinking out of the box*, and its analogue *blue-sky thinking*, reflect both the value attached to the features of creativity mentioned above and dissatisfaction with contemporary modes of perception. As Richards (2011) has put it, there is a need to build personal narrative, biography and identity from authentic, creative, alternative tourism experiences. Taylor (1988) examined the definitions of creativity available at the time and grouped scientific approaches according to their focus on four objects of study: the creative person, the creative process, the creative product, and the creative environment. These four conceptual elements intermingle in the following broad depiction of the creative tourist.

Profile of the creative tourist

The creative tourist belongs to what Florida (2002) has termed the creative class, a cosmopolitan highly mobile class from the middle and upper strata of society, from both developing and developed countries, which shares higher levels of education. This creative class is attracted to places that offer a combination of amenities and tolerance of difference. Elaborating on Florida's theories, Maitland (2007) specifies these amenities as being areas that offer low crime rates, good public transport, good architectural design, bars and restaurants, and a vibrant street life. Creative tourists establish friendship networks, especially through social networks, and choose destinations 'off the beaten track' rather than the standard tourist attractions. They like to meet the locals and come to some understanding of the mundane details of everyday life, such as shopping in regular street markets or supermarkets and being part of the 'real life' of their hosts, in anticipation of an authentic experience.

This type of tourist wants to escape the tourist bubble created by cities, regions and countries that have replicated venues of proven success for tourists unable to travel to original destinations. This creative person craves new experiences (Raymond, 2007) and is looking for transformation both of himself/herself as an individual and of the places of destination, not only visiting the places, but 'making' them. The ability of such tourists to engage in the activities on offer will depend on their motivation, skill and capacity to face challenges. According to Richards and Wilson (2007c: 263), 'When the challenge of an experience is in balance with our skill levels, this is when we experience Csikszentmihalyi's (1990) "state of flow" or achieve an optimum experience. Too little challenge is boring, too much induces discomfort'. The goal of the creative destination should therefore be to achieve this kind of balance.

Being open-minded and passionate about learning, creative tourists respect other cultures and are willing to interact with them imaginatively, in order to contribute to a new tourist product, of which they are co-owners, and to ensure 'co-makership' happens through an exchange of skills and knowledge with those who are visited (Richards, 2011). Given the right environment, the creative process may also lead them to routes where instead of accumulating experiences, they remake themselves by discovering hidden features of their personality, new facets of their identity.

Having very diversified ways of life, the creative class enjoys participating in a wide range of authentic experiences; indeed, they are characterised by being more interested in being participants than in being spectators (Florida, 2002). This active aspect had already been explored by Ray and Anderson (2000), who divided this creative class into two segments: the cultural creatives and the green cultural creatives. The former are said to include writers, artists, musicians and the like who combine a focus on spirituality with social activism. The latter segment, who include people representing most of the professions, share, among many other characteristics, a strong love of and respect for nature and the planet and its natural balance; they are quite proactive on environmental issues and are believers in the principle of cradle-to-cradle instead of cradle-to-grave. Respectful of other people's cultures and their natural gifts, they are also defenders of more funding for education and community sustainability and are optimistic and willing to get involved in creating a new and better way of life.

Research undertaken in two pilot creative tourism events in the UK, in 2009, showed that participants were predominantly female, aged 45 plus and likely to have children who are teenagers or who have now left home. The other large group was made up of younger women, aged between 22 and 30, with busy full-time jobs and no children. The participants also included creative professionals looking to add to their other existing artistic practices and teachers wishing to 'be on the other side for a change' (Campbell, 2010).

There would appear to be many millions of people corresponding to this profile all over the world, if we give credence to the figures presented by Ray and Anderson (2000) (50 million in the USA alone in the year 2000 and also another 80–90 million estimated to exist in Europe). These figures, however, have been contested (Maitland, 2007). Whatever the real numbers may be, this creative class has to be quite large, owing to the exponential increase in the availability of creative environments and destinations globally. These new environments are looked at next.

Developing a creative offer

Perhaps due to our constant mobility and the fleeting nature of the present, due to our liquid modernity according to Bauman (2000), research sponsored by EnjoyEngland (2005) revealed that people feel that the resources they most lack in their lives are time, space, energy and a greater sense of well-being; people have a growing desire to connect with each other and feel more in touch with local communities. A creative tourism break can provide this and also provide people with a sense of achievement through learning a new skill. In addition, by creating their own souvenir, whether a painting, crafted object, poem or even a recipe, people are more likely to have a lasting emotional attachment to the creative tourism destination, to talk, blog or tweet about it in a positive way and to return to it (EnjoyEngland, 2005).

In Jonesborough, Tennessee, in 1973, the first North American Story-telling Festival was hosted. Recognised as the world's first public event devoted exclusively to storytelling, the Festival ignited a renaissance of the storytelling tradition that has spread throughout America and beyond and transformed Jonesborough into the storytelling capital of the world. Its founding member, Jim Neil Smith, recounts how quite by accident he read *Creative Tourism: A Global Conversation*, edited by Rebecca Wurzburger and others, in 2010, and how he was thus given a new perspective on cultural tourism. Since then, and through Wurzburger's guidance and insight, Jonesborough has become one among the most successful destinations for creative tourism. Meeting the expectations of travellers who 'wanted to get closer to their vacation community and its people, to engage in inter-active learning experiences that are true to the community's culture, and to develop their personal creative potential' (Smith, 2012), after 40 years of activity Jonesborough began to provide a new experience by experimenting with various approaches to helping visitors, through brief, but powerful, interactive workshops, to discover crafts, and share their personal and family stories. This example, not particularly prominent in bibliographical reviews of this field, is perhaps a good general illustration of how creative tourism has sprung up worldwide.

An uncommon feature of creative tourism is reflected in McNulty's remark 'Tourism is too important to be left to the marketers. It needs to be managed and owned by the community to ensure that the benefits are realized' (McNulty, 2010: 72). As a founder of Partners for Livable Com-munities in 1977, McNulty envisioned tourism as a form of community development, since 'cities have needs that visitors can financially support. By balancing the tourism infrastructure with existing city services, the year-round resident has a higher quality of life'. The goal of creative tourism is to engage visitors more completely, by encouraging a deeper understanding of a place, increasing the vitality of the local tourism industry and eliminating mediators, such as marketers, as dream providers of the authentic experience.

This existential authentic experience[5] is an ideal that the self seeks in order to let emotion and spontaneity overcome reason and self-constraint. Tourism, and nature tourism in particular, is therefore seen as a space of freedom outside the dominant institutions of modernity (Wang, 1999: 361). In other words, individuals might want to be de-rooted from their routine, to be in touch with 'primitive' unconstrained emotions that may surge from, say, agritourism activities in Portugal, cookery workshops in Barcelona, tango lessons in Argentina, basket weaving with the Maori people, watercolour painting in stately houses in Britain, bone carving with the Inuit, and to find new roots with the living communities they embrace.

One of the most celebrated destinations for creative tourism has been New Zealand, particularly the little city of Nelson, where it all started. As the region has attracted around 400,000 international overnight visitors a year from New Zealand's 2.4 million annual international visitors, plus a further 800,000 domestic overnight visitors, and is home to many of New Zealand's artists, Nelson is a promising example of well managed creative tourism for others to learn from (Richards & Wilson, 2007b). Beginning with 20 tutors as founding members of CTNZ, this initiative was later to become a national network. The activities offered by local artists ranged from bone carving to flax weaving to seafood cookery. Tourists could engage in propagating native plants, appreciate the local olive oil, take a Maori journey or make a woolly scarf.

Today, Nelson is still a thriving city, with crafts shops where both foreigners and natives are very welcome because, besides the natural gracefulness of New Zealanders, competition for the Top Shop prize consisting of 'one on one experience' is fierce. The city is proud of its arts festival, which takes place each October and dates back to 1995. In the words of one of the festival directors:

> The Nelson Arts Festival grows stronger each year as a community event that celebrates creativity and helps to shape our identity. We are grateful to all the wonderful people who help bring our events to life, the hard working crew who put in tireless hours, and the artists for sharing their stories and songs. (See Miccio & Kelly, 2012)

Although just two examples of creative tourism destinations, Jonesborough and Nelson, are highlighted here, many more can be discovered throughout the world. Niche marketing is vital for such destinations, which are then easily promoted using targeted advertising, internet sites, social networking pages, online profiles and special-interest groups that are the specific target for a creative tourism product. Word of mouth can be the best publicity, but the web amplifies it exponentially, and has a paramount role in endorsing recommendations. An illustration of this is TripAdvisor, where the ratings are experience based, that is, based on the recommendations of friends and therefore not on the reviews of experts. Hence, creativity has its applications to the tourist industry as a broad concept and not just to creative tourism; it also applies to other niches of tourism that can only prosper from the inventiveness of the people able to design the dream experiences that visitors desire.

Creativity in the Tourism Business

Travel narratives have always fascinated people, ever since the earliest stories about heroes and the travails met on their journeys. From such different works as *The Odyssey* and *The Canterbury Tales*, the reader could always imagine what it would be like to be the wandering Ulysses or one of Chaucer's pilgrims. Indeed, it is hard to imagine tourism without the creative use of seductive imaginaries about people and places. Literature and narratives about travelling to enticing places have been in the imaginary of people for millennia. However, with the advent of television in the 1950s, people have been able to see in their living rooms moving images of the distant places they had only heard or read about. The allure of travelling to distant places was made possible by disposable incomes and wide-bodied planes; at about this time the dreams of 'going places' became affordable to the many rather than an elite few (Holloway, 1998; Lickorish & Jenkins, 2000). However, by the beginning of the 21st century, everywhere seems to have been already explored; few isolated bastions remain to be discovered by bold adventurers, new discoverers with a large income. Unless, of course, tourism service providers put all their creativity into realising promises of fulfilment for a wider constituency of individuals.

Film-induced tourism

Films are made of images and images of places abound in films. As Portegies (2010) puts it, images of places 'are ubiquitous and most often serve as a backdrop to the storyline'. These places viewed in films sometimes leave an indelible impression on the viewer, who, often unconsciously, formulates the wish to visit them. Study of the impact of films on destinations and their potential to promote them has paved the way for a body of published work on film as a generator of tourism (e.g. Beeton, 2006, 2010; Gjorgievski & Tropka, 2012; Heitmann, 2010; Portegies, 2010).

The two thriving industries that can satisfy the drive for creative experience and personal growth are those of entertainment and tourism. One can experience a wide variety of sensations without leaving one's home, given the large supply of television and film series, or enjoy the latest special and 3D movie effects at a cinema, or can have the best of both worlds, if on one's next holiday one chooses to visit a film location.

To give only a few examples of how film has influenced travellers in their choice of destination, Danny Boyle's 2000 movie *The Beach*, dramatising Alex Garland's novel set on the Thai island of Phi Phi Leh, has popularised the Phi Phi islands as a destination internationally. The film itself can be understood as a form of vicarious tourism (Heitmann, 2010; Hudson & Brent Ritchie, 2006). Regrettably, however, due to intensive tourist exploitation of a highly sensitive ecosystem, movie tie-in interest has resulted in extensive environmental damage to Phi Phi Leh island (Croy, 2010; Macionis & O'Connor, 2011).

Tourism organisations can use marketing campaigns as springboards if a film is seen as appropriate for the destination. Additional businesses and services can be created through film tourism, which in turn can extend the visiting season. Such is the case with Tourism New Zealand, whose management strategies had been centred on nature and the passive and active experiences in these environments (Croy, 2010). The government of New Zealand then invested millions of dollars to support Peter Jackson's effort to create Tolkien's Middle Earth at the bottom of the world. Though the tourism figures were less than sensational, that is, there was only an increase of 3% in international tourism (Beeton, 2006; Croy, 2010; Buchmann, 2010), probably due to the remoteness of New Zealand from most Tolkien fans, after the release of the *Lord of the Rings* films in the early 2000s there was peak usage of the Tourism New Zealand website, where the films and tours were overtly connected, as is clear from the examples given below.

Only a few *Lord of the Rings* tours are endorsed by Ian Brodie, author of *Lord of the Rings Location Guidebook*. Our tours are among them. Each tour booking receives a complimentary collectible souvenir. (Lord of the Rings Tours and Experiences)

Walk beside Mt Doom, see Orc country, Mordor, EmynMuil, Meads Wall, walk on the Orc road and encampment. See the spot where Sauron lost the ring on the Whakapapa side of the mountain. (Wades Landing Tours in New Zealand Tourism Guide, 1 of 30 sites recommended)

The *Lord of the Rings* trilogy were not the only films to be supported by the Tourism New Zealand organisation: *The Chronicles of Narnia* (directed by Andrew Adamson, 2005) also received great support from the authorities in New Zealand, where parts of the film were shot (Hudson & Brent Ritchie, 2006; Karpovich, 2010). The world has also more recently witnessed the *Hobbit* phenomenon (another trilogy directed by Jackson, 2012–14), where once again almost an entire nation volunteered to become Middle Earth. New Zealand devised an array of ingenious tricks to lure in Tolkien and Jackson fans. With Air New Zealand forming a partnership with Weta Workshop, Jackson's production company, they created a special in-flight safety video with a Middle Earth theme, and painted planes with images of Jackson's actors, thus engaging in an aggressive marketing campaign before the films' release (Driscoll, 2012). Creative energy can be used to raise your spirits and exalt ordinary actions, such as watching an in-flight safety video, but it can also cater to our interest in more negative experiences.

Dark tourism

Another niche tourist activity soaring both in popularity and in the research it is engendering is 'dark tourism'. As stated by Stone (2006: 159): 'Dark tourism is the act of travel and visitation to sites, attractions and exhibitions which have real or recreated death, suffering or the seemingly macabre as a main theme.'

The journeying to and experiences associated with death are not new phenomena: people have long been drawn to sites associated with death, suffering, violence or disaster (Stone, 2006, 2010; Stone & Sharpley, 2008; Tarlow, 2005; Yuill, 2003). Among the most popular destinations are war-related attractions, holocaust camps, graveyards, former prisons, slavery heritage sites and sites of atrocities. The list grows each year due to the increasing demand for this tourism product. The academic who started the study of this phenomenon was Rojek, who developed the concept of 'black spots' in 1993, but Lennon and Foley coined the expression 'dark tourism' in 1996, which Seaton labelled 'thanatotourism' in the same year (see Yuill, 2003). It has been suggested that there are different shades of dark tourism, notably by Sharpley, who divided the field of dark tourism, in respect of both supply and demand, into pale, grey and black (Sharpley, 2005, quoted in Stone, 2010: 80). In the present chapter, the focus will be on the lighter shades of this tourism typology, particularly as it relates to the entrepreneurial creativity of certain endeavours.

One of the largest sub-genres of dark tourism is grief tourism and two of the most prominent examples of grief sites are Auschwitz-Birkenau in

Poland and Ground Zero in New York, where natives and tourists flood to confront the inevitability of death and grieve as a people or as a nation stricken by events that seem to stand beyond human control. In many cases, the tourism business has responded sensitively to a desire that seems to spring out of what is a basic human need, by supplying the logistics for visiting the site or the mementos people want to acquire to commemorate these dark events. There are others, however, who clearly see an opportunity to exploit this human desire by charging exorbitantly for such experiences, as is the case with the Pennsylvania farmer who offered for $65 per person a tour of the crash site of hijacked Flight 93 from the 9/11 attacks (Bly, 2003; quoted in Stone & Sharpley, 2008: 577).

Another example of creativity in dark tourism (and examples abound) was the *Titanic* experience offered by some cruise liners in 2012, during the centennial commemorations of the disaster. Some were bold enough to promise *Titanic* keepsakes for the cruisers included in the steep prices of the ticket or to recommend the unique experience of replicating the original menu or the music played at the time of the sinking, which proved to be an irresistible lure for gullible fans (Callahan, 2012). This kind of inventiveness explores the thin line between healthy curiosity and the macabre.

In 2008, an online poll commissioned by the Czech Tourist Board discovered and then went on to promote the top 10 darkest places of interest to visit in the Czech Republic (Šindelářová, 2008). In Scotland, 'ghost tourism' seems to be a commercial reality, and an important source of revenue, with Edinburgh Underground Ghost Tours (Auld Reekie Tours, 2013) and paranormal activity tours with 'Ghost Events: A truly haunting experience', as well as others. There are indeed numerous sites around the world, 'dark destinations', which provide unique experiences such as visiting a recent disaster site and help rebuild it or just gawking at how people have been able to survive in the aftermath (Stone, 2006, 2010; Stone & Sharpley, 2008; Yuill, 2003). The former case is an illustration of the complexity inherent in dark tourism. If, on the one hand, it is possible to belittle the dupe tourist who engages in creative scams to pursue a fantasy, on the other hand, it is also possible to comprehend the need individuals feel to help rebuild not just the damaged site but also their own 'damaged' identities. Such persons may yearn to contribute and find a new purpose in these experiences. Dark tourism, and creative tourism in general, are far more complex than just being themed domains where the dichotomous roles of the 'tourist as sovereign chooser or unfortunate dupe' (Richards, 2011) are played out. They are relatively recent practices involving an array of different actors, contexts and experiences, the scrutiny of which is still in its infancy.

Conclusion

The business of tourism thrives in part due to the entrepreneurial capacity of creative business people who are often clever dream providers, who know how to pitch adventure tours to peripheral destinations involving risk and danger, when individuals are exposed to the unpredictable and the unknown, as in the Arctic (Gymóthy & Mykletun, 2004; Notzke, 1999; Weber, 2001) or inside a storm (Buckley, 2012; Xu *et al.*, 2012), in a thrill-seeking quest that threatens to obliterate both being and identity.

Furthermore, as competition is fierce among recreation enterprises fighting to provide these unique experiences, it is the surprise factor, the personal touch in all details, which will reinforce the bond with tourists, who are to be treated as friends if they are to remain regular customers. The element of creativity remains fundamental, whether in film-induced tourism, dark tourism, adventure tourism, ecotourism or any other niche that strives to provide that unique ingredient of authenticity or danger, in which we may either find or lose ourselves.

Notes

(1) Not all types of holiday fall into the intangible category, however. When discussing consumptive and non-consumptive tourism, Weaver (2001: 81) points out that the activities of hunting and fishing (except perhaps for 'catch and release' fishing) are commonly identified as being consumptive, and therefore tangible, though nowadays hunting has largely been replaced by photographic safaris.

(2) Travellers and tourists are usually considered two distinct categories. The traveller is perceived as more independent, adventurous, active and usually spends more time travelling than the tourist, more passive, more sightseeing. See Boorstein, quoted in Richards (2010: 4). Although the definition of 'tourist' encompasses the person who leaves his/her environment for more than 24 hours and less than 12 months, one hardly arrives at the idea of mass travellers from this. Nevertheless, because it is the most commonly used word it will also be employed in this chapter.

(3) In the 1990s the EUROTEX project involved countries such as Portugal, Greece and Finland and its main goal was to rediscover and enhance the textile industry of the 19th and 20th centuries, providing identification and valorisation of the European textile heritage. It had an impact in the rural areas of Alto Minho in Portugal, where traditional crafts still survived in some villages. The project has expanded and still aims to promote long-term cooperation among cultural, institutional and economic agents, encouraging creative reinterpretation processes and the circulation of young artists and their project works. See http://www.acte.net/projects#.U5mEyvldXh4.

(4) Richards has used the expression 'routes and roots' in *Leisure in the Network Society: From Pseudo-events to Hyperfestivity?*, when he asks questions about the routes from the roots of leisure research (Richards, 2010: 8).

(5) Wang, who has widely discussed the concept of authenticity, considers existential authenticity as a potential existential state of being that is to be activated by tourist activities. Correspondingly, authentic experiences in tourism are to achieve this

activated existential state of being within the liminal process of tourism (see Wang, 1999).

References

Auld Reekie Tours (2013) Scotland underground ghost tour. At http://thosecrazyschuberts. com/2012/01/scotland-underground-ghost-tour.html (accessed June 2014).

Bauman, Z. (2000) *Liquid Modernity*. Cambridge: Polity Press.

Beeton, S. (2006) Understanding film induced tourism. *Tourism Analysis* 11 (3), 181–188.

Beeton, S. (2010) The advance of tourism film. *Tourism and Hospitality Planning and Development* 7 (1), 1–6.

Bradburne, J.M. (2002a) Not just a luxury: The museum as urban catalyst. In OECD *Urban Renaissance. Glasgow: Lessons for Innovation and Implementation* (pp. 214–226). Paris: OECD.

Bradburne, J.M. (2002b) The museum time bomb: Overbuilt, overtraded, overdrawn. *The Informal Learning Review*. At http://www.informallearning.com/archive/Bradburne-65.htm (accessed June 2014).

Briggs, S. (2005) *Cultural Tourism. How You Can Benefit. A VisitBritain Advisory Guide*. London: VisitBritain.

Brunnermeier, M. (2009) Deciphering the liquidity and credit crunch of 2008–2009. *Journal of Economic Perspectives* 23, 77–100.

Buchmann, A. (2010) Planning and development in film tourism: Insights into the experience of *Lord of the Rings* tour guides. *Tourism and Hospitality Planning and Development* 7 (1), 77–84.

Buckley, R. (2012) Rush as key motivation in skilled adventure tourism: Resolving the risk recreation paradox. *Tourism Management* 33, 961–970.

Callahan, M. (2012) Cruisers left with a sinking feeling. At http://nypost.com/2012/04/16/ cruisers-left-with-a-sinking-feeling (accessed June 2014).

Campbell, C. (2010) Creative tourism providing a competitive edge. *Tourism Insights*, February, unpaginated.

Croy, W.G. (2010) Planning for film tourism: Active destination image management. *Tourism and Hospitality Planning and Development* 7 (1), 21–30.

Csikszentmihalyi, M. (1996) *Creativity – Flow and the Psychology of Discovery and Invention*. New York: Harper-Collins.

Driscoll, M. (2012) 'Hobbit' in the skies: Air New Zealand creates a Middle-Earth-themed safety video. At http://www.csmonitor.com/Books/chapter-and-verse/2012/1106/ Hobbit-in-the-skies-Air-New-Zealand-creates-a-Middle-earth-themed-safety-video (accessed June 2014).

EnjoyEngland (2005) What is the future of domestic tourism to 2015? At http://www. visitengland.org/Images/Domestic%20tourism%20trends%20to%202015-%20 2005_tcm30-19732.pdf (accessed June 2014)

Florida, R. (2002) *The Rise of the Creative Class*. London: Basic Books.

Franken, R.E. (2007) *Human Motivation*. Stanford, CA: Thomson/Wadsworth.

Gjorgievski, M. and Trpkova, S.M. (2012) Movie induced tourism: A new tourism phenomenon. *UTMS Journal of Economics* 3 (1), 97–104.

Gymóthy, S. and Mykletun, R. (2004) Play in adventure tourism: The case of Arctic trekking. *Annals of Tourism Research* 31 (4), 855–878.

Hall, C.M. (2010) Crisis events in tourism: Subjects of crisis in tourism. *Current Issues in Tourism* 13, 401–417.

Hall, C.M., Timothy, D.J. and Duval, D.(2003) Security and tourism: Towards a new understanding? *Journal of Travel and Tourism Marketing* 15 (2/3), 1–18.

Heitmann, S. (2010) Film tourism planning and development: Questioning the role of stakeholders and sustainability. *Tourism and Hospitality Planning and Development.* 7 (1), 31–46.

Holloway, J.C. (1998) *The Business of Tourism.* Harlow: Longman.

Hudson, S. and Brent Ritchie, J.R. (2006) Promoting destinations via film tourism: An empirical identification of supporting marketing initiatives. *Journal of Travel Research* 44, 387–396.

Karpovich, A.I. (2010) Theoretical approaches to film-motivated tourism. *Tourism and Hospitality Planning and Development* 7 (1), 7–20.

Lickorish, L.J. and Jenkins, C.L. (2000) *An Introduction to Tourism.* Oxford: Reed Elsevier.

Macionis, N. and O'Connor, N. (2011) How can the film-induced tourism phenomenon be sustainably managed? *Worldwide Hospitality and Tourism Themes* 3 (2), 173–178.

Maitland, R. (2007) Tourists, the creative class and distinctive areas in major cities: The roles of visitors and residents in developing new tourism areas. In G. Richards and J. Wilson (eds) *Tourism, Creativity and Development* (pp. 73–86). London: Routledge.

Miccio, A. and Kelly, S. (2012) Nelson Arts Festival brochure. Nelson: Nelson City Council.

McNutly, R. (2010) Creative tourism and livable communities. In R. Wurzburger *et al.* (eds) *Creative Tourism: A Global Conversation. How to Provide Unique Creative Experiences for Travelers Worldwide* (pp. 70–77). Santa Fe, NM: Sunstone Press.

Notzke, C. (1999) Indigenous tourism development in the Arctic. *Annals of Tourism Research* 26 (1), 55–76.

Portegies, A. (2010) Places on my mind: Exploring contextuality in film in between the global and the local. *Tourism and Hospitality Planning and Development* 7 (1), 47–58.

Ray, P.H. and Anderson, S.R. (2000) *The Cultural Creatives: How 50 Million People Are Changing the World.* New York: Random House.

Raymond, C. (2007) Creative tourism New Zealand: The practical challenges of developing creative tourism. In G. Richards and J. Wilson (eds) *Tourism, Creativity and Development* (pp. 145–157). London: Routledge.

Richards, G. (2001) Cultural tourists or a culture of tourism? The European cultural tourism market. In J. Butcher (ed.) *Innovations in Cultural Tourism. Proceedings of the 5th ATLAS International Conference* (pp. 1–10). Tilburg: ATLAS.

Richards, G. (2010) *Leisure in the Network Society: From Pseudo-events to Hyperfestivity?* Tilburg: Tilburg University.

Richards, G. (2011) Creativity and tourism: The state of the art. *Annals of Tourism Research* 38 (4), 1225–1253.

Richards, G. and Raymond, C. (2000) Creative tourism. *ATLAS News* 23, 16–20.

Richards, G. and Wilson, J. (2006) Developing creativity in tourist experiences: A solution to the serial reproduction of culture? *Tourism Management* 27, 1209–1223.

Richards, G. and Wilson, J. (eds) (2007a) *Tourism, Creativity and Development.* London: Routledge.

Richards, G. and Wilson, J. (2007b) Tourism development trajectories. From culture to creativity? In G. Richards and J. Wilson (eds) *Tourism, Creativity and Development* (pp. 1–33). London: Routledge.

Richards, G. and Wilson, J. (2007c) Creativities in tourism development. In G. Richards and J. Wilson (eds) *Tourism, Creativity and Development* (pp. 255–288). London: Routledge.

Robinson, M. and Novelli, M. (2005) Niche tourism: an introduction. In M. Novelli (ed.) *Niche Tourism: Contemporary Issues, Trends and Cases* (pp. 1–11). Oxford: Elsevier Butterworth-Heinemann.

Šindeláøová, L. (2008) Terezín: The darkest places of interest in the Czech Republic. At http://www.4hoteliers.com/features/article/3491 (accessed June 2014).

Smith, J.N. (2012) The history of the International Storytelling Center of Jonesborough. At http://www.storytellingcenter.net/learning/the-story-revolution (accessed June 2014).

Stone, P. (2006) A dark tourism spectrum: Towards a typology of death and the macabre related tourist sites, attractions and exhibitions. *Tourism* 54 (2), 145–160.

Stone, P. (2010) Death, dying and dark tourism in contemporary society: A theoretical and empirical analysis. PhD thesis, Central University of Lancashire.

Stone, P. and Sharpley, R. (2008) Consuming dark tourism: A thanatological perspective. *Annals of Tourism Research* 35 (2), 574–595.

Tarlow, P. (2005) Dark tourism: The appealing 'dark' side of tourism and more. In M. Novelli (ed.) *Niche Tourism: Contemporary Issues, Trends and Cases* (pp. 47–58). Oxford: Elsevier Butterworth-Heinemann.

Taylor, C. (1988) Various approaches to and definitions of creativity. In R.J. Sternberg (ed.) *The Nature of Creativity: Contemporary Psychological Perspectives* (pp. 99–121). Cambridge, MA: Cambridge University Press.

Thakara, J. (2002) Trophy buildings are over: French turn attention to arts de la rue. At http://www.doorsofperception.com/locality-place/trophy-buildings-are-over-french-turn-attention-to-arts-de-la-rue (accessed June 2014).

UNESCO Creative Cities Network (2006) *Towards Sustainable Strategies for Creative Tourism*. Discussion Report of the Planning Meeting for 2008 International Conference on Creative Tourism. Paris: UNESCO. At http://unesdoc.unesco.org/images/0015/001598/159811e.pdf (accessed June 2014).

Wang, N. (1999) Rethinking authenticity in tourism experience. *Annals of Tourism Research* 26 (2), 349–370.

Weaver, D.B.(2001) Ecotourism in the context of other tourism types. In D.B. Weaver (ed.) *The Encyclopedia of Ecotourism* (pp. 73–83). Oxford: CABI Publishing.

Weber, K. (2001) Outdoor adventure tourism: A review of research approaches. *Annals of Tourism Research* 28 (2), 360–377.

Weiseberg, R. (1993) *Creativity: Beyond the Myth of Genius*. New York: W.H. Freeman.

WTO (2012a) *Tourism Highlights* (2012 edn). Geneva: WTO.

WTO (2012b) International tourism strong despite uncertain economy. At http://www2.unwto.org/en/press-release/2012-11-05/international-tourism-strong-despite-uncertain-economy (accessed June 2014).

Wurzburger, K., Aageson, T., Pattakos, A. and Pratt, S. (eds) (2010) *Creative Tourism: A Global Conversation. How to Provide Unique Creative Experiences for Travelers Worldwide*. Santa Fe, NM: Sunstone Press.

Xu, S., Barbieri, C., Wilhelm Stanis, S. and Market, P.S. (2012) Sensation-seeking attributes associated with storm-chasing tourists: Implications for future engagement. *International Journal of Tourism Research* 14, 269–284.

Yuill, S.M. (2003) Dark tourism: Understanding visitor motivation at sites of death and disaster. Master of Science thesis, Texas A&M University.

2 Negotiating Mobility: On the Slow Move

Marzena Kubisz

> *To tour, to stop, to drive slowly, to take the longer route,*
> *to emphasise process rather than destination....*
> John Urry, *Mobilities*

> *To really know why San Francisco is not Paris, you must sense it.*
> Joy Monice Malnar and Frank Vodvarka, *Sensory Design*

The Return of the Repressed: Travelling in the Travelless Age

Analysed in the context of the history of tourist experience, the present cultural moment can be defined in terms of transition from a travel*free* to a travel*less* age. I propose to use the term 'travelfree' for it points to the sense of celebration of the liberation of an individual from the burden of travel. Seen on the one hand as hard work (the word 'travel' comes from Old French *travail* and means to work) and on the other as a waste of time in the culture of rush, travel has been represented as an unnecessarily burdensome practice, or, as Nicky Gardner in 'A manifesto for slow travel' puts it, 'a minor inconvenience' (2009: 10), whose elimination has been cast as a marker of a modern sense of comfort and maximisation of efficiency, the value central for Western axiological reality. The sense of comfort and pleasure in the travelfree age originates, largely, in the act of annulment of the experience of travel.

The transition from a travelfree to a travelless age is marked by the rise of the phenomenon of slow travel. Illustrative of the sense of yearning for the experience of travel, systematically and successfully erased from the spectrum of contemporary experience, slow travel tells the story which is underwritten by the sense of deprivation and lack, the story of the quest for something that is believed to have been lost. Seen in this light, slow travel can be approached as a form of Kate Soper's 'alternative hedonism' (2008), with its roots in the sense of displeasure and dissatisfaction with the models of life promoted by hyper-consumerism. As Soper points out: 'the affluent lifestyle is generating its own specific forms of disaffection, either because of its negative by-products or because it stands in the way of other enjoyments' (2008: 571). The description of the character of the present cultural moment in terms of its 'travellessness' registers a meaningful change in the Western conceptualisation of travelling experience and allows issues to be addressed as diverse as agency, environmental consciousness and 'other pleasures' (see Soper, 2000b) as the forms of contestation of acceleration and the 'supposed blessings of consumerism' (Soper, 2008: 571).

'A manifesto for slow travel' by Nicky Gardner, the editor of *Hidden Europe* magazine, is one of the most explicit representations of slow travel ideas. Regardless of the character of the cause – be it social, political, cultural or artistic – a manifesto[1] is always an expression of a certain ontological certainty which is constructed by means of accentuating a difference. In her analysis of the 'Slow food manifesto', Wendy Parkins refers to Janet Lyon's *Manifestoes: Provocations of the Modern* (1999), whose insightful reading of the nature of manifestoes provides her with the theoretical framework to emphasise that manifestoes are 'the means by which movements articulated their own identity by rhetorical denunciation of their enemies' (Parkins, 2004: 372). Lyon emphasises that, since its inception, a manifesto has been the forum for the expression of the needs of those who felt they had been marginalised, oppressed and enslaved: 'to write a manifesto is to announce one's participation, however discursive, in a history of struggle against oppressive forces' (Lyon, 1999: 10).

Two main components of a manifesto which play a significant role in the process of the creation of a certain vision of the world include a representation of the world/community/movement seen as desirable or beneficial for a group, community or the whole of mankind, and a counter-representation which involves a critical representation of the status quo. Each manifesto stems from the sense of dissatisfaction with the present (or some aspects of it) and recommends a method by which to eliminate negative aspects of the present.

The iconography of slow travel is spread between two extremes: at one end there is a donkey, 'an indispensable asset of the would-be slow traveller', while at the other we find planes, those 'fragile aluminum tubes which … shoot through the sky at slightly less than the speed of sound' (Gardner, 2009: 11). Both planes and high-speed trains are represented as a slow traveller's enemies for the effect they have on the mind and the body of a person on the move. The speed at which they move disconnects a traveller from the physical space he or she travels through and activates the process of disappearance of the landscape, which becomes 'untouchable' (Illich, 1974: 25) and as such is no longer seen as an indispensable part of the travelling experience. A description of the experience of travelling by fast train provided by Gardner in her manifesto abounds with expressions that reflect the state of disintegration, disconnection and fragmentation: the trains 'slice' the space, 'defying the warp and weft of the landscape' and produce 'distracted passengers' who are exposed to 'flashes of light between tunnels, angled glimpses of the sky and plenty of scope for headaches'. In contrast to the unnerving experience of fast travel, any travel by a slow train is represented as a source of radically different emotions, as 'the train follows the meandering course of the river, affording wonderful views of gabled villages, precipitous vineyards and romantic gorges' (Gardner, 2009: 12).

According to Gardner (2009: 12), slow travel is 'about having the courage not to go the way of the crowd'; while mass tourism is represented as consisting of an unending repetition of tourists schemes, whose stability is guaranteed by the creation of tourists' needs which the schemes are supposed to satisfy, 'the slow traveller does not play the same dangerous game'. The opposition thereby erected positions a slow traveller as a cultural rebel and anarchist, not likely to be manoeuvred into traps set up by culture, which erases any traces of individual taste and instead produces a homogenised mass of tourists doomed to participate in the spectacle of 'numbing boredom'.

Gardner (2009: 10) says: 'travel has somehow slipped out of fashion.... The pleasure of the journey is eclipsed by anticipation of arrival. To get there fast is better than to travel slow'. Devaluation of travel is seen as symptomatic of the acceleration of everyday life. Gardner (2009: 11) has no doubts that 'Modernity comes at a cost', and these words acquire a new dimension when we inscribe them in the context of Lyon's analysis of a manifesto as 'the form that exposes the broken promises for modernity' (Lyon, 1999: 3). It is not too much to say that one of the promises of the technologically advanced culture of modernity was the comfort of everyday life, which consists, among other things, in the acceleration of what used to be slow. 'The acceleration of just about everything', to refer to James Gleick's study (1994), is the promise that has been kept, but it turned out to be a double-edged sword.

Slow covering of the distance is a factor which situates a traveller in the space *between*: between a place a traveller has just left and his or her destination. Contemporary culture, with its focus on the instant gratification of man's every need, reckons such a state of 'in-betweenness' to be worthless and in need of immediate shortening. The 'impatience complex', as Bauman calls it, is emblematic of what he sees as a 'new life strategy of instant joy' (Bauman, 2010: 23) and underlies a vast segment of contemporary cultural production. Annihilation of 'in-betweenness', manifest in almost all spheres of contemporary life, is framed by two equally powerful factors: an obsession with speed and the concern with the product rather than process. Ranging from television commercials which promote products that are thought to bring desired results – alleviate pain or guarantee fat reduction – in less than a second to advertisements of cosmetic surgeries where before and after are miraculously deprived of the 'in-between' stage, and courses which promise to teach any foreign language or to sail in a weekend, all these products are framed by a similar conviction that what matters is the achievement and not the process. The conviction strikes a chord with Tim Ingold's claim that one of the most characteristic features of Western thought is the tendency to 'privilege form over process' (2000: 198).

Slow travel is a challenge to task-oriented mass tourism, whose offer includes maximisation of the tourist experience and often introduces a sense of accomplishment that is realised by the imposition of the imperative to see everything that *has to* be seen. Slow travel and slow tourism move against the flow with their celebration of 'other pleasures' and challenge the authoritarian rule of the consumerist model of a good, sustainable life, by prioritising models of non-commodified gratification and emphasising the ideas of exchange, reciprocity and co-responsibility and the role they play in the process of marking the contours of post-consumerist pleasure. The rhetoric of slow travel makes its way against the flow of market-oriented tourist practices by encouraging the rise of structures of feeling with roots in the growing sense of displeasure generated by the side-effects of the domination of models of life promoted by contemporary culture. Slow travel situates itself in the new, hedonist imaginary, the aim of which is to 'subvert current perceptions of the attractions of a consumer material culture' (Soper, 2008: 567). Approached from the perspective of an 'alternative hedonist' dis-enchantment with consumerism, slow travel becomes emblematic of such a concept of sustainable life which is marked by a decisive departure from the idea which conflates it with high-consumption and the immediate satisfac-tion of needs. As an act of alternative hedonism, it aims to 'accommodate the goods that are currently being lost or marginalised' (Soper, 2008: 572). Soper believes that the quest for an alternatively defined pleasure should involve 'very different conceptions of consumption and human welfare from those promoted under capitalism' (Soper, 2000a: 271). Gardner's description of slow travel, with its stress on redefinition of the nature of basic elements of tourist experience, is informed by similar attitudes:

Slow travel is about making conscious choices. It is about deceleration rather than speed. The journey becomes a moment to relax, rather than a stressful interlude imposed between home and destination. Slow travel re-engineers time, transforming it into a commodity of abundance rather than scarcity. And slow travel also reshapes our relationship with places, encouraging and allowing us to engage more intimately with the communities through which we travel. (Gardner, 2009: 11)

The advocates of the idea of slow travel see it as a 'deeper type of travel' (Slow Travel, undated) which is not only slower but also easier and simpler. Two main components of slow travelling include spending at least one week in one place, preferably in a vacation rental and not in a hotel, and using the 'concentric circles' theory for day trips (Slow Travel, undated). Such a model of slow leisure assumes liberation from the pressure of the model of standard tourism, which is task-and-quantity oriented and whose framework is defined by the 'must-sees', which often entail racing through the trip. Slow travel replaces the standard model of European leisure, which is seen not only as most popular but also most 'natural', with models of slow leisure oriented towards quality time. What turns out to be one of the most characteristic features of the phenomenon is the fact that slow travel is often a natural extension of lifestyles practised at home. It is not so much a two-week experiment carried out during leisure time but rather a consequence of lifestyle choices made with reference to ethically oriented definitions of sustainable life in the context of hyper-consumerism. More often than not, it is a manifestation of a certain mode of thinking about the world and the role one plays in the world's system of interdependency.

Such an approach to travelling makes a distinction between 'staying' and 'living' in a given destination a fundamental principle of slow travel philosophy. 'Living' in a place assumes that a traveller has the time and a willingness to discover the specificity of a place and is ready to become a part of the locality for a short period. 'Living' assumes connection, while the idea of 'staying', as seen by slow travel enthusiasts, is underlined by disconnection, superficiality and an unmarked passing through. Living in a place assumes integration into the cityscape rather than being 'merely a passing observer' (Gardner, 2009: 12).

Slow travel in the age of acceleration is about a connection: to a place, to its people and to culture (Slow Movement, undated). It is the awareness of mutual dependency that informs the ideological ramifications of slow travel. A dedication to the cause of the welfare of the planet and its in-habitants dismantles the boundaries between 'us' and 'them' when, as Soper (2008: 572) puts it, 'the individual acts with an eye to the collective impact of aggregated individual acts of affluent consumption for consumers themselves'. Those committed to the idea of consuming differently do not perceive themselves as 'innocent and passive victim[s] of industrialism'. Rather, they are motivated by a belief in the power of the choice:

> as consumers they opt wherever possible for fair trade and more environmentally-friendly goods or services, to cut down on packaging and plastic use wherever possible, to spend time cooking rather than use fast food, to avoid whenever possible the more ecologically damaging forms of holiday and leisure activity, and so on. (Soper, 2008: 572)

Environmental consciousness forms an essential dimension of slow mobility, which can be seen as a form of 'green pleasure', defined by Richard Kerridge (2009: 131) as the type of pleasure that 'follows the logic of environmentalism – by using less carbon, deepening one's love of things already at hand, appreciating cycles of growth and renewal in the local and global ecosystems, understanding and taking delight in interdependency'. Soper's alternative hedonism and Kerridge's green pleasures are informed by a sense of reciprocity. The quest for a redefined pleasure is emblematic of a desire to see oneself in the broader context yet still making space for one's individual sense of 'self-interested concerns' (Soper, 2008: 571–572). Slow travel is thought to be the source of 'other pleasures', which flow from the sense of co-responsibility for the place and locality and from the readiness to engage with the local, not only by accepting but also by giving and sharing, which often takes the form of ecologically oriented modes of behaviour, as well as support for the local economy and agriculture.

Smelling the Roses: From the Occular-centric to the Multisensory

> In Gardner's 'A manifesto for slow travel' we read:

> It is easy to practice slow travel. Start at home. Explore your immediate locality. Leave the car at home and take a local bus to a village or suburb that perhaps you have never visited. Plan expeditions that probe the jungles and traverse the deserts of your home neighbourhood. Visit a church, a community centre, a cafe, a library or a cinema that you have passed a thousand times but never entered. (Gardner, 2009: 13)

It comes as no surprise that, in the wake of the recent explosion of interest in anything slow, slow guidebooks have started to appear and reveal a growing appetite for slowness in tourism. For instance, published in 2010 by Affirm Press in Melbourne and Hardie Grant Books in London, *Slow London* is described by the publishers on its website (http://www.affirmpress.com.au/slow-london) as 'an inspirational lifestyle guide for Londoners who want to live more and fret less'. The companies offer a range of guidebooks which 'celebrate all that's local, natural, traditional and sensory in each great city' (http://www.affirmpress.com.au/slow-guides). The corners of the world covered include Melbourne, Sydney and Dublin, and in the wake of the 2009 Slow Down London Festival the year 2010 witnessed publication of *Slow London*, by Robin Barton and Hayley Cull. The webpage for the book claims that this is the right book if you want to 'rise up – in your own time, of course – against the culture of speed and uniformity' and explicitly suggests that the integration of slowness and tourism is not so much about physical movement to far-away and exotic places but rather is a form of inner journey, the prerequisite for which is slowing down. All the books published in the series have a similar design, in the centre of which there is a man on a donkey, a donkey being another symbol – next to the snail – enthusiastically adopted worldwide by the promoters of slow living, below which we read the motto of the series: 'Live more, fret less'.

As a guide to London it is untypical, for it is directed primarily at those who actually *live* in the city (although the guide can be used by all non-Londoners who are interested in discovering the slow metropolis). The act of addressing Londoners and turning them into the book's target audience is indicative of the assumption behind a decision to write a guide to the city for the city's inhabitants: it redefines them as strangers to the city and the city itself as a *terra incognita*, the place that needs to be rediscovered and renamed and whose invisible slow side is there for those who know where to look for it. *Slow London* redraws the cartography of the city and, while doing so, it deprives it of the sense of familiarity which has served to draw an invisible curtain over the city since, as Bauman (2010: 3) says, 'Nothing escapes scrutiny so nimbly, resolutely and stubbornly as "things at hand", things "always there", "never changing".... Their ordinariness is a blind, discouraging all scrutiny'. When not taken for granted and approached in a slow adventure mood, slow London displays its uniqueness and teaches that 'After all, even in the city of eight million people, it's possible to slow down and smell the roses'(Barton & Cull, 2010: 83).

Slow food's endorsement of 'the primacy of sensory experience' – which allows for the treatment of 'eyesight, hearing, smell, touch, and taste as so many instruments of discernment, self-defence and pleasure' (Petrini, 2001: 69) – turned out to be slow travel's epistemological foundation. The *Slow London* guide follows the main assumptions of Petrini's project of the rehabilitation of the senses by splitting the second part of the book, entitled 'Be – slow down and smell the roses', into five sections entitled 'See', 'Hear', 'Smell', 'Taste' and 'Touch', where the five senses are represented as the tools of embodied perception. Slow guidebooks challenge the hegemony of sight so successfully established in the Western sensorium. The guide's shift towards the wide spectrum of sensory experience of the urban space can be seen as an element of the new sensitivity to urban space, the essence of which is focused on the mobilisation of urban designers to 'disregard their occularcentric perspectives and reconceptualise the city as a multisensory space' (Pink, 2007: 65).

The turn towards sensory experience opens new cognitive spaces and creates new exploratory possibilities. To illustrate the way the senses can be reactivated through slow tourism, let us take a look at the two sections of the guidebook entitled 'Hear' and 'Touch'.

The sense of hearing engaged in the process of getting to know London rediscovers a variety of 'soundscapes' and makes it possible to create an 'aural archive of London' (Barton & Cull, 2010: 83). Ian Rawes, the founder of the London Sound Survey, registers the diversity of the sounds of London, which include, among other things, the sound of traffic, the sound of people, as well as bird song, and thereby reveals the potential of the sound to tell the story of continuity and change. Under 'Rhythms, riffs and recording', Hayley Cull writes that

> sounds can represent fashion, from singing canaries and wind chimes to boom-boxes and car horns that play the first eight notes of 'colonel Bogey'. They reflect developments in trade, industry and technology; growth of the city itself; demographic and social change; even shifts in the scattering of wildlife, like the raspy squawk of the ring-necked parakeet as it becomes astonishingly prevalent here. (Barton & Cull, 2010: 83)

Under 'Schedule of sounds' there is a calendar of 'aural events' which includes the 'cascading chimes of Big Ben' on 1 January, 'the lazy drone of bumblebees' in May and fireworks in November (Barton & Cull, 2010: 85–89). The sonic aspects of city life included in the guidebook correspond with David Pocock's study in which he says that 'sounds play a crucial role in the anticipation, experience and remembering of places' (quoted in Malnar & Vodvarka, 2004: 140) and he emphasises the role they play in the process of transformation of environments to places.

The re-creation of the city's soundscape is represented as a source of un-commodified pleasure, one that allows for the rediscovery of the ability to hear, which paradoxically has been lost in the culture of noise. Similarly, touch, 'the first sense we experience and the last we lose' (Malnar & Vodvarka, 2004: 127), undergoes rehabilitation as an important tool of cognition which, when revalued, opens the door to 'the other London' and invites one to connect with time and tradition as 'through marks of touch we shake the hands of countless generations' (Pallasmaa, quoted in Malnar & Vodvarka: 145). Inviting us to touch our way through London, the authors of *Slow London* say:

> A smooth, polished feel dominates the ancient hardwood pews of St Paul's, while the battered timber bars of our old pubs are equally sacred.... Running your hand over the beautiful vines today is to connect with both a time and a tradition.
>
>   Metal can feel colder but it's an equally good conductor of memories and stories. In places like the National Gallery and the Royal Courts of Justice, the banisters and handrails have been burnished by countless palms. Running soft hands along the worn railings is a timely illustration of how billions of tiny actions can have an effect on something as hard and intractable as metal or stone. (Barton & Cull, 2010: 131)

The above fragment suggests an interesting parallel with the Preface to the October 1991 issue of the *Architectural Review*, in which we read:

> We appreciate a place not just by its impact on our visual cortex but by the way in which it sounds, feels and smells. Some of these sensual experiences elide, for instance our full understanding of wood is often achieved by a perception of its smell, its texture (which can be appreciated by both looking and feeling) and by the way in which it modulates the acoustics of the space. (Quoted in Malnar & Vodvarka, 2004: 23–24)

Two things demand emphasis. What both excerpts have in common is the revalorisation of sensory experience underwritten by the conviction, stated by Yi-Fu Tuan, that 'Taste, smell, and touch are capable of exquisite refinement. They discriminate among the wealth of sensations and articulate gustatory, olfactory and textural worlds' (1977: 10). Both *Slow London* and the *Architectural Review* invigorate the sensuous discourse by recasting senses as valid 'ways to knowledge' (Synnott, 1993: 128). In Western culture the senses have always been the subject of scepticism and ambivalence, and Western thought has always been permeated by an oscillation between 'the superiority or inferiority of the senses with respect to reason, and the ratio or balance of the sensorium' (Synnott, 1993: 128). The rehabilitation of the sensory in the epistemological process, generated, among other things, by the explosion of interest in slowness as a valid cultural and social idea and practice, inscribes itself in the long history of Western ambivalence towards the senses and locates itself on the side of eulogising their utility and validity.

What *Slow London* proposes is cognition on an intimate scale based on sensory perception. While Molnar and Vodvarka (2004: 239) claim that 'we need to revalue the nonvisual senses and learn a new vocabulary as well', Juhani Pallasmaa (2005: 142–143) observes that 'the city of the gaze passivates the body and the other senses, the alienation of the body again reinforces visibility'. *Slow London* reimagines the capital as a sensory city – the sense of pleasure is achieved by enhanced sense-oriented experience and overturning of the hegemony of vision. The 'primacy of sensory experience' that Petrini talks about can be seen as one of the defining features of the slow tourist experience, which thus can be understood as 'multisensorial and as such *neither* dominated *nor* reducible to a visual mode of understanding' (Pink, 2009: 64). In the words of Yi-Fu Tuan (1977: 18), 'An object or place achieves concrete reality when our experience of it is total, that is through all the senses as well as with the active and reflective mind'.

The turn towards sensory experience of slow travel corresponds with Soper's analysis of 'other pleasures' when she says that it 'does not reside exclusively in the desire to avoid or limit the un-pleasurable by-products of collective affluence, but also in the sensual pleasure of consuming differently' (Soper, 2008: 572). *Slow London* can be seen as advocating such a form of experiencing of the metropolis, which is based on the engagement of all the senses, thus giving rise to the 'alternative urban "sensescapes" that implicitly critique the visual, olfactory, gustatory, sonic and haptic experiences that are associated with global consumer capitalism' (Pink, 2009: 66). The awakening of the redefined pleasure and the rise of 'alternative hedonism' are deeply rooted in the realm of sensory experience.

The cognitive perspective adopted and promoted by the authors of *Slow London* correlates interestingly with a phenomenological view, the validity of the parallel, supported by an explicit claim made by Gardner (2009: 13) in her manifesto when she describes travelling as a 'phenomenological process' and claims that 'Slow travel reinvigorates our habits of perception'. The city, Gardner writes, 'deserves more than a casual glance – cityscapes are there to be studied and observed in detail. They are spurs to meditation and only much later can words flow'. The phenomenological character of the slow travel experience consists in the rehabilitation of the role the senses play in the process of learning. The world immediately experienced through the senses does not aspire to objectivity – sensory perception does not seek to *explain* London in an objective, universally accepted manner but it rather seeks to illustrate the manner in which 'the world makes itself evident to awareness through direct, sensorial experience' (Malnar & Vodvarka, 2004: 24).

The phenomenological tradition, with its reorientation of the senses, has turned out to have a special appeal for environmentalists. Considering slow travel's concern with ecological issues, it seems only natural that sensory perception should embrace 'the perception of the environment', to refer to Tim Ingold's work (2000), thus giving rise to eco-phenomenological readings of the position and role of a human being in the world. David Abram, the author of *The Spell of the Sensuous*, writes:

> Our bodies have formed themselves in delicate reciprocity with the manifold textures, sounds and shapes of an animate earth – our eyes have evolved in subtle interaction with *other* eyes, as our ears are attuned by their very structure to the howling of the wolves and the honking of geese. To shut ourselves off from these voices, to continue by our lifestyles to condemn these other sensibilities to the oblivion of extinction, is to rob our own senses of their integrity, and to rob our own minds of their coherence. We are human only in contact, and conviviality, with what is not human. (Abram, 1997: 22)

Seen from the perspective of phenomenology, perception is always reciprocal and dialogic. As such, seen in the light of eco-phenomenology, perception of the environment re-establishes the broken connection with the natural world by engaging the perceiving self in 'silent conversation' (Abram, 1997: 22) with the perceived, thus allowing for the reconstruction of the integrity of the senses and illustrating the ways in which 'self-identities and environments are coproduced' (Pink, 2007: 61).

The English poet Jeremy Hooker (1999) has provided environmentalists and eco-critics with a very useful and hence often used metaphor of 'ditch vision', whose essence consists in the ability and readiness of the perceptive mind to see the unusual in the familiar, the mode of perceiving reality which came to dominate his childhood spent in rural England. Following this mode of perception it is clear that

> natural spaces do not necessarily have to be large wilderness areas, they could even exist inside a city, and that fields, when viewed from ditches, can appear to be endless. What is important about these spaces is not their extension but the perceived difference of social control and the possibility for alternative perspectives, in other words their openness for signification and individual appropriation. (Bigell, 2006: 52)

Slow London takes up this challenge and enables the quest for the unknown in an environment which seems to be all too well known. What it reveals is that the other dimension is always there: hidden, not exposed to immediate consumption, requiring an effort to be made; not imposing itself ostentatiously yet already there as long as the fact of 'our sensuous immersion in the world' (Kerridge, 2009: 136) is acknowledged. An excerpt from *Slow London* may serve as an illustration of the ways in which the urban environment is transformed in the act of 'individual appropriation' into an alternative space. This is how one of the authors of *Slow London* describes her encounter with the natural world in Morden Hall Park:

An irresistible giant oak launched me into the tour: its trunk had branched into two, one half showing off familiar rough bark, the other cloaked shyly behind dried, wooded vines. Like light and dark, the tree had formed a perfect dichotomy of texture. This set me off, barefoot on the dewy grass under the full force of the sun....

A fallen tree became an, admittedly slightly lumpy, bench but it did the job as I watched a duck dart and dive in the river and wondered what it must feel like to skim water. My attention drifted to a tree that had been allowed to die naturally, a rare thing these days. (Barton & Cull, 2010: 130)

A walk through one of London's numerous parks becomes, as 'A manifesto for slow travel' suggests, an expedition 'that probe[s] the jungles' of the local environment. For David Lindo, Hooker's metaphor of 'ditch vision' might be a useful tool in the process of appropriation of the natural environment and turning it into a realm of discovery and adventure. He says: 'You have to imagine that this is a wilderness, that people don't exist and the buildings are the cliffs. There's more to life in cities than people realise' (quoted in Barton & Cull, 2010: 130). The approach requires re-orientation to the natural and, although performed in the urban setting, it can still be achieved, even if by more purely imaginative means.:

'Ditch vision' names the imaginative habit of playing with scale in order to discover wildness and infinity in small spaces; the genre of daydreaming that sees in an overgrown railway bank the principle and possibility of wildness. (Kerridge, 2009: 133)

The vision of the world sought by the advocates of slow tourism, as exemplified by *Slow London*, rests upon Abram's 'other sensibilities', which can be seen as helping to reconstruct the connection long lost in the process of alienation of our bodies from the natural world. Following Abram's rereading of Merleau-Ponty's phenomenology of perception, it is possible to adopt the idea of perception as a 'dynamic relationship in which the perceiving body is constituted in the act of perception' (quoted in Kerridge, 2009: 135). Such an approach to sensuous immersion in the world corresponds with the stress put on the relation between sensuous perception and the acts of self-identification/self-creation by urban designers and social anthropologists.

The phenomenon of slow tourism inscribes itself in the context marked by John Urry's analysis of the tourist's gaze, in the sense that a slow traveller can be described as a semiotician who performs the act of 'reading the landscape for signifiers of certain pre-established notions' (Urry, 1990: 12) or, pushing the analysis further, as an eco-semiotician who engages the senses in the act of reading the natural environment and lets them create a wide spectrum of 'senscapes'. However, it seems that slow travel destabilises the opposition between the ordinary and the extraordinary, which Urry sees as a fundamental condition of tourist experience:

> Tourism results from a basic binary opposition between the ordinary/ everyday and the extraordinary. … potential objects of the tourist gaze must be different in some way or other. They must be out of the ordinary. People must experience particularly distinct pleasures which involve different senses or are on a different scale from those typically encountered in everyday life. There are many different ways in which such a division between the ordinary and the extraordinary can be established and sustained. (Urry, 1990: 11–12)

In the case of the slow tourism experience, as illustrated by *Slow London*, the presence of the extraordinary is not the effect of the introduction of the division into working time and leisure time, which thus allows for the experience of the 'out of ordinary', but is represented as a natural extension or continuity of everyday and ordinary practices. Since slow travel is described by Gardner as 'a state of mind', the suggestion is that what underlies a slow traveller's sensitivity is the erasure of the opposition between the ordinary and the extraordinary. A slow traveller is represented as the one who seeks the extraordinary not only 'outside the normal places of residence and work' (Urry, 1990: 3) but in the everyday, the mundane and the familiar.

Conclusions

Although it seems tempting to look for the pioneers of slow travel in ancient Rome or among medieval pilgrims or participants of the Grand

Tours, the question of whether slow travel has its antecedents in past forms of travel remains disputable. To see the phenomenon of slow travel in terms of continuity suggests a readiness to take the risk of reducing slow travel to a one-dimensional phenomenon, the essence of which is a preference for slow modes of transport over fast ones. Slow travel is a phenomenon whose ideological ramifications cannot be limited to a preference for slower modes of transport, but, as a dialectical phenomenon, it should be viewed in the context of its opposite, lest its contestative and resistant character be eclipsed. Slow travel is about agency and individuality in the age of mass production of cultural practices and meanings, and it is only in contrast with the mainstream models that the ideological framework of slow travel can display its subversive potential:

> Slow travel … represents a way of consumer thinking about tourism, where there is synergy between experiential aspects of travel and, for some tourists, discourses about the environment, in particular climate change. By travelling slowly, people are not just choosing a mode of transport, but they are also negotiating with place, the environment, their personal identity as a tourist, and in some cases, expressing certain ethical and ideological values. (Dickinson *et al.*, 2011: 282)

Urry's study of leisure and tourism in contemporary culture leaves no doubt as to what it is that forms the foundation of tourist experience: the gaze. Says Urry (1990: 1): 'we gaze at what we encounter. And this gaze is as socially organised and systematised as is the gaze of the medic'. Urry's approach is shaped by the conviction that the tourist's gaze is a construct which has its own history, a history which reflects changing patterns of Western cultural practice. Following this mode of thinking about the constructed nature of the tourist's gaze, it is possible to reproduce slow travel as emblematic of 'changing … distinctions of taste within the potential population of visitors' (Urry, 1990: 4).

What most slow travel publications, whose popularity illustrates the change of 'distinctions of taste', have in common is that their rhetoric is visibly marked by the logic of binary oppositions, according to which what is slow is deeper, easier and more rewarding than anything that is not slow, the logic emblematic of what might be seen as an example of *slowwashing*. Slowness is seen as a remedy and recipe for a change: slow travel emerges as a means of metamorphosis, which is very likely to happen when a tourist spends a week living with the locals and following the rhythm of life of a place he or she has chosen to spend slow time in. Having spent a week or more in this way, the slow traveller is expected to 'come away from … [a]

trip rejuvenated and changed' (Urry, 1990: 4), although the quality of change is never specified on this level in advertising publications. The change is taken for granted as part and parcel of the influence of slowing down, which is illustrative of the huge transformation the very concept of slowness has undergone in the last two decades. Slowness becomes synonymous with change and, what is often implied, with spiritual rebirth.

Bill Newlin, Avalon Travel publisher, says:

> They [contemporary tourists] are valuing time over money, looking for ways to make educated decisions. People want to find something new, have stories to tell, but what that means has changed.... The unknown is harder to find today but the craving for adventure survives. (Quoted by Parkes, 2006)

Since the world has shrunk radically and there are hardly any unexplored places left, the sense of adventure undergoes redefinition and entails the rise of a novel approach to places which are already well known on the surface but are still capable of offering the possibility of diving deep beneath what is customarily highlighted by traditional tourist description, satisfying travellers' hunger for novelty. The object of tourist exploration does not have to change; what changes is the mode of tourist experience.

Note

(1) In the chapter I refer to Janet Lyon's analysis of the character of manifestoes in *Manifestoes: Provocations of the Modern*. Since the use of the indefinite article is required when the author discusses manifestoes from the perspective of their general characteristics, in order to avoid confusion I will be referring to 'a manifesto for slow travel' as 'Gardner's manifesto', while 'a manifesto' will be reserved for Lyon's analysis. The analysis of 'a manifesto for slow travel' from the perspective of Lyon's study of manifestoes as an ideologically framed genre owes its general shape to Wendy Parkin's reading of the 'slow food' manifesto (Parkin, 2004).

References

Abram, D. (1997) *The Spell of the Sensuous*. New York: Vintage.
Barton, R. and Cull, H. (2010) *Slow London*. Melbourne: Affirm Press; London: Hardie Grant Books.
Bauman, Z. (2010) *44 Letters from the Liquid Modern World*. Cambridge: Polity Press.
Bigell, W. (2006) Distinction but not separation: Edward Abbey's conceptualization of nature. Dissertation for the degree of doctor philosophiae, Department of English, Faculty of Humanities, University of Tromsø. At http://munin.uit.no/bitstream/handle/10037/1227/thesis.pdf?sequence=1 (accessed 30 May 2012).

Dickinson, J., Lumsdon, L.M. and Robbins, D. (2011) Slow travel: Issues for tourism and climate change. *Journal of Sustainable Tourism* 19 (3), 281–300.

Gardner, N. (2009) A manifesto for slow travel. *Hidden Europe* 25 (March/April), 10–14.

Gleick, J. (1999) *Faster: The Acceleration of Just About Everything.* New York: Pantheon Books.

Hooker, J. (1999) Ditch vision. *Powys Journal* 9, 14–29.

Illich, I. (1974) *Energy and Equity.* New York: Harper and Row.

Ingold, T. (2000) *The Perceptions of the Environment.* London: Routledge.

Kerridge, R. (2009) Green pleasures. In K. Soper, M. Ryle and L. Thomas (eds) *The Politics and Pleasures of Consuming Differently* (pp. 130–153). Basingstoke: Palgrave Macmillan.

Lyon, J. (1999) *Manifestoes: Provocations of the Modern.* New York: Cornell University Press.

Malnar, J.M. and Vodvarka, F. (2004) *Sensory Design.* Minneapolis, MN: University of Minnesota Press.

Pallasmaa, J. (2005) Lived space: Embodied experience and sensory thought. In P. MacKeith (ed.) *Encounters: Juhani Pallasmaa – Architectural Essays.* Hämeenlinna: Rakennustieto Publishing.

Parkes, C. (2006) Travel writers. The history of travel guides. Blog at http://travelwriters.blogspot.com/2006/04/history-of-travel-guidebooks.html (accessed 5 November 2013).

Parkins, W. (2004) Out of time: Fast subjects and slow living. *Time and Society* 13 (2/3), 363–382.

Petrini, C. (2001) *Slow Food: The Case for Taste.* New York: Columbia University Press.

Pink, S. (2007) Sensing Cittàslow: Slow living and the constitution of the sensory city. *Senses and Sociology* 2 (1), 59–77.

Pink, S .(2009) *Doing Sensory Ethnography.* London: Sage.

Slow Movement (undated) What is slow travel? At http://www.slowmovement.com/slow_travel.php (accessed 23 August 2013).

Slow Travel (undated) What is slow travel? At http://www.slowtrav.com/vr/index.htm (accessed 20 July 2013).

Soper, K. (2000a) *What Is Nature?* (2nd edn). Oxford: Blackwell.

Soper, K. (2000b) Other pleasures: The attractions of post-consumerism. *Socialist Register 2000: Necessary and Unnecessary Utopias* 36, 115–132.

Soper, K. (2008) Alternative hedonism, cultural theory and the role of aesthetic revisioning. *Cultural Studies* 22 (5), 568–587.

Synnott, A. (1993) *The Body Social: Symbolism, Self and Society.* London: Routledge.

Tuan, Y.-F. (1977) *Space and Place: The Perspective of Experience.* Mineapolis, MN: University of Minnesota Press.

Urry, J. (1990) *The Tourist Gaze: Leisure and Travel in Contemporary Societies.* London: Sage.

3 Mein Mallorca: A German–Spanish Love Affair

Petra M. Bagley

This chapter explores how Mallorca has become much more than an island of refuge for exiled German writers, much more than a popular holiday destination for German tourists; instead, Mallorca provides a setting for what could be termed a new form of 'immigrant' fiction, namely, tales of relocation, of second-home ownership. The descriptive terminology for exile proves to be inadequate for this body of contemporary writing, as this is voluntary relocation. Worthy of discussion is the way in which the experience of living between two languages, between two cultures, has inspired such narratives, which are difficult to categorise in literary terms, since they could also be considered a sub-genre of travel writing, an expatriate literature. At the same time, they could be associated with 'immigrant literature' in terms of theme, since a common feature of such texts is the way in which these authors convey the struggle to create a home community and a sense of belonging, in this case a Mallorcan *Heimat*. Moreover, in their detailed study of the concept of *Heimat*, Boa and Palfreyman (2000: 195) argue that, over time, the word *Heimat* has distanced itself from attachment to a fixed place and has instead become 'a frame of mind: the commitment of citizens to the process of making a liveable social space'.

This is a new field of research, which is still in search of definitions that can guide the process of enquiry, because some would argue that these narratives of relocation have their 'home' in travel literature, while it is also possible to borrow elements of the descriptors of 'axial', 'post-national', 'postcolonial', 'exophonic', 'grey zone', 'settlement' literature, due to the fact that the narrators/authors have relocated to another country and draw attention to the differences between their own and their host culture. They also continue to write in their mother tongue. The extent to which this creation of a new homeland has happened and is happening suggests that Mallorca has undergone a form of German colonisation, both factual and fictional; whether it will continue to be the focus of relocation is another story.

The Germans' long 'love affair' with the Mediterranean island of Mallorca is undeniable, but not unequivocal. Their first 'date' can be traced back to around 425 AD, when the Vandals, a Germanic tribe, invaded the Balearics and, having defeated the Romans, remained for 70 years, until they themselves were conquered by the Byzantines (Bott et al., 1999). This tumultuous and aggressive start to their relationship eventually blossomed into a romance, so that by the start of the 20th century a number of Germans, in particular the wealthy elite and artists seeking sanctuary, had already settled in Mallorca and had made a home for themselves alongside the islanders. In 1903 the island's first hotel was opened by the Austrian archduke, Ludwig Salvator; in the same year the tourist board was established 'as an instrument for stimulating cultural and intellectual activity' (Bull, 1997: 141). The relationship became more earnest in the 1930s, as the island provided refuge for exiled German writers, such as Erich Arendt (1903–84), Harry Graf Kessler (1868–1937) and Karl Otten (1889–1963).[1] German hotels and pensions, as well as English and American ones, started to appear. *Majorca Sun*, a foreign-language newspaper, was also published in German and French; there was even a German lending library. With the arrival of the first charter plane in 1952, the nature and simplicity of this peaceful paradise was about to shift to hedonism and sensual adventures. The once refined relationship was replaced by fun-filled, passionate, one-night stands, when, from the late 1960s onwards, Mallorca became the number one holiday destination for sun, sea, sand and sex.

The Germans, like the British, came in their droves, with cheap package holidays resulting in mass tourism. By the beginning of the 1980s, due to the mass tourism and corresponding reports in the media, the image of Mallorca had turned into that of an island of cleaning ladies (*Putzfraueninsel*), because even they could afford two weeks in the Mallorcan sun, as Wachowiak (2009) explains in his discussion of the trip patterns of German tourists. According to Heilmann (2005), the boom hit an all-time high in 1998, when more than 4.5 million German tourists 'invaded' the island, overwhelming the 610,000 local inhabitants to such an extent that they believed the Vandals had returned. In August 1999 the German weekly news magazine *Der Spiegel* ran as its cover story 'Wem gehört Mallorca: Spanier gegen die Germanisierung' ('To whom does Mallorca belong: Spaniards against Germanisation').[2] The Germans were no longer just visiting: they wanted commitment in the relationship. They showed this initially by buying holiday homes – 20% of the island's property was now in German hands – and then by choosing to live permanently on the island. By the end of the 1990s, approximately

100,000 Germans had relocated and opened up businesses, thus investing both emotionally and financially in their dream of paradise.[3]

For the Mallorcans, however, the relationship had already turned sour. While it was true that tourists had transformed the island from a rural backwater into the richest province in Spain, there was talk of the island being 'sold out' to Germany. Already in 1994 an MP from Germany's Christlich-Soziale Union (CSU, Christian Social Union), Diony Jobst, had indeed made the incredible suggestion should either purchase Mallorca or lease it for 99 years, thus making the island Germany's 17th federal state (see Heilmann, 2005).

Situated about 90 km to the east of the Spanish mainland, Mallorca is by far the largest of the Balearics, an archipelago, which also comprises Menorca, Ibiza and Formentera, and forms one of the autonomous regions of Spain. In German parlance *Malle* is still affectionately referred to as Germany's southernmost state, while the Castilian-Catalan spelling of 'Mallorca' in English is 'Majorca' and has given rise to a long-standing Spanish joke of there being a fifth Balearic island. As in the case of Germany, Majorca is Britain's favourite holiday destination, though each nationality frequents different areas: the British tourists tend to stay in Magaluf and Palma Nova in the west, the Germans are in the east, in Arenal, where this geographical segregation is broken down even further into regional segregation, such as 'Hamburg hill' or 'Düsseldorf hole'.

As noted above, the island has for many centuries lured visitors on account of its favourable climate, extensive coastline, attractive, white sandy beaches and endless blue skies. Its beautiful seas and scenery, as well as the tranquillity, gave rise to Mallorca's dominant image as 'la isla de la calma'. The British artist Francis Caron lived there in the 1930s and drew attention to the common perception that time almost stood still on the island:

The air here is hot, and quite still. It smells of leaves and all sorts of spices, and they say that strangers when they first come to the island are drugged by it. The nights are slower and more spacious than they are at home – and that is because the sky is larger too. (Caron, 1939: 1)

Sixty years later the drug is sangria and binge drinking among many pleasure-seeking tourists. Their summer holiday is a hothouse of nationalistic fervour, of pub crawls and discos: 3000 people can fit into the German disco Bierkönig in Arenal. The last thing they want is peace and quiet. To accommodate the multitude of visitors, the coastal landscape in the south has been transformed by high-rise apartment blocks. Each week some 400 aircraft from Germany land in Mallorca. The German language can be heard everywhere: German beer gardens, restaurants, supermarkets dominate the main streets; most German television networks are available via satellite; three German newspapers are readily available, and the German tabloid *Bild* even has an island edition, *Mallorca Zeitung;*[4] and a proliferation of German signs and menus is evident. 'Beach section 6' has been renamed *Ballermann 6* and is synonymous with non-stop alcohol consumption. It has become the epicentre for the plague of new German 'vandals': a sub-culture which presents the worst possible picture of young Germans. Is it any wonder then that the Mallorquins fear a Germanisation of their island and perceive a threat to their identity?

But it is not just the young who come in large numbers: elderly Germans are taking advantage of the healthy climate and the cheaper cost of living, and they want something more exotic than butter trips on the Baltic. In winter 2003/04 the German travel firm TUI Club Elan opened three hotels on the island to cater specifically for this market. The over-50s have access to German doctors and chemists; they have their own website and club newspaper. Many choose to retire to the island and live in planned settlements with their own restaurants and shops. The infrastructure is custom-built to meet the needs of retirees. To live comfortably on the island there is also no need for them to speak the language, since translators abound and local German-language newspapers advertise numerous types of services provided by German-speaking entrepreneurs. For these 'residential tourists', creating a *Heimat* abroad does not involve integration into the host country's lifestyle and culture. As Huber and O'Reilly (2004: 348) conclude in their study of Swiss and British elderly migrants in Spain, what counts in the construction of a new *Heimat* in a new environment 'is a functioning network of good friends and neighbours (regardless of nationality and background), and solid links with the home of origin'.

Back in the winter of 1838, friends and neighbours were very few and far between according to George Sand's account of her three-month stay on the island together with her lover, Frederic Chopin, and her two children. For health reasons they too had sought the warmer climate of the Mediterranean island: the composer was ill with bronchitis and Sand's son, Maurice, was suffering from rheumatism. However, after a month of hot weather, the rains started and turned that particular winter into an unusually severe one: as a consequence, Chopin's bronchitis worsened and he became feverish. The family moved from Palma to Valldemossa, where they stayed in the cells of the Carthusian monastery. The local inhabitants believed Chopin had tuberculosis and stayed away from the family. They also frowned upon the facts that the couple were living in sin and that Sand never went to mass, that she smoked cigarettes and dressed herself and her daughter in masculine clothes. Two months later the visitors returned to France, and within two years Sand published *Un Hiver à Majorque* (1841), a book in which she praised the natural beauty of the island but condemned the Mallorcans as barbarians, cheats and thieves, who lied, abused and plundered. In her words:

> [the islanders] found the idea of selfless service to a stranger as incomprehensible as that of behaving honestly or even obligingly to a foreigner.... We nicknamed Majorca 'Monkey Island' because when surrounded by these crafty, thieving and yet innocent creatures, we grew accustomed to defending ourselves against them. (Sand, 1956: 144–146)

It might be surprising to learn, therefore, that this book is still printed and sold in Mallorca in English, German and Spanish, without comment on its errors and slanders. Moreover, it has been described by the *Encyclopaedia Britannica* as one of the great travel books. Certainly, Sand does describe in great detail aspects of 19th century life on the island but her observations are blurred by personal experience. From the perspective of the Mallorcans, it may be that by continuing to make the book readily available they are playing a joke on the author, for the book illustrates the extent to which the island has developed since she wrote her scathing account.

Prejudices, however, remain. In her recent account of her year working on the island, journalist Marie Roth (2009: 128) notes:

> Vorurteilen begegnet man auf der Insel zwischen den Kontinenten wie Sand am Meer. Die Deutschen meinen, die Mallorquiner seien provinziell, verschlossen und geizig. Die Mallorquiner meinen, dass die Kultur der Deutschen aus Bratwurst, Bier und sentimentalen Schunkelliedern bestehe. Und dass die Deutschen glauben, alles kaufen zu können und *caps cuadrads* seien.

> On the island you come across prejudices between continents like the sand along the sea. The Germans think the Mallorcans are provincial, reserved and miserly. The Mallorcans think that German culture consists of sausages, beer and sentimental songs to which you rock to and fro arm in arm; and that the Germans believe they can buy everything and they are stubborn and inflexible.

Criticism should of course be part and parcel of any good travel guide or travel narrative. Michael Böckler adds a new twist not only to the genre of travel writing, but also to Sand's description of Mallorquin villains. Published in 2002, *Sturm über Mallorca* (*Storm over Mallorca*) has features typical of a crime story. For two years the German police had been searching for a German stockbroker, who had embezzled millions on the stock exchange and then vanished. Felix Reiter has assumed a new identity and is living on a yacht in one of Mallorca's many bays. The story begins with the yacht crashing about in the waves of a sudden storm; the young German girl on board finds herself alone, unable to steer the yacht. Her companion, whom she had met just two weeks before, has seemingly fallen overboard and disappeared. The reader then learns in retrospective flashbacks about how they met, as well as how the press, a private detective and the Spanish mafia are all hunting for this man.

What makes the style of this crime story so different from others is that Böckler also provides information about the island within the story and in an appendix, so that the reader knows about the best restaurants, the places to visit and even learns about the history of the island, including the visit of Chopin and Sand. The subtitle, *Ein Roman als Reiseführer*, which is not on the book's cover, but on the title page, makes it clear that this is a novel as well as a travel guide. In my opinion it is a very odd combination of fact and fiction, and unsuccessfully tries to combine the twofold purpose of a gripping crime story and an informative guidebook for tourists, who are already on the island. As a reader of crime stories, you want to progress with the story, instead of being interrupted with what are sometimes pages of historical detail not at all relevant to the plot. While its appeal and target market must therefore be limited, it does add another dimension to forms of travel writing, as well as crime writing. Like the exiled writers of the 1930s, Böckler's protagonist seeks refuge in Mallorca, and like the holidaymakers he, too, is fleeing reality.

For Ulrich Stefan's first-person narrator, it is employment which brings him to the island. Written in 2004, *Hüte dich vor den Bergen und dem Wind und den Deutschen, die im Ausland sind! Eine deutsch-mallorquinische Episode* (*Beware of the Mountains and the Wind and the Germans, Who Are Abroad! A German –Mallorcan Episode*) focuses on how German entrepreneurs make a living in Mallorca. Stefan does not portray life on the island through rose-tinted spectacles; like Sand and Böckler, he too includes Mallorcan history in his account, but he relates the events to the current situation of his narrator and at the same time he expresses his criticism, not of the Mallorcans, but of the German tourists and residents who have created enclaves called the Düsseldorfer Loch (Düsseldorf Hole) around Port Andratx and Hamburger

Hügel (Hamburg Hill) between Felanitx and Santany, as noted earlier. He points out that within these communities the people who can fit a light bulb describe themselves as electricians, while a trained hairdresser runs a health spa. Many soon find themselves facing financial crises; their dream of living the good life turns into a nightmare. This narrator's observations are supported by sociological studies of expatriates abroad as well as statistics: over 29,000 resident Germans experienced more money problems than any other group of islanders in 2007 (Anonymous, 2007b). A number are choosing to return home to Germany, as has been documented in a German weekly television programme called *Die Rückwanderer* (*The Returnees*), which features people giving up on their dream of living in the sun. In the case of the many retirees, old friends have also moved back home, usually due to severe health problems, or they have passed away. Loneliness and isolation are not uncommon. One of the greatest taboos is that of alcohol consumption among the residential tourists. With time on their hands one in two Germans are reported to have turned to alcohol to deal with depression (Bott *et al.*, 1999). After five years, Stefan's protagonist leaves Mallorca because his skills are no longer required; the work has dried up in the building trade. According to him, the new German Eldorado will be the islands of Cape Verde, where another paradise awaits the intrepid entrepreneur and tourism is in its infancy. A peripatetic migrant, he will recreate his home wherever there are money-making opportunities.[5]

Today, at least half of the foreigners who live permanently or semi-permanently on Mallorca are Germans, another 40% are Britons and the remainder Scandinavians. Germans own about 60% of the island's holiday homes. The author Elke Menzel is one of these owners, a German-Mallorcan residential tourist. In *Eine Finca auf Mallorca oder: Geckos im Gästebett* (2006) (*A Finca on Majorca or: Geckos in the Guest Bed*), an autobiographical novel, she describes with much humour the renovation of her *finca*, her holiday home, as well as her contact with the local inhabitants and other Germans. We hear about the festivities celebrated on the island; the survival of the Mallorquin language; the harvesting of almonds; the problems of infestations of ants, flies and even rats. Her account aligns itself with narratives of relocation/settlement, since the reader is privy to all the ups and downs of her experiences of creating a new home in a new environment.

Humour is also a characteristic of more recent German stories about Mallorca. Peter Knorr's *Mallorca: Insel der Inseln* (*Island of Islands*) and Stefan Keller's *Papa ante Palma: Mallorca für Fortgeschrittene* (*Daddy before Palma: Mallorca for Advanced Learners*) both appeared in 2011; both are semi-autobiographical. Knorr, a satirist and journalist, has been migrating between his homes in Frankfurt and Mallorca for more than 20 years, while

Keller, a musician and writer, moved with his Spanish wife and young twin daughters from Cologne to Palma in 2007, and then moved to the Mallorcan countryside.

These authors have followed in the footsteps of many other Germans, and if the media and budget airlines have their way others will follow them and will make the island their home, their *Heimat*, by joining an established community, which includes German private health clinics, a German radio station and even German bakeries. Television programmes such as *Goodbye Deutschland. Die Auswanderer (The Emigrants)*, *Mein neues Leben (My New Life)* and *Lebe deinen Traum. Jetzt wird alles anders (Live Your Dream. Now Everything Is Going to Change)* document how ordinary people have followed their dream of starting a new life, after selling up and moving abroad.[6] On the one hand, these series are tempting audiences with images of warmth, beauty, tranquillity and cheap property; on the other hand, they show how dissatisfied these people are with life in Germany. Soap operas, including *Hotel Paradies*, set in Deià, and *Mallorca – Auf der Suche nach dem Paradies (In Search of Paradise)* further fulfil the fantasies of the German viewer. The figures suggest that never before in the history of the Federal Republic have so many people opted to leave the country, totalling 155,000 in 2006, an increase of 7% compared with the previous year.[7] While Switzerland is the most popular destination for German emigrants, Spain is ranked sixth out of a list of 20 countries (Anonymous, 2007a). Many are seeking the sun, a relaxed way of life, almost always in the countryside, improved employment prospects, culminating in a better standard of living, and, above all, happiness in a foreign land, where they retain their own culture and can construct transnational communities that transcend place.

In *Sunset Lives*, King *et al.* (2000: xi) employ the term 'residential tourists' 'to describe retired (and other) people who have settled permanently or semi-permanently in the same areas as those visited by large numbers of tourists'. They discuss how the problem of differentiating migrants from visitors is illustrated by the number of possible labels, which alternate according to the extent of long-term commitment to and contacts with the country of origin: permanently settled emigrants, dual residents, seasonal migrants, second-home owners, long-stay tourists. They point out that the influx of such groups into southern Europe has resulted in the 'creation of cultural enclaves with familiar, northern European types of services, where languages such as English and German are widely understood, and the deterioration of the quality of life in these enclaves' due to the congestion caused by the increased numbers (King *et al.*, 2000: 49). Mallorca is clearly a prime example. In a similar vein, Bousta's study of French retirees in Marrakesh shows how 'the impact on the socio-cultural environment could lead to the disappearance of the very atmosphere and lifestyle that the tourists come to find' (Bousta, 2007: 166).

In conjunction with this phenomenon, there has been a noticeable increase in the number of autobiographical novels as well as fictional tales of relocation and migration to sunnier climes, both in English and in German, so much so that it could be argued that this type of narrative has become a genre in its own right, and therefore warrants some form of labelling other than 'travel books'. These narratives of relocation have their 'home' in travel literature but their authors are not on a 'Grand Tour', nor are they imparting factual knowledge or advice for its own sake. While they or their protagonists have indeed migrated to another country and draw attention to the differences between their own and their host culture, it could be regarded as marginalising to employ a concept such as 'literature of migration', which is very broad and might suggest a negative outlook, attitude or experience. Recently, Tita Beaven has used the term 'settler narratives' to describe the autobiographical texts of English writers who now live in Spain and who explore their new sociocultural identity as well as offer the reader the possibility of imagining a life abroad through their writing (Beaven, 2007).[8] Tom Cheeseman refers to 'literature of settlement' and 'hyphenated writers' to explain the writings of third-generation Turkish immigrants living in Germany (Cheeseman, 2007). In my opinion, using the words 'settler' or 'settlement' is problematic due to the historical links to the writings of American, Australian and South African pioneers of the 19th century. Two centuries later, writings about life from outside a homeland may well be simply encapsulated in 'literature of place'. In this case Mallorca.

The German literary works featured in this chapter illustrate how the once casual attitude of a visitor towards a place or country, for instance the brief sojourn of a holidaymaker, or of someone on the run from their problems back home, becomes something much more meaningful, no longer a protracted love affair, but a serious relationship in terms of new job prospects, new friendships, a new lifestyle. Both the fictional and the factual literature about Germans in Mallorca does suggest that the island has undergone a form of colonisation, since so many young and elderly Germans choose to live as one community and create a Mallorcan *Heimat*, however negatively this might be regarded. At the same time, they blur the distinction between migration and tourism, because they oscillate in physical and psychological terms between their home and host country. Their migration may ultimately be seen as a migration to the concept of freedom, escape and new beginnings.

Notes

(1) For a detailed discussion of German exile writers living on Mallorca during the period of the Third Reich, see Reinhard Andress (2001).

(2) The impact of Germans on the lives of Mallorcans continues to this day. The German magazine *Mare: Die Zeitschrift der Meere (92)* had as its cover story in July 2012 'Mallorca und die Deutschen. Kellner, Gärtner, Zimmermädchen sagen uns, wer wir sind' (Mallorca and the Germans. Waiters, gardeners, maids tell us who we are), in which ordinary Mallorcans were able to express their opinions of German tourists and residents.

(3) The figures show that approximately 10 million tourists visited Mallorca in 2007, of whom 3.9 million were Germans. Officially 29,094 Germans live on the island; unofficially the figure is around 100,000. Stella Bettermann's article on Germans living on Mallorca features both their good and bad experiences (Bettermann, 2008).

(4) According to Roger Munns (2012), the German tabloid sells 65,000 copies a day, illustrating how strong the German network is on the island.

(5) Stefan's protagonist is typical of the 'flexible people' (coined by Richard Sennett in 1998) the global economy promotes. They repeatedly take on new tasks and are always ready to change their job, profession and residence. The promise of immediate satisfaction, such as lower living costs, becomes more important than religion, language and even family.

(6) Within the past decade there has been a boom in relocation programmes on British television. Among the many are *A Place in the Sun, Living in the Sun, Living the Dream, No Going Back, Get a New Life, Home from Home, Dream Holiday Home* and *There's No Place Like Home?*, in which expatriates reconsider returning to Britain.

(7) Further figures are available from the Federal Office of Statistics' press release of 30 May 2007 at http://www.destatis.de. Germany in 2009 was considered a country of emigration, with more exits than new entries registered.

(8) I am indebted to Tita Beaven for sending me a copy of her paper 'A life in the sun: Accounts of new lives abroad as intercultural narratives', which has since been published (Beaven, 2007).

References

Andress, R. (2001) Deutschsprachige Schriftsteller auf Mallorca (1931–36) – ein ungeschriebenes Kapitel in der deutschen Exilforschung. *German Studies Review* 24 (1), 115–143.

Anonymous (2007a) Besser leben im Heidi-Land. *Focus*, 17 February. At http://www.focus.de/magazin/archiv/auswanderer-besser-leben-im-heidi-land_aid_218355.html (accessed 30 September 2012).

Anonymous (2007b) Mallorca, die Insel der Schuldner. *Hamburger Abendblatt*, 15 August. At http://www.abendblatt.de/vermischtes/article874487/Mallorca-Die-Insel-der-Schuldner.html (accessed 30 September 2012).

Beaven, T. (2007) A life in the sun: Accounts of new lives abroad as intercultural narratives. *Language and Intercultural Communication* 7 (3), 188–202.

Bettermann, S. (2008) Mallorca für immer? *Focus*, 14 July. At http://www.focus.de/finanzen/karriere/perspektiven/arbeiten-im-ausland/tid-11348/lebensart-mallorca-fuer-immer_aid_317653.html (accessed 30 September 2012).

Boa, E. and Palfreyman, R. (2000) *Heimat. A German Dream: Regional Loyalties and National Identity in German Culture 1890–1990*. Oxford: Oxford University Press.

Böckler, M. (2002) *Sturm über Mallorca*. Munich: Knaur.

Bott, H., Ihlau, O. and Wiedemann, E. (1999) Rückkehr der Vandalen. *Spiegel Online*, 2 August. At http://www.spiegel.de/spiegel/print/d-14115464.html (accessed 30 September 2012).

Bousta, R.S. (2007) From tourism to new forms of migration: Europeans in Marrakesh. In C. Geoffroy and R. Sibley (eds) *Going Abroad: Travel, Tourism and Migration. Cross-cultural Perspectives on Mobility* (pp. 158–166). Newcastle upon Tyne: Cambridge Scholars Publishing.

Bull, P. (1997) Mass tourism in the Balearic Islands. An example of concentrated dependence. In D. Lockhart and D. Drakakis-Smith (eds) *Island Tourism: Trends and Prospects* (pp. 137–151). London: Pinter.

Caron, F. (1939) *Majorca: The Diary of a Painter*. London: Cassell.

Cheeseman, T. (2007) *Novels of Turkish German Settlement: Cosmopolite Fictions*. New York: Camden.

Heilmann, A. (2005) Das 17 deutsche Bundesland. *Spiegel Online*, 29 June. At http://www.spiegel.de/reise/europa/0,1518,362532,00.html (accessed 2 September 2010).

Huber, A. and O'Reilly, K. (2004) The construction of Heimat under conditions of individualised modernity: Swiss and British elderly migrants in Spain. *Ageing and Society* 24, 327–351.

Keller, S. (2011) *Papa ante Palma: Mallorca für Fortgeschrittene*. Berlin: Ullstein.

King, R., Warnes, T. and Williams, A. (2000) *Sunset Lives: British Retirement Migration to the Mediterranean*. Oxford: Berg.

Knorr, P. (2011) *Mallorca: Insel der Inseln*. Reinbek bei Hamburg: Rowohlt.

Menzel, E. (2006) *Eine Finca auf Mallorca oder: Geckos im Gästebett*. Westerstede: Reise Know-How.

Munns, R. (2012) Majorca residents fed up with Germans. At http://www.abcarticle directory.com (accessed 10 June 2012).

Roth, M. (2009) *Ein Jahr auf Mallorca: Reise in den Alltag*. Freiburg: Herder.

Sand, G. (1956) *Winter in Majorca*. London: Cassell.

Sennett, R. (1998) *The Corrosion of Character: The Personal Consequences of Work in the New Capitalism*. New York: Norton.

Stefan, U. (2004) *Hüte dich vor den Bergen und dem Wind und den Deutschen, die im Ausland sind! Eine deutsch-mallorquinische Episode*. Aachen: Karin Fischer.

Wachowiak, H. (2009) Trip patterns of German tourists. *Advances in Hospitality and Leisure* 5, 185–203.

4 Commercial Cinema, Location Shooting and 'the Tourism Effect'

Anthony David Barker

In the 2008 English-language film version of Jose Saramago's *Ensaio sobre a Cegueira*, entitled *Blindness*, directed by Fernando Meirelles, the exteriors of Saramago's unnamed city were played by parts of São Paulo, Montevideo and Toronto. No realist protocols were breached by this and no one seems to care; *anyplace* could be composed of many places. Indeed, Vancouver in Canada has been playing specific, *named* Northern American cities now for over 40 years in so-called 'runaway productions' and US television crime series because of its 'relatively generic urbanity' (Walls, 2013: 9). Films are shot in locations which are filming-friendly (that is, open, cooperative and either economical or providing tax breaks), regardless of the name of the place in the shooting script. Iconic cities like New York and Washington, London, Paris and Rome have been the exceptions to this rule. But in most other instances, the look of a location has always served, and been subordinate to, the narrative and/or aesthetic requirements of the movie or the economics of movie-making. In relatively few cases and only relatively recently have the images obtained directly served the commercial interests of the places and locations used. I use the word *directly* advisedly because it is impossible to quantify the effect of images and references that are constantly and multifariously before us.

The established distinction between 'organic' sources of information about destinations (word of mouth, photos in circulation, general reference in the media, etc.) and 'induced' sources – those which are essentially targeted and promotional in nature (Campo *et al.*, 2011: 141) – is not an easy one to apply where film-making is concerned. A film may work strenuously to glamorise a setting but have no ulterior motive beyond the film's own internal priorities for doing so. The *effect*, however, may be little different from the directly promotional. In the general sense of these terms, very little in the movie-making process is 'organic'; nearly everything is 'induced'. What might make the distinction valid is when one can identify a clear pecuniary motive (budgetary contributions, low-cost services, easy access, tax breaks, etc.) for the producers of these film images to make them in particular ways and in particular places.

In this chapter I will offer a historical perspective on how criteria for the use of location shooting came into being and will look at some of the instances where a film has gone on to provide benefits for the locations featured. This is most clearly the case when a relatively unknown place comes to touristic prominence. Many films show the Taj Mahal in India or the Eiffel Tower in Paris but it has hardly been decisive for these landmarks that they have done so, for they have consistently been popular places to visit and familiar images, even for those who do not travel. The particular object of my attention is the deliberate intention to exploit exotic or charismatic locations for their ability to attract visitors; one assumes that this strategy only has much meaning in an age of mass tourism. Aristocratic Grand Touring can be found from the 17th century onwards and bourgeois travellers with their *Baedekers* and railway timetables are plentiful in the 19th century. But the mass movement of people internationally is largely a 20th-century phenomenon (and a post-mid-century phenomenon at that).

Filmmakers from their earliest days out on the west coast of America during the silent era were aware of a movie's capacity to generate revenues apart from those simply accruing from cinema ticket sales. The moguls who took over the American film industry in the second and third decades of the 20th century were businessmen from scrap metal trading, second-hand clothes dealing and the running of amusement arcades and vaudeville theatres. Of the four Warner brothers, two were film-men and two were salesmen. It was therefore second nature for them to try to sell other commodities along the way, most notably food and drink to accompany the movie-going experience. But it was not long before it was realised that what is in a movie may have a profound effect on consumer behaviour. The domains of fashions in clothing, make-up, hair products, jewellery and smoking requisites are perhaps the most obvious examples of cinema's ability to influence.

The film which perhaps best encapsulates the advantages and disadvantages of using exotic locations in commercial film production in the early years of sound cinema is RKO's *Flying Down to Rio* (1933). The thing for which the film is best known, its original pairing of Fred Astaire and Ginger Rogers, is not of interest here. Indeed, the title alone foregrounds all that one might need to think about in the early exploitation of glamorous locales. The first thing to observe is that virtually no one did fly down to Rio in 1933, inside or outside the film. The film was shot almost in its entirety in the USA. RKO would have dispatched a second unit to get some general street scenes, public buildings and monuments; more importantly, that same crew would have obtained aerial shots of Rio to accompany arrival sequences and to use as back-projections for the film's musical finale, which has been described as 'the famous aerial ballet climax … with scores of chorus girls, anchored to the wings of airplanes, dancing and doffing their clothes for all of Rio to see' (Jewell & Harbin, 1982: 69). In fact, none of the performers or the main crew left Hollywood.[1] As a classic Depression-era movie, the title evokes the need for escape ('flight' in the other sense of the word). Rio/Brazil is far enough away from the experience of ordinary Americans to constitute a fantasy land of dance, music and permanent partying. Indeed, cultural difference between North and South America in the film is wholly understood as an affectionate competition between jazz/swing and samba/carioca. The real and thoroughly modern nexus between north and south, however, is not music but flight in its other sense, that of modern aviation. The promise of being able to fly to and away from places is what is being held out and that would only increase over the coming decades.

RKO had attempted an extravaganza uniting musical performance, mass transportation and escape in *Melody Cruise* earlier that year (Barrios, 1995: 405). This film had limited appeal but when the same producer, Lou Brock, transferred his ideas to the 'sexier' medium of aviation, the formula became a big success. Flying had been a central preoccupation of film since the Oscar success of William Wellman's *Wings*[2] (1927) and the spectacular effects of Howard Hughes's *Hell's Angels* (1930). These films had been about fighter pilots and aerial combat; what is new in 1933 is the attention given to commercial aviation. *Flying Down to Rio*'s plot begins in Miami, which was the hub for transportation flights to the islands of Cuba, Haiti, etc., and the film was made a few short years after the founding of the company Pan Am. The head of production at RKO, former military pilot and explorer Merian C. Cooper,[3] sat on the board of Pan Am from the beginning. Some of the men who bankrolled RKO and other studios, notably Cornelius and Jock Whitney, were stakeholders in Pan Am. Howard Hughes, who bought into RKO at the end of the decade and who briefly was its sole owner, was a dominant shareholder in Trans World Airlines (TWA). These were the only two US aviation companies to operate internationally, and which came to dominate long-distance plane travel, especially the transatlantic routes, for over three decades after the Second World War.

The conditions for mass tourism were laid during the 1930s. At first it was all fantasy. Pan Am was set up to compete for airmail contracts, delivering to the islands and to Central America. Aviation travel was very expensive and could really only press its speed advantage over water. Over land, the train was still the safer and cheaper option. Ironically, the plane which we see Gene Raymond pilot in *Flying Down to Rio*, the two-seater Monocoupe 90, could not reach Haiti, much less Brazil. When routes did begin flying after 1931, it was by seaplane, with refuelling, using the Sikorsky S-38 and S-40. Scheduled services coast to coast in America began in 1930, but the journey took 36 hours with an overnight stop in Kansas. The putting into service of the Douglas DC1 in 1934 cut the time to around 13 hours. Transatlantic routes began in 1937 but either by circuitous and expensive routes (via Newfoundland and Ireland) or by seaplane (via Bermuda and the Azores) to Lisbon. Regular flights from the USA to the UK began in 1939 but were halted almost immediately by the Second World War. It is estimated that relative to contemporary purchase prices, a transatlantic flight in 1939 cost 10–15 times more than it does today.

Why provide all this information on early plane travel? Well, without a means to deliver tourists in large numbers to foreign destinations, there was little or nothing for the film studios to be promoting. It did not matter how attractive Rio was; hardly anyone could afford to fly down there, except for those doing big business. This situation continued to persist until the end of the war, and even beyond that. There was one illuminating exception, however. Orson Welles flew down to Rio to make his documentary *It's All True* in 1941, as part of a State Department-sponsored 'good neighbour' policy where, during wartime, it was felt that North and South Americans should learn more about each other and public money should be put into promoting this exchange of knowledge and mutual respect. Welles began to shoot footage for RKO on schools of samba, carnival and incidentally on the favellas of Brazil.[4] The Brazilian government became suspicious of what looked like socialist sympathies, RKO was irritated by the costs and Welles was sacked. Although he continued with his picture using a skeleton crew, the footage was impounded, some of it was dumped in Santa Monica Bay and the rest was placed unedited and unreleased in a vault in Salt Lake City (Leeming, 1989: 328). Welles hoped to buy it back, edit it and release it himself, but even by hiring himself out on acting assignments he could never raise the money. A film with the worthy intention of promoting Brazil and Rio de Janeiro to Americans was junked because the political priorities that had inspired it shifted and there was no pecuniary motive to compensate for this. *It's All True* (1941/42) became a tax write-off for RKO.

Merian C. Cooper is a man whose name keeps cropping up in this history. So does that of Lowell Thomas. There was a form of cinema which existed to promote places around the world: the travelogue. Indeed, it is older than cinema. Burton Holmes had pioneered touring slide-show travelogues in 1893 and continued to exhibit them until 1914. These took the form of an evocative commentary delivered over a series of well composed images. Eventually, as motion picture technology improved, short passages of moving images were incorporated. Lowell Thomas (journalist, travel writer and broadcaster famous as the man who turned T.E. Lawrence into 'Lawrence of Arabia'[5]) worked as a radio broadcaster with CBS in the 1930s and was simultaneously the voice of Fox Movietone newsreels until 1952. Within Fox Movietone, Thomas made innumerable films about exotic faraway places, all rendered in his authoritative upbeat voiceover style, a style, I should say, which became very vulnerable to parody in the 1950s and '60s. These were all relatively cheap programme-fillers but they had what are now unquantifiable effects in stimulating an interest in the outside world for mass American audiences. The devastation of the war (1939–45) and its aftermath in Europe meant that it was difficult to exploit that interest until the 1950s. But, with rising affluence in the USA during that decade, it then became possible to do so.

Before addressing the general situation in the 1950s, I would like to review one fascinating business cul de sac. Thomas, Cooper and impresario/ filmmaker Mike Todd got together in the early 1950s to produce films in Cinerama. With two exceptions and despite all appearances to the contrary, Cinerama was to become the apotheosis of the film travelogue. It is axiomatic about widescreen cinema that it exists to display landscape to best effect. The first five films in Cinerama were essentially travelogues: *This Is Cinerama* (1952), *Christmas Holiday* (1955), *Seven Wonders of the World* (1956), *Search for Paradise* (1957) and *Cinerama South Sea Adventure* (1958). Needless to say, they were all shot expensively in three-strip format with cumbersome equipment on location and they required cinemas showing them to be customised to maximise the widescreen effect. This reduced audiences and increased costs, at a time when other studios were expanding the use of cheaper widescreen colour processes. Mike Todd himself jumped ship to film, in his own Todd-AO format, the blockbuster *Around the World in 80 Days* (1956). Todd's big-budget adaptation of Jules Verne's globe-trotting novel-turned-travelogue in the mid-1950s is hugely indicative of a rising appetite for foreign travel, the cinema's ability to glamorise destinations in Technicolor and the provision of transport systems to satisfy it. Many films which use extensive world travel as their subject have become stories about their own logistics. Ironically for a narrative about earthbound travel (Verne's balloon-travel being the exception), the final credits of *Around the World in 80 Days* acknowledge the assistance of no less than 22 airlines in its making. A second irony is that the film celebrates 'Anglo-European global mobility … through a combination of technology and tenacity' (Grant,

2005: 158) at exactly the time many of the countries visited had just achieved, or were struggling for, independence from European colonialism.

The breakthrough film for promoting European venues to Americans was William Wyler's *Roman Holiday* (1953). It succeeded more effectively than the Cinerama films precisely because the promotion is artfully woven into a compelling romantic narrative. Perhaps surprisingly, but wisely, the decision was taken to shoot it in black and white so that the stunning Roman backgrounds would not overwhelm the performances of the romantic leads, Gregory Peck and Audrey Hepburn. It is still the case, however, that Paramount did not gain from promoting Rome as a travel venue as such. After the war, American companies found that they had large amounts of revenue trapped in European countries, generated by their huge backlog of unreleased-in-Europe films from the war years, and as a direct consequence of recovering nations not allowing so much foreign exchange to exit their territories. At the same time, living standards and labour costs were rising sharply in America. It therefore made sense to shoot pictures in Europe for international audiences using this money, in this particular case on a modest budget of $1.5 million. *Roman Holiday* is the pure product of this logic, as well as that of an unequal distribution of wealth whereby many Americans could afford to holiday in Europe whereas few Europeans could holiday in America. As you watch the film, it is clear that liberated Italy provided full cooperation to the filmmakers, as 10 of its most famous squares and monuments are paraded in the film; roads were cleared for Hepburn and Peck's famous scooter-rides around Rome and all the interiors were shot on Rome's Cinecittà Studio sound stages at relatively low rental cost. Now, *Roman Holiday* takes its place alongside the films of Frederico Fellini as works which have helped to form the popular imagination about Rome. Stills from the film are on sale all over Rome and tourists can easily purchase a *Roman Holiday*-illustrated calendar for any given year.

A similar kind of logic informs Hitchcock's comedy thriller *To Catch a Thief* (1955), starring Cary Grant and Grace Kelly, also made by Paramount in Europe but for around $2.5 million. This film foregrounds two things: the French Riviera around Cannes and Monaco; and Paramount's new wide-screen VistaVision filming process. In 1950s cinema, the need to compete with the dingy black and white images of television meant that money was made available for both widescreen and colour shooting on location. Television of the 1950s had the very greatest difficulty in leaving purpose-built studios. Making things deliberately big is reflected in the range of titles of 1950s films (*The Big Country, Giant, South Pacific,* etc.) as well as the often biblical and epic subjects chosen. Historical subjects, however, were dubiously useful for promoting travel – generally only contemporary stories could do that. As an old-school filmmaker, Hitchcock valued Hollywood and its studio facilities as his place of work and so only half of *To Catch a Thief* was shot in Europe. All interiors were mocked up back in California. The film is, however, remarkable for being one of the first to use extensive helicopter shooting. Hitchcock's talented second unit collected these aerial establishing and chase scenes in France, after principal shooting had finished, using doubles for the star performers. Lush colour, attractive costumes and locations and charismatic performances, together with the high-profile marriage of Grace Kelly and Prince Rainier following the making of the film (which helped to superimpose a *Roman Holiday*-like fairytale over the film) made the Riviera a destination for a generation of visitors from America. As Joel W. Finler writes:

> *To Catch a Thief* … was one of the first widescreen pictures to be filmed abroad, and this was naturally considered to be an important selling point by Paramount. Thus, the posters for the film stated, 'You'll feel that you're actually on the beautiful Riviera in Vistavision.' (Finler, 1992: 105)

Cary Grant's follow-up romantic film, with Deborah Kerr, *An Affair to Remember* (1957), similarly travels between America and the French Riviera, both as narrative and as a film in production.

It may seem something of a side issue but it has some relevance here: inward tourism has always been more important for America. Most Americans do not leave America; they do not own passports. Among the world's 20 most visited places, 9 are in America (6 in the top 10). These tend to be customised, man-made holiday venues (Disneyland, Las Vegas) with highly developed corporate and promotional structures rather than historical or naturally occurring phenomena (Niagara Falls, the Great Wall of China). Another important factor which shaped the 1950s was the Cold War, when it was felt in Washington that Americans were insufficiently enthusiastic about or interested in their own American landscape. Being a frontier nation, Americans had not always had the leisure to appreciate nature while fighting with it for survival. In the 1950s, certain agencies in Washington felt that a campaign should be launched to make Americans more patriotic about their countryside. The main agent of this campaign was to be the National Geographic organisation, based in Washington, which would photograph, enhance and bring to the attention of Americans the glory that is their country. Hollywood also had a role in this. Some of the films representing America as big and beautiful (*The Big Country, Shane, Raintree County, Niagara, Cimarron*, leading into the Cinerama classic *How the West Was Won* (1962)) also had a part to play in this campaign. In particular, the films of John Ford were valued for their celebration of Monument Valley in Colorado; Cornelius Whitney himself was the producer of Ford's most celebrated western *The Searcher* (1956), which makes extensive use of Monument Valley. Many epics of the mid-1950s and early 1960s had a nation-uniting sub-theme, as the USA attempted to weather the difficult and divisive civil rights period. The sense of a loved and shared homeland was integral to the ideology of 'one nation under God' and this is very clearly reflected in the way America put its own landscape up on the screen. Clearly, the images were 'induced' for a wider political purpose but that would not have prevented them from having a significant effect on inward tourism in the USA.

The 1960s saw a more genuinely internationalist cinema emerging, with Europe regaining both its confidence and its prosperity. Part of that prosperity was the promise of and greater access to holiday travel. The greater mobility in people's lives is reflected in the greater mobility in film production: directors like Truffaut (*Fahrenheit 451*), Antonioni (*Blow-Up*) and Polanski (*Repulsion*), for example, came to England to make films, and subsequently made films in the USA. We can see this greater mobility at work in British cinema of the 1960s too. The film *The Italian Job* (1969) has extended sequences filmed in the mountains of northern Italy and on the streets of Turin (its famous chase scenes). The James Bond film franchise began in the 1960s and to some extent represents the *Zeitgeist*. The Cold War/spy film took audiences to glamorised locations around the world, with the specific intention of promoting a globe-trotting lifestyle. The fifth Bond film for example, *You Only Live Twice* (1967), as well as having principal filming in Pinewood Studios and at English and Scottish locations, takes its audience to Malaga, Gibraltar and Andalusia, Bermuda and the Bahamas, Norway, Hong Kong and the main site of its action, various locations in Japan. To be sure, the locations were a background to action in a plot-driven narrative form, but it is clear that part of Bond's mystique was his propensity to pop up in many of the world's most attractive places. The marker of this is the use of onscreen place captions to assist the fast-paced narrative and slick scene changes. Other elements have modified over the years with this franchise but the compulsion to snapshot the world's beauty spots has not. *Moonraker* (1979) is set in Venice, Paris, Argentina, Amazonia in Brazil and Florida, as well as London. *Quantum of Solace* (2008) makes extended visits to Chile, Panama, Mexico, Tuscany and the Italian lakes, Madrid and London. In this sense, the right to travel and experience the world was placed alongside the Bond series' licensing of a right to easy sex and violence beyond the law. Thus, in the more conflict-driven 1960s, the Riviera adult fairytales of the previous decade were replaced by a more narcissistic, even sadistic, sense of entitlement to do as one wished in places that ravish the senses. The final sequence of *From Russia with Love* (1963), for example, pulls back from an implied sex scene in a gondola to reveal the splendour of the canals of Venice.

American cinema of the 1970s vacated the studio in search of the mean streets of US cities. These films, however, are permeated with a sour social outlook; they exhibit so powerful a desire to find the dirty underside of public and private life that they deliberately court a negative 'ugly' aesthetic. A founding text for the 1970s is Hopper's *Easy Rider* (1967), where the protagonists set off on what might easily become a travelogue, a journey to discover America. But what they see from their motorbikes is poverty, injustice and repression. For a decade, the counterculture commanded the heights in Hollywood and the counterculture saw as its mission finding fault, not to praise. Such beauty as can be found in the 1970s insidiously glamorises the Mafia in the *Godfather* films (1972 and 1974) or ambiguously criticises war in *Apocalypse Now* (1979). This wholesale rejection of cinema as business was as far as one could get from the promotion of people, places and products. Nicolas Roeg's *Don't Look Now* (1974) is one of the great film evocations of a European city, Venice. Yet filmed in autumnal half-light out of the visiting season and containing haunted characters recovering from the loss of a child by drowning, no film has ever striven so hard indirectly to dissuade its audience from going to its location. Death, decay, danger, violence and indifference are in every carefully composed shot. Also, it is worth observing that one of the dominant forms of 1970s cinema was the disaster or collective jeopardy movie, in which planes crashed, ships sank, imposing buildings collapsed and weather threatened the lives of people, often when they were in holiday mood. Big-budget, lavishly photographed mayhem was not likely to promote either travel or luxury accommodation; indeed, it made *abroad* in general seem very dangerous, and therefore was in consonance with the wave of terrorist activity in the 1970s, where ships, planes, airports and railway stations were preferred targets, as they have once again become today.

In the 1980s, the deregulation of communications and media industries started the process of synergising the production, distribution and exhibition of entertainment products. In the first instance it was cable delivery and new forms of home entertainment that hastened this process, but it was further accelerated by rapid market saturation in telecommunications and the internet. The business consequence of this was the formation of huge multimedia conglomerates that held assets in all the various leisure industries. The logic of their position was that they could use one business to promote another. For example, holdings in the newspaper and magazine publishing domain could ensure that reviews of new films made by their own film production divisions were largely favourable, as would be chat show discussion and promotion on owned television channels and affiliates. According to Janet Wasko (1994: 41–65), by the 1990s, conglomerates like Time–Warner, Paramount Communications, the Disney Corporation, News Corporation/Fox, Sony/Columbia and Matsushita/Universal began to acquire entertainment portfolios which included resorts and hotels in holiday and leisure destinations. Finally, the film industry was achieving the synergy of owning both locations in which to shoot and venues to promote. When Billy Wilder shot *Some Like It Hot* (1959) at the Coronado Hotel in San Diego, masquerading as a Miami hotel, it was near impossible for the Coronado, San Diego (or Miami for that matter) to benefit from the deception. By the time we get to Spielberg's *Castaway* (1997), the logo of the real delivery company FedEx is all over the picture (FedEx allowed the brand to be used although it equivocated about the picture and put no money into it because it did not want to be associated with the plane-crash which initiates the drama). By the time of the film comedy *Forgetting Sarah Marshall* (2008), we have all our protagonists decamping to Hawaii and staying in a real and routinely named holiday venue, the Turtle Bay Resort, owned by Benchmark Hospitality International, an influential US hotel and resort chain which must have paid handsomely for so much publicity.

Yet, in another sense, the ability to exploit movie exposure for touristic ends depends upon the general enthusiasm and/or the movie literacy of audiences. What makes a person want to follow up on a pleasurable movie experience to the extent of visiting places where movies are shot? Hellmann and Weber-Hof's 2006 publication *On Location: Cities of the World in Film* and the Intellect books series 'World Film Locations', which has individual volumes on a dozen cities, including London, New York, Los Angeles and Paris, strongly suggests that they do. In 1995 the British Tourist Authority and BAFTA (the British Academy of Film and Television Arts), in association with General Motors/Vauxhall, produced a movie map of Britain (Liddall, 1995). This map reveals 186 locations in Britain where films and television shows were shot. Once again, the map hails itself as a triumph of synergy:

> The British car industry and the British cinema both celebrate their centenaries in 1996. As they have grown up together, the two industries have had an enormous impact on our society and on each other. Cars are the stars in many films and the cinema provides a wonderful record of the car's growing and changing role in all our lives....

As we look forward to the next 100 years of motoring and movie-going, we hope you will enjoy visiting the locations on the Vauxhall Movie Map.

The cover of the map contains pictures from the movies *Loch Ness*, *Jack and Sarah* and *Carrington* (all 1995 productions and therefore able to benefit from the publicity the map afforded) and from *Four Weddings and a Funeral* (1994), the film that had put the British film industry back on the map (pun intended) after a period of relative international anonymity. *Four Weddings* had been an enormous and unexpected international success precisely because it had revived an interest in British pageantry, architecture, landscape and social ritual. It is fair to say that this is done in a cleverer way than is commonly found in movie productions. The funeral in the north-east is followed by a scene contemplating the sea which purports to be the local coastline but is in fact the Essex estuary near London, some 200 miles south. A careful reading of the map will not give you this information, nor will it lay bare much of film-making's other sleights of hand. The map contains a disclaimer by the British Tourist Authority about the accuracy of some of the information it might contain. To offer a more cynical view of this caveat, we might reflect that movies construct imaginary places, and the tourist industry is more than happy to collude with these (partial) falsifications.

Four Weddings and a Funeral initiated a decade-long sequence of movies which Paul Dave has written about as a cycle of 'London fairytales and idylls' (Dave, 2006: 45–60). These films, which include *Sliding Door* (1998), *Notting Hill* (1999), the *Bridget Jones* films (2001 and 2004) and *Love Actually* (2003) are mostly made by Working Title Pictures, written by Richard Curtis and exploit London venues as places of communitarian harmony and romantic possibility. *Love Actually*, in particular, selectively films London at Christmas time as a place of enchantment, encapsulated by the film's title and theme tune 'Love Is All Around Us'. Following 9/11 (but before 7/7), London could claim to be one of the (few) places abroad where American tourists could feel nearly at home and totally safe. The film is therefore appropriating a brief window of opportunity. After *Four Weddings*, Working Title and its partner Universal began a strategy of targeting US audiences with British product, to the extent of using American stars and releasing British films there before London itself. This cycle also provides an interesting and current example of the ambiguous power of movie fandom. The travel bookshop featured in the movie *Notting Hill* announced in early August 2011 it was to close, for lack of customers interested in travel literature. Various celebrities and well-wishers organised themselves to keep the shop open. Because it featured in a movie, the campaign achieved a measure of popular support and media coverage. This was not enough, however, according to Laura Bly (2001), to prevent its final closure on 10 September that year. Apparently, the shop had many visitors drawn to it by the film but few interested in purchasing a book. Indeed, both parties were disappointed by the interaction, for the interior of the shop was wholly different from the one appearing in the film. That had been constructed on an altogether different site just for the film. The fate of print culture, now more than ever, seems to rest upon the life support of film adaptation, but sometimes not even this is enough.

By the time we get to the 1990s, we are in the era of the Travel Channel and like-minded shows on television. A vast amount of (not usually dis-interested) information about where to go, how to get there and what it is like to be there is being piped into people's living-rooms. The final examples of the way movies have been used to promote the tourist potential of specific places are the well known ones of *Mamma Mia!*, *Vicky Cristina Barcelona* and *In Bruges* (all made in 2008). It has to be said that whatever one's view of them as works of film art, they have been tremendously successful in that precise area of delivering relatively low-cost publicity to places of touristic interest.

The Greek islands are a very well known and appreciated tourist venue but they have not been exhaustively promoted in the cinemas of other nations. There was an American movie *Summer Lovers* (1982), starring Peter Gallagher and Daryl Hannah, which managed a fusion of romantic tryst and gorgeous locations on Crete, Delos and Mykonos. No data is forthcom-ing but one imagines it helped to bring many young backpackers to the Greek islands. *Shirley Valentine* (1989), adapted from Willy Russell's stage play, repeated the experience on Mykonos for the disaffected, middle-aged and unhappily married. *Mamma Mia!*'s production team of Tom Hanks, Rita Wilson and Gary Goetzman had been extremely successful in making all things Greek popular in America with *My Big Fat Greek Wedding* (2002), which briefly became the most lucrative wholly independent movie produc-tion of all time. *Mamma Mia!*, adapted from a stage musical showcasing the music of Abba, is a more tongue-in-cheek confection, appealing not just to the holiday-seeking set but also to those wishing to relocate or retire southward. It therefore offered itself to a vast constituency of people who consume the television kitsch of travel, lifestyle and home-swap shows. There is a lucrative real estate industry selling retirement homes in southern Europe, especially Spain, to moneyed and ageing northern Europeans. *Mamma Mia!* appeals to both the romantic young and the property-minded middle-aged. The island of Skopelos has been quick to rebrand itself on websites as the *Mamma Mia!* island, with Kalokairi beach (used in the film) given prominence. The photogenic Agios Iaonnis Chapel at the end of a long promontory, employed in the film for the climactic wedding scenes, now has to sift numerous applications from couples who want to get married there. There are around 20 'Getting married in Greece' websites catering for people who may feel this desire, many of which are adapted or disguised travel agencies. These websites do not neglect to mention the movie in their first paragraph and have many links to other sites discussing and showing appropriate clips from the film. It is doubtful whether Greece as a nation had to put any money into the film; the pre-existing musical with its plot set on a Greek island must have forced the producers to scout locations there. But Greece has nonetheless reaped a rich reward.

Although one imagines the phrase was meant positively (and surely could equally well be applied to *Mamma Mia!*), one blogger, Luke Ford, perceptively described *Vicky Cristina Barcelona* as 'spectacular real estate porn':

> Ultimately, though, Vicky Christina Barcelona is still a worthwhile endeavor. An enjoyable romp filled the requisite angst and passion of Woody Allen's better efforts. Best of all, there's Spain and Barcelona. The landscapes, people and architecture provide even more spectacular real estate porn than Melinda & Melinda. Not only does it make you want to go to Barcelona, it will make you feel like you've lived there and loved it. (Ford, 2008)

Never has a narrative been more lavishly moulded to show off the assets of its host culture. This is a new form of the Americans-in-Europe film of the 1950s. Here, the initiative was taken by the Generalitat of Barcelona, which, according to various sources,[6] put up around $1.5 million to have the film shot in its locality and thereby to give greater visibility to Catalan culture. It also provided general access to the resources of the region for the purpose of seeing it promoted in an internationally distributed feature film. The closing credits of the film also list a cornucopia of Catalan and Spanish branded products which appear in the film. No doubt the stimulus for the film was the sincere mutual admiration of Catalan officials for Woody Allen's film achievements and of Allen for a less stuffy and judgemental approach to art and life which he found and celebrates in Europe in general, and Spain in particular. It is easy to believe that the film's extended detour to Oviedo was marked by a similar mutual admiration, which had led that city to place a life-size statue of Woody Allen in the streets there in 2002. The filmic result, however, is the mismatching of attractive or cloying (depending on your point of view) creative people against a background of indiscreet product placement and naked cultural boosterism. In particular, the character of Antonio's father, who is so high-minded that he will not allow his poetry to be read, much less translated, is grating and sits badly with a highly capitalised art form like cinema, where you have to find huge sums of money to begin production, usually with many commercial strings attached, and where you have to hop on a publicity carousel in order to have your film seen widely. This is why few of *Vicky Cristina Barcelona*'s self-styled artists, like the shepherds who rarely actually tend to sheep in pastoral, have to concern themselves with selling anything and so can devote their time to love-making and flattering each other. Perversely, there may be more coherence in a work like Michael Bay's *The Island* (2005), where Scarlett Johansson's character looks at a real advertisement of herself promoting the Calvin Klein fragrance Eternity Moment. Bay is an acknowledged master of saturation product placement – his recent *Transformers* (2009) has 47 paid-for products in it, contrasted with the more modest 35 in *The Island*. In these films, there is no pretense that it is not all about the money, or that one can find a context in which to create without these sorts of consideration.

In Bruges seems to me to be the most artistically successful of the three films of 2008, although it performed the worst at the box office. Bruges possesses many medieval treasures and architectural delights, yet it is probably the least well known and visited of the three locations. What makes the film work is that it finds an appropriate narrative justification for the extended exploration of Bruges (criminals lying low in an unlikely hiding place) but does not sacrifice characterisation to location. The film proves to be a contemporary morality play set against the backcloth of works by earlier moralist/creators like Bruegel and Hieronymus Bosch. Bruges is an interesting discovery but remains modest about its assets, and indeed the film maintains a running critique on the ennui of sight-seeing as Ray (the character played by Colin Farrell) shows limited interest in the city in which he is unwillingly holed up. *In Bruges* piques our interest in the city without trying to hype it (it is filmed out of season and often at night), and it does so, remarkably, in a low-key thriller without winning characters, that is, those normally found in romantic comedy.

Finally, it is worth referencing the recent Peter Weir film *The Way Back* (2010). Weir's career (and the international recognition of Australian film culture) began with his haunting *Picnic at Hanging Rock* back in 1975. Perhaps no single film has ever catapulted a national landscape into international prominence as comprehensively as Weir's photography of the Australian outback and Ayers Rock has done. His 2010 work was financed in part by National Geographic; it deals with the escape of prisoners from a wartime Siberian gulag and their tortuous journey southward across the Asian mainland via the steppes, forests, tundra, desert and the Himalayan mountains to reach India. Ostensibly a true-life narrative (although the honesty of its literary source has been strenuously contested[7] and in any event the movie treatment is not especially faithful to it), the story is unvaried and harrowing; one by one the fugitives die off until the few hardy survivors arrive in India. Its *raison d'être* seems to be displaying expansive scenery, human figures splendidly photographed moving through a vast landscape, hence the involvement of National Geographic. Hoberman (2011) identifies it as one of a newly emergent film genre, the 'movie as ordeal', like *The Passion of the Christ* (2004), *United 93* (2006), *Hunger* (2008) or *127 Hours* (2010). One might think that the one thing such an attritional movie would lack is touristic appeal; nor would such torturous experience have enjoyed the cooperation of the tourist authorities of Siberia, the ex-Soviet republics, Tibet and China. As I suggested, it is usually only romantic comedies that sell holidays, and preferably widescreen or musical movies at that. So, because there was no commercial interest in any of these places, nor they in the film, Siberia could be mocked up by Bulgarian locations and the Gobi desert substituted by camera-friendly Morocco. Only the Himalayas could not be faked. Not even carrying the National Geographic imprint is enough to guarantee authenticity.

Travel and tourism is becoming such big business for all international players irrespective of their political ideology that we can look forward to a time when no parts of the world are shut off to the location shooter, and when film crews will come expecting local subsidies and other benefits for choosing to shoot in these sites. What began purely as the logic of fantasy to sell cinema tickets is being conscripted as compelling and original marketing to sell the four corners of the world, alongside those cinema seats. Media synergy, as is its wont, is going global.

Notes

(1) Likewise, the scenes of Rio de Janeiro in Hitchcock's *Notorious* (RKO, 1946) are studio stock footage.
(2) *Wings* contains one of the earliest and most notorious instances of branded product placement, when one of the pilots eats Hershey's chocolate, puts the bar down and for no very good reason the camera gives us a close-up of it.
(3) Planes figure prominently in the climactic scenes of Cooper's own directorial triumph *King Kong* (1933).
(4) Ironically, it appears there are now popular tours run through the favellas in which the savagely violent *Cidade de Deus* (2002) was shot.
(5) The character Jackson Bentley, played by Arthur Kennedy, in David Lean's *Lawrence of Arabia* (1962) is based on Lowell Thomas.
(6) There is no general agreement about how much money the production received from Spanish public sources. This instance highlights the difficulty in obtaining financial details about investment in films for largely promotional purposes. Chris Evans

(2010) writes that the Catalan government invested \$21 million in film production in 2009.

(7) Slavomir Rawicz's *The Long Walk* was an international best-seller when published in 1956. A BBC radio show suggested in 2006 that there was not a shred of evidence to support what is described in the book and documents which suggest that it did not happen, at least to Rawicz (see Levinson, 2006).

References

Barrios, R. (1995) *A Song in the Dark: The Birth of the Musical Film*. Oxford: Oxford University Press.

Bly, L. (2011) Final chapter for Hugh Grant's Notting Hill travel book store. *USA Today*, 8 September.

Campo, L.R., Brea, J.A.F. and Muniz, D.R.T. (2011) Tourist destination image formed by the cinema: Barcelona positioning through the feature film *Vicky Cristina Barcelona*. *European Journal of Tourism, Hospitality and Recreation* 2 (1), 137–154.

Dave, P. (2006) *Visions of England: Class and Culture in Contemporary Cinema*. Oxford: Berg.

Evans, C. (2010) The celluloid city. *Metropolitan – Barcelona*, 29 March. At http://www.barcelona-metropolitan.com/articles/the-celluloid-city (accessed 21 October 2013).

Finler, J.W. (1992) *Alfred Hitchcock: The Hollywood Years*. London: B.T. Batsford.

Ford, L. (2008) Review of *Vicky Cristina Barcelona*. At http://lukeford.net/blog/?p=4939 (accessed 21 October 2013).

Grant, B.K. (2005) 1956: Movies and the crack of doom. In M. Pomerance (ed.) *American Cinema of the 1950s* (pp. 155–176). Oxford: Berg.

Hellmann, C. and Weber-Hof, C. (2006) *On Location: Cities of the World in Film*. Munich: Bucher.

Hoberman, J. (2011) The way back is a grueling trip. *The Village Voice*, 11 January. At http://www.villagevoice.com/2011-01-19/film/the-way-back-is-a-grueling-trip (accessed 21 October 2013).

Jewell, R.B. and Harbin, V. (1982) *The RKO Story*. London: Octopus Books.

Leeming, B. (1989) *Orson Welles: A Biography*. London: Penguin Books.

Levinson, H. (2006) Walking the talk? BBC News website, 30 October. At http://news.bbc.co.uk/2/hi/6098218.stm (accessed 21 October 2013).

Liddall, J. (ed.) (1995) *The Vauxhall Movie Map: Film & TV Locations in Britain*. London: British Tourist Authority.

Walls, R. (ed.) (2013) *World Film Locations: Vancouver*. Chicago, IL: University of Chicago Press.

Wasko, J. (1994) *Hollywood in the Information Age*. Cambridge: Polity Press.

5 Nature, Culture and the Genesis of the Concept of Travel

Silvio Lima Figueiredo

Introduction

In more recent discussions and studies in the field of human sciences, the theme of travel has not been given its due importance. If, on the one hand, the study of tourist activity has led research into the phenomenon of travel to be conducted with more rigour, it has also tended to equate the latter with the concept of tourism, without paying attention to the fact that they are actually different. There are two aspects that differentiate these categories: the ontological characterisation of travelling presupposes the dislocation of man in space and time; but since this is insufficient to explain the category 'travel', the ontological meaning must be expanded to contain the perception of a space–time dislocation of man, who leaves the place where he lives to arrive in a place where he does not live or might live in the future.

So, the concept of travel goes beyond the idea of a simple spatial dislocation and involves a dislocation between the same and the different. In this case, the study of tourism would be the study of a specific kind of travel, one that involves leisure, the experience of returning, and the travel package: tourism as a good (Figueiredo, 2010; Figueiredo & Ruschmann, 2004; MacCannell, 2003). Just as the concepts of travel and tourism are confused with one another, scholars have been speculating for a long time on the possibility that travel is a human need. Many studies, following what is said by sellers of touristic products, have associated vacations with travel, causing consumers to believe that it represents a real need and that the Western (and later globalised) population as a whole should take a touristic trip at least once a year to get to know fashionable and idyllic places. This important marketing discourse about travel destinies and touristic products has ended up generating the idea that travelling is a human need, which is justified by the fact that every person should indulge in sophisticated leisure activities, such as travelling to famous tourist destinations, as if an individual's résumé must be improved by recordings of the trips he or she has gone on. This perhaps explains how photography and filming have become so salient in tourist experience.

By understanding the tourism product as a touristic experience (Uriely, 2005), it has been possible to identify the differences between the traveller and the tourist (Figueiredo, 2010; Lévi-Strauss, 1984; Urbain, 1983, 1986, 1993, 2002a, 2002b, 2003a, 2003b) and to notice that there are some characteristics that would help to identify travel as a basic need. However, and above all, it is noticeable that the elements that constitute a trip and could serve as examples of this inherent need are actually cultural and specific categories that are part of symbolic processes that exist in certain cultures and groups. It would, therefore, seem impossible to think of them as something natural. This is the case with the search for adventure and risk, which considers different types of adventure – from a love affair to a trip – as a rupture from everyday life (Simmel, 2002). The search for the exotic, for what is different, and curiosity about discovering the Other, as observed in Christin (2000) and Segalen (1999), might lead us to a universal truth for all human beings. Would any human group deny this affirmation? According to Michel (2000), only the desire to get to know other places, to go *ailleurs* (elsewhere), is left to us. So, it is possible to think of human beings as people essentially eager to get to know other places and avid for the experience of spatial dislocation, for going and coming. As Michel (2000) argues, this is a primary desire. Maffesoli (2006) also observes the desire for roaming.

This chapter lays forth some thoughts on the characterisation of travelling as something both natural and cultural, based on studies undertaken by three extremely important thinkers in the field of human sciences: Claude Lévi-Strauss, Clifford Geertz and Bronisław Malinowski.

Travel, Nature and Culture

Travel and its counterpart, tourism, are currently characterised by their possibility for representing post-modern man. The huge quantity of leaflets and propaganda that try to compel people to take trips is testimony to our latent desire to travel at least once a year – often to places that one has never visited before. Travelling would therefore appear not to be something superfluous. It creates possibilities for a better life because it heals and relaxes from the stress of everyday life and represents the endless possibilities of life experiences and (why not?) of educating the traveller/tourist, offering a transformation in his or her perception of life. Travel provides knowledge. We might conjure up famous and brave travellers as examples. So, it is possible to look at the act of travelling as something associated with a need which has to be fulfilled, as its lack will be harmful to man. This might make man miserable and perhaps physically and spiritually ill. So, in this respect, travelling is seen as something natural. No one mentally healthy should in principle refuse to travel. Some anthropology researchers have closely studied the relationship between nature and culture, so it is possible to try to review how the act of travelling is situated in this discussion.

Nature and Culture in Claude Lévi-Strauss

Man is a biological being and a social individual at the same time. In affirming this, Claude Lévi-Strauss (1969: 3–4) presents a basic discussion of this dichotomy in his study *The Elementary Structures of Kinship*. To him, culture can be considered neither simply juxtaposed with nor simply superimposed on life. In one sense, it replaces life, and in another sense, it uses it and transforms it in order to synthesise a new order. By means of these arguments, Lévi-Strauss proposes two forms of analysis in order to understand how the formation of culture and the relationship with the natural takes place. One of them concerns the regression of man to a state outside society, involving experiments or otherwise, in which children were raised by apes, wolves or baboons. With the child being raised isolated from society, and based on the most varied studies, the author demonstrates that this type of individual becomes a complete idiot, one who is not capable of reasoning. Therefore, the author notices that there is no point of regression that refers and attaches itself to a previous natural state of what is commonly known as man and his culture, 'since the species has no natural behaviour to which an isolated individual might retrogress' (Lévi-Strauss, 1969: 5). The 'wild children', originating from a method of isolation either the product 'of chance or experimentation ... may be cultural monstrosities, but under no circumstances can they provide reliable evidence of an earlier state' (Lévi-Strauss, 1969: 5). So, the search through regression for a previous, incipient and initial state, in which a man without culture and in his natural state could be observed, is a fruitless search, because this state does not exist and the only thing experimentation and accident can offer is the identification of unhealthy beings.

The other form of analysis, a way of looking for answers and finding the 'natural man', is to invert the study: instead of searching for inferior stages of man, by trying to find out the behaviour of superior stages of animal life, in which – putting aside complex societies of bees, ants and other insects, for they are perfect examples of the natural state in instinct and in the anatomical equipment that transmits hereditary features for the survival of the colony – it is feasible to see the impossibility of finding elements of what he calls a universal cultural model. But, before arguing with Lévi-Strauss and conceptions of inversion, we should identify in these elements what would characterise culture or the 'cultural man': languages, tools, social institutions and systems of aesthetics, moral and religious values. Thus, it is possible to better 'hunt out' the natural man in some mammals, such as anthropoid apes (gorillas, chimpanzees and orang-utans) (Lévi-Strauss, 1969: 5–6). For Lévi-Strauss, this pathway is equally frustrating. Chimpanzees may use elementary instruments and tools, show signs of solidarity and subordination, have experiences with the sacred, and present a diversity of eating and sexual habits, but these acts, these sketches of culture, do not go much beyond this even in terms of rudimentary language because, even though there is no biological hindrance, apes are not able to attribute any kind of sign to the few sounds they emit. Sense does not exist.

Such behaviours demonstrate a versatility that could be natural or cultural, but then there would be two models that, associated with the notions of nature/culture and diversity/versatility, would be within the scope of nature, while universal rules and patterns would be within the field of culture. In a clearer and more acceptable way, this means that the universals are found in the category 'nature'. Regulation and rule indicate culture and are relative. So, universality should be contained in nature: 'what is constant in man falls necessarily beyond the scope of customs, techniques and institutions whereby his groups are differentiated and contrasted' (Lévi-Strauss, 1969: 8), and is characterised by spontaneity. Culture would be within the domain of the private and the relative.

Clifford Geertz and the Interpretations of Culture

Another important contribution was made by the North American anthropologist Clifford Geertz, who carried out studies on the relationship between nature and culture and the definition of mind. According to Geertz (1973: 34), 'the Enlightenment view of man was, of course, that he was wholly of a piece with nature and shared in the general uniformity of composition which natural science, under Bacon's urging and Newton's guidance, had discovered there', that is, laws of a human nature. This conception has gradually been turned over, in the sense that studies on non-Western societies started to be carried out so that they would be understood as units in themselves. Thus, the search for universal units of man has been progressively put aside – making, in the words of the anthropologist, 'the drawing of a line between what is natural, universal, and constant in man and what is conventional, local, and variable extraordinarily difficult' (Geertz, 1973: 36) – and has contributed to the 'decline of the uniformitarian view of man', in line with the following maxim: 'man may be so entangled with where he is, who he is, and what he believes that he is inseparable from them' (Geertz, 1973: 35).

Geertz explains this recurring concept in the analysis of nature and culture in man as being based on a stratified conception of culture: when the life of man is interpreted as natural, then we have relationships between biological, psychological, social and cultural factors, as if they were different levels, and man is characterised in his essence by what he is biologically. Based on that, layers are formed until the cultural man and culture itself can be reached. This conception has influenced theories disseminated through-out human sciences, such as the famous 'Maslow's pyramid'. Maslow, a theoretician of the psychology of motivation, says that man is formed by various levels of needs and that some of them are more 'urgent' than others. It is necessary to first satisfy the most basic needs and then satisfy the less basic ones. These needs are described as a pyramid, whose base is formed by physiological needs, followed by needs for safety and security, needs for love and belonging, esteem needs, self-actualisation needs, until the top is reached with aesthetic needs (Maslow, 1970). Physiological needs represent nature, which means that hunger is a basic need and is attached to instinct. The other needs would be attached to culture, because they represent the information and instruments needed to live in society; and when put in layers, one by one, they must be met completely.

In short, if the life of man is set up in layers, we only need to remove the layers attached to the social, cultural and psychological aspects in order to find the lost connection. Geertz appropriately reminds us, as Lévi-Strauss did, that this interpretation was built based on the search for a concept of a universal man, which, according to Geertz, existed only in the Enlightenment, in the obvious formation stage of scientific knowledge and in the search for cultural universals. Therefore, some aspects are really necessary for human life and others are peripheral. This is the concept of *consensus gentium* (consensus of all humanity).

Malinowski's Theory of Culture and Universal Institutional Types

Anthropologist followers of functionalism, especially Malinowski, who carried out very important studies in works such as *Argonauts of the Western*

Pacific (1953) and *The Sexual Life of Savages in North-Western Melanesia* (1941), which describe his trip to the Trobriand Islands and are classic examples of an anthropological trip – the first of all anthropologists' fieldwork – have an obviously functional interpretation of the relationship between nature and culture. Malinowski produces a relationship between what he calls universal institutional types, which are found in his *The Scientific Theory of Culture* (1944). Among these types (Malinowski, 1944: 62–65), there are –

* *in reproduction* (bonds of blood defined by a legal contract of marriage and extended by a specifically defined principle of descent): the family, as the domestic group of parents and children; courtship organisation, the legal definition and organisation of marriage as a contract binding two individuals and relating two groups; the extended domestic group and its legal, economic and religious organisation; groups of kindred, united through the unilateral principle of descent; the clan, matrilineal or patrilineal; the system of related clans.
* *in voluntary associations*: primitive secret societies, clubs, recreational teams, artistic societies; at higher levels, mutual aid and benefit societies, lodges, voluntary associations for recreation, uplift or the fulfilment of a common purpose.
* *in principles of rank and status*: states and orders of nobility, clergy, burghers, peasants, serfs, slaves; the caste system; stratification by ethnic (i.e. racial or cultural) distinctions at primitive and developed levels.

Taking Malinowski's family category as an example, it is possible to notice that its characterisation as a 'domestic group of parents and children' is a universal categorisation, which obeys the typology of human universals, with the concept of marriage 'a more or less durable connection between male and female lasting beyond the mere act of propagation till after the birth of the offspring' (Durham, 1978: 17).

It is necessary to highlight the functionalist characteristics in Malinowski's text, which is based on the following observation: there are a large number of human impulses – biological and natural – which individuals and groups transform into cultural matters. However, some of these impulses are found in many cultures and seem universal. In Malinowski, the understanding of groups and cultures is based on minutely empirical research, to do which he lived at a particular place for a particular period of time. And *Argonauts of the Western Pacific* makes explicit exactly this feature, especially in the chapter 'The Subject, Method and Scope of This Enquiry' (Malinowski, 1953).

The author also seeks to elaborate concepts of permanent and vital importance, which exist in all cultures and are present in: the impulse to breathe (*act*, intake of oxygen; *satisfaction*, elimination of CO_2 in tissues); hunger (*act*, ingestion of food; *satisfaction*, satiation); thirst (*act*, absorption of liquid; *satisfaction*, quenching); sex appetite (*act*, conjugation; *satisfaction*, detumescence); fatigue (*act*, rest; *satisfaction*, restoration of muscular and nervous energy) (Malinowski, 1944: 77).

Culture, Nature, Travelling and Tourism

According to Geertz, the first issue about these kinds of interpretation concerns the substantial or non-substantial forms of universal concepts, dealing with concepts such as marriage, religion or property (taking us back to Malinowski with *family* and to Lévi-Strauss with *kinship*). The author affirms that 'if one defines religion generally and indeterminately – as man's most fundamental orientation to reality, for example – then one cannot at the same time assign to that orientation a highly circumstantial content'. Using other examples, this orientation among the Aztecs is not the same as among the Zunis, the Kayapós or Brazilian Catholics. Thus, the concepts end up becoming general information that loses its rigour. On the other hand, exaggerated relativism has limitations in terms of its contribution to the understanding of man based on the relationships between nature and culture.

So, debates on universals attached to important categories are present in the relationship between cultural and universal phenomena and the universal categories of understanding. According to Lévi-Strauss, the universal and cultural phenomenon observed in all cultural or human groups is incest. In *The Elementary Structures of Kinship* (Lévi-Strauss, 1969: 3–25) the author, within his concept of culture as something normative and specific, and nature as something universal, finds in incest the prime example of something normative and universal. The communicational aspect (of exchanges) that is so important in Lévi-Strauss's structuralism is actually his explanation of incest, neither exclusively biological nor exclusively social:

> We have been led to pose the problem of incest in connection with the relationship between man's biological existence and his social existence, and we have immediately established that the prohibition could not be ascribed accurately to either one or the other. (Lévi-Strauss, 1969: 24–25)

Going further in the discussion, the concept of culture will appear as a key concept, which is obviously the result of its relationship with nature. Man is diverse, thus his answers to environmental configurations are also diverse. According to Geertz, the study of man is not only the study of recurrence, but also of anomalies and alternations; and more important than looking for different identities among similar phenomena is looking first for systematic relationships among different phenomena. In order to achieve this, the author proposes two ideas for the study of man. The first is the characterisation of culture not as a complex of concrete behaviour patterns (customs, usages, traditions, habit clusters) – which it is usually associated with – but as a set of control mechanisms (plans, recipes, rules, instructions) for the governing of behaviour. The second is that this group of control mechanisms is necessary to complete, or to shape, man. So 'undirected by culture patterns – organized systems of significant symbols – man's behaviour would be virtually ungovernable, a mere chaos of pointless acts and exploding emotions, his experience virtually shapeless' (Geertz, 1973: 46).

Thus, there has not been a moment in which the biologically complete man has needed culture in order to transform him into what he is. This lost connection did not appear in this way, since culture was not added to a finished animal: it was an essential ingredient for the production of this same animal. From an interactive perspective, there has been the passage of nearly one million years between the beginning of culture and the appearance of man as we see him today. Man depends more and more on the systems of signifying symbols (language, art, myth, ritual) for orientation and communication. Culture increasingly shows that it is responsible for what man currently is. According to Geertz, this suggests that what is usually called human nature does not exist independently from culture. Anyway, these systems of signifying symbols that characterise culture show themselves as a group of specific systems, which means that man is not completed by general culture, but mainly by specific forms of culture, as may be noticed in a Javanese or Balinese person, who is different from a Western person (Geertz, 1983).

However, we should not forget that this system of signifying symbols is created by man himself and it is in this attribution of sense to actions where culture expresses itself: 'that man is an animal suspended in webs of significance he himself has spun, I take culture to be those webs, and the analysis of it' (Geertz, 1973: 30). These definitions allow for an understanding of how travelling is expressed as an attribute of man. Travelling is understood as a human phenomenon, and it should appear as such. However, the main issue here is to understand how something that apparently occurs in all human cultures, in various groups and historical moments, can be considered a product of culture and not of nature, since travelling shows itself as something universal (as Lévi-Strauss suggests about incest).

Therefore, summarising the main point of the discussion, the difficulties are many: one of them is the characterisation of travel as a basic need, appearing to be an aspect of nature that expresses itself in the behavior of man, that is, as an instinct. Celestino Domingues's *Technical Dictionary of Tourism* describes travelling as 'the dislocation of one person or group of people between two points, with or without return, who use any means of transportation and are absent from their residence for a considerable amount of time' (Domingues, 1990: 285). This displacement can be from one place to another, and can happen by different means of transportation (air, land, sea) and for the most different of reasons (business, leisure, studies, health, family visit, etc.) (Pellegrini Filho, 2000: 289).

In Fernandez Fuster's (1978: 565) words:

> man has always met on his slow path the 'travel demon' and has been possessed by it. It is likely that, on many occasions, the very existence of this 'human being' is confirmed by the Cartesian principle: 'I travel, therefore I exist'; in which the dislocation is related to all other vital needs.

A series of other authors have agreed with Fernandez Fuster, who wrote the seminal book *Teoria y técncia del turismo*. The book's basic premise is to see travelling as a fundamental and vital need. Some theories found in tourism texts make us believe that the desire to travel, to get to know other places, was inherent to man from the moment that he acquired culture, according to Castelli (1990), or as both Feifer (1986) and Rouanet (1993) suggest. Such a conception might lead to the unfounded belief that man may have in his genetic make-up some kind of information about travelling, and that the desire would actually be a basic, almost physiological, need.

Referencing Maslow and his pyramid once more, it is possible to see travelling as a basic need, somewhere near the bottom of the pyramid (and thus attached to nature), behaviour that proceeds from instincts that make man commit to dislocation to ensure his reproduction. This issue is demystified by biologism and its immediate answers, because the need for dislocation occurs firstly due to the need for food and shelter when the place of origin does not offer these items anymore. The nomadism of man is, in its origin, attached to these basic needs:

> By traveling, they have completed a process of hominization: the *homo viator* is in the origin of the *homo sapiens*. Traveling is an act of freedom. (Rouanet, 1993: 7)

Michel Maffesoli, in his work *Du nomadisme*, presents a category that alludes to travelling: nomadism as an 'anthropological constant', present in many peoples, religions and cultures, such as in the Guarani Indians' rituals (Maffesoli, 2006). The characteristics of travelling, which are part of the nomadic instinct, are found in many peoples and cultures. The desire for circulation, change and mobility is age old and present even in contemporary patterns of migration.

Travels and Mythologies

Elemental forms of displacement are seen in different forms of travel, which in their turn have different purposes. Migratory displacements, wars of conquest and adventures are narrated as the first manifestations of displacement. The nomad, usually found in groups and tribes, is a common figure and category in displacements, whose aim is to find better means of subsistence. Nomadism is an elementary form present in the origins of travel, displacements and migrations (Feifer, 1986); groups, families and tribes practised it when they needed to look for food, better housing or to engage in communication and commercial exchanges. Today, it is possible to find peoples who still manifest these characteristics, such as the Tuareg and other nomadic pastoralists in North Africa, in India or in Mongolia.

The encounter with and exploration of new realities bring challenges with them, constituting emblematic situations which we find witnessed by earlier societies, such as the Phoenicians, the Sumerians, the Greeks, the Romans and the Vikings. Ancient Greece, and later Rome, evoke the most widely known travel stories that correspond to great heroic adventures: the narratives of Homer's *Iliad* and *Odyssey*. Epic narratives are actually the most admired form through which the imaginary of the search for knowledge and challenges is expressed (both in literature and in Greek/Roman mythology). The adventure, which entails the courageous taking of personal risk, merges with the drama of displacement, travel and exploration.

Simultaneously with the myth of Hercules and his 12 labours, the adventures of Ulysses and of Prometheus, Greek society was also responsible for the emergence of new social rituals, such as the Olympic Games, which was a sporting event that attracted many Greeks from different cities like Sparta, Athens and Thebes. In this case, it was athletes and some spectators who travelled. Today, the Olympic Games, as a sports event, have become explicitly part of the television, leisure and tourism industries. The Roman elite travelled quite often and in relative safety (Feifer, 1986); in some periods of the Roman Empire it was to go to bath complexes, which attracted many visitors. However, it was after the territorial conquests, especially during the late expansion of the Empire, that displacements began to include other parts of Europe, the north of Africa and other regions.

Since those times, it is clear that one of the reasons for such displacements becoming so much more urgent and dynamic involves particular political and economic aspirations. These factors drove European maritime expansion in the 15th, 16th and 17th centuries. An intense cycle of displacements came mainly with the development of new means of transportation. The great age of sail gave an impulse to travel and subsequently the entire world was explored and 'discovered'. Since then, modern technology has gone on improving the economic, social and technical conditions that enable increased travel around the world. From this perspective, the displacement of whole communities, families and people, that is, the migration phenomenon, has taken place within unprecedentedly short periods of time. This has included the migration of refugees, displaced people and economic migrants.

Tourism, on the other hand, which is characterised as a trip that includes the intention to return and has broadly leisure-oriented purposes, has become one of the main forms of displacement in contemporary times. Touristic travel emerged as the preferred form of travel of late capitalist society and particularly as a post-modern phenomenon (Boyer, 1982, 2003). One may notice that in literature, mythology and history, the characteristics of the traveller are very different from those of the tourist, in terms of both motivation and behaviour. The understanding of tourism as a form of extra-domestic leisure for the individual, which is presented in detail in Cazes (1992), suggests that tourism is related to concepts of leisure which have emerged in modernity. Stendhal's *Mémoires d'un touriste* (1868) accurately enumerates these ideas. Tourism is leisure, and the tourist traveller is a very different category of person from that of the ancient, romantic or adventurous traveller. I would argue that in both cases, however, the desire to travel is fundamental.

Finally, it is important to understand that, although displacement and travel are present in many peoples and cultures, travel cannot be understood as something natural, universal or a rule in the process of formation of modern societies. Different motivations – migrations for economic reasons, sociability and the persistence of nomadism, business trips, military displacements, religious and philanthropic missions and ultimately tourism – cannot be equated, cannot be seen as being of equal value, even though they have displacement as a common active element.

Conclusion

Are we therefore justified in saying that the action of travel and its symbology have nothing to do with nature? Taking into account the manifestations of travel within this discussion, it is possible to observe that geographic displacements occur in several different forms; therefore, travel, as it is approached in this study, cannot be understood as something instinctive or natural, because what motivates displacements varies according to the culture of a people, as well as to their social, economic and environmental needs. There are currently over 200 million immigrants in the world (according to the International Organization for Migration, IOM, 2013); as for tourism, over 1 billion people are estimated to have travelled around the world in 2012 (according to the United Nations World Tourism Organization, UNWTO, 2013).

Therefore, in view of the fact that the action of travel is present in several cultures and across various historical moments, it is noticeable that although there is a clear tendency to understand travel as something natural, several types of displacements are seen as taboos among some groups. In other cases and at other times, trips have been taken very rarely, as in medieval societies, for example. Fear has always been an important factor, reducing its incidence.

Literature, mythology and history have praised travel, but they have also shown that it is circumstantial in nature; certain elements need to come together for it to occur. In any event, this cultural trait, which formerly characterised only certain groups, has become global with the emergence of tourism. Conversely, at the same time that the virtues of travel have been widely praised, the figures of 'the bad traveller' and 'the bad trip' have emerged, represented by the tourist and his/her journey. It should be added that in nearly all cases, this is a class-based prejudice, because the tourist is just the common man who travels.

References

Boyer, M. (1982) *Le tourisme*. Paris: Du Seuil.
Boyer, M. (2003) *História do turismo de massa*. Bauru-SP: Edusc.
Castelli, G. (1990) *Turismo, atividade marcante*. Caxias do Sul: Educs.
Cazes, G. (1992) *Pour une geographie du tourisme et des loisirs*. Paris: Breal.
Christin, R. (2000) *L'Imaginaire voyageur ou l'expérience exotique*. Paris: L'Harmattan.
Domingues, C. (1990) *Dicionário Técnico de Turismo*. Lisbon: Dom Quixote.
Durham, E. (1978) *A reconstituição da realidade*. São Paulo: Ática.
Feifer, M. (1986) *Tourism in History: From Imperial Rome to the Present*. New York: Stein and Day Publishers.
Fernadez Fuster, L. (1978) *Teoria y Tecnica del Turismo*. Madrid: Nacional.
Figueiredo, S.L. (2010) *Viagens e Viajantes*. São Paulo: Annablume.
Figueiredo, S.L. and Ruschmann, D. (2004) Estudo genealógico das viagens, dos viajantes e dos turistas. *Novos Cadernos NAEA* 7(1), 155–188.
Geertz, C. (1973) *The Interpretation of Cultures: Selected Essays*. New York: Basic Books.
Geertz, C. (1983) *Local knowledge: Further Essays in Interpretative Anthropology*. New York: Basic Books.

International Organization for Migration (2013) *World Migration Report 2013*. Geneva: IOM.

Lévi-Strauss, C. (1969) *The Elementary Structures of Kinship*. Boston, MA: Beacon Press.

Lévi-Strauss, C. (1984) *Tristes Tropiques*. Paris: Plon.

MacCannell, D. (2003) *El Turista, uma neuva teoria de la clase ociosa*. Barcelona: Melusina.

Maffesoli, M. (2006) *Du nomadisme*. Paris: Table Ronde.

Malinowski, B. (1941) *The Sexual Life of Savages in North-Western Melanesia*. New York: Halcyon House.

Malinowski, B. (1944) *The Scientific Theory of Culture*. Chapel Hill, NC: University of North Carolina Press.

Malinowski, B. (1953) *Argonauts of the Western Pacific*. London: Routledge & Kegan.

Maslow, A. (1970) *Motivation and Personality*. New York: Harper & Row.

Michel, F. (2000) *Désirs d'ailleurs, essai d'anthropologie des voyages*. Paris: Armand Colin.

Pelegrini Filho, A. (2000) *Dicionário enciclopédico de ecologia e turismo*. Barueri: Manole.

Rouanet, S. P. (1993) *A razão nômade: Walter Benjamin e outros viajantes*. Rio de Janeiro: UFRJ.

Segalen, V. (1999) *Essai sur l'exotisme*. Paris: Fata Morgana.

Simmel, G. (2002) *La philosophie de l'aventure*. Paris: L'Arche.

Stendhal (1968) *Mémoires d'um touriste*. Paris: Slatkine Reprints.

United Nations World Tourism Organization (2013) *World Tourism Barometer, Vol. 11, January 2013*. Madrid: WTO.

Urbain, J.D. (1983) Sur l'espace du Touriste: un voyage en Tunisie. Elements pour une sémiotique de l'espace touristique des Français. *L'espace geographique* 2, 115–124.

Urbain, J.D. (1986) Sémiotiques comparés du touriste et du voyageur. *Semiótica* 58 (3–4), 269–279.

Urbain, J.D. (1993) *L'idiot du voyage: histoires de touristes*. Paris: Payot.

Urbain, J.D. (2002a) *Sur la plage*. Paris: Payot.

Urbain, J.D. (2002b) *Les vacances*. Paris: Le Cavalier Bleu.

Urbain, J.D. (2003a) *Ethnologue mais pas trop*. Paris: Payot.

Urbain, J.D. (2003b) *Secrets de voyage*. Paris: Payot.

Uriely, N. (2005) The tourist experience, conceptual developments. *Annals of Tourism Research* 32 (1), 199–216.

Part 2
Narratives of Travel and Identity

6 The Appeal of Otherness: Reconstructions of Self in Contemporary Travel Writing

María del Pino Santana Quintana

> *Abroad, we are all Titanians, so bedazzled by strangeness that we comically*
> *mistake asses for beauties; but away from home, we can also be Mirandas, so*
> *new to the world that our blind faith can become a kind of higher sight.*
> Pico Iyer, *Video Night in Kathmandu*

Travelling is the perfect experience to discover the other, but also to encounter your own self. Perceiving the difference and assimilating the other are travelling practices firmly attached to the transformation of one's identity. The genre of travel writing has proved to be especially good at testifying to this process of the self. Travel writers draw considerably on their own personal experiences; the first-person account that arises from their journeys proves the significance of the self in foreign surroundings; the confidence of the narrative voice makes the journey revolve around the particular adventures of the traveller abroad, wandering around far-off places, lost in his or her own thoughts.

But travellers are not alone. They never are, not even in the remotest corners of the earth; and so their narratives are not determined by the sole expression of an isolated self. Their own relations to the landscape and the place and the people that surround them are in constant interaction. Far from remaining static, the traveller's identity takes an active part in the cross-cultural process that travelling itself entails; it is an identity that is nourished from the perception of difference and the encounter with the other. In travel narratives, the inner development of the travel writer and the temporal progression of the journey go hand in hand. By exploring the world, the traveller explores his or her own identity, so each new place she or he observes opens enriching possibilities for a new self. How different sounds the voice of the traveller who sets out on the journey from that of the one who returns home, refreshed and highly influenced by the encounter with otherness.

In the process of journeying into and out of the self, the traveller goes through a series of stages: the first contact scenes are followed by the traveller's initial impressions, which, in turn, develop into his or her willingness to convert the unfamiliar into the ordinary; such willingness requires total immersion, which, if successful, opens the way to the experience of going native, and finally concludes with the traveller's return home, which may not be a definitive one. This phase of evolution of the self shows the traveller's gradual identity development in a foreign territory.

In first contact scenes, otherness initially operates on the basic principle of language. For those travellers who want to experience diversity to its limits and who avoid moving around places where their mother tongue might be spoken, foreign-language encounters play a decisive role. They highlight the physical and emotional distance from home and generate that self-conscious, yet illuminating feeling of landing on a different planet. It is for good reasons that the American travel writer and Peace Corps volunteer Moritz Thomsen established as a golden rule for his journey to the Amazon 'No hanging around places where English might be spoken', as Paul Theroux points out in his anthology of journeys *The Tao of Travel* (2011: 242). Not knowing the language of the country you are travelling in is, in Michel Butor's words, like 'learning to read once more' (1992: 60). Travellers must interpret the sounds and gestures of the native and simplify the language that constitutes their sense of place and belonging. To accomplish a simple task, like finding the way back to the hotel, deciphering street signs or trying to deal with a menu at a street stall, becomes a series of deductions and misunderstandings.

The traveller and global soul Pico Iyer gives us a good example of the kind of sudden strangeness experienced when approaching a distant land where native populations speak languages other than the mother tongue of the traveller. In his brilliant book of journeys to the Far East, *Video Night in Kathmandu* (1988), Iyer recounts his frustrated attempt to get a train ticket to Beijing. Hopelessly lost in Canton Station, in the city of Guangzhou, Iyer reports:

> Anxious to find anyone or anything that I could understand I began walking – around the hall, and through it, up the stairs and down a corridor, into an empty room, and out of it again. I walked along the length of corridors and around a balcony and through the garden, back around the hall, into waiting rooms and out of them, back up the sweeping staircase and down again. Everywhere it was the same: no English, no help, no good. I went back to a duty free shop and around again, and back to the waiting hall, and out. Nowhere any English,

nowhere any help. I walked up, and down, and up once more. No English. No use. No good. (Iyer, 1989: 105)

In this passage, Iyer is explicit about his feeling of displacement in his first contact with foreignness. Unable to read the Chinese characters and to communicate with locals, he is confused and guideless in what seems to be a maze of corridors and stairs that lead nowhere.

Language barriers may lead to discouraging encounters during a trip abroad or in everyday interaction with foreign speakers. Even the polyglot Paul Theroux, who learnt Mandarin Chinese before setting out on his epic journey through China, had problems at the time in assimilating the country's language. In his account of train travel through China in the years 1986–87, *Riding the Iron Rooster* (1988), Theroux relates that on every occasion he heard the Chinese word for railway, he assumed his name was being mentioned. As he explains: '*Tielu* ("iron road") sounds something like a Chinese person attempting the French pronunciation of Theroux. The word never failed to turn my head. What were they saying about me?' (Theroux, 1989: 55).

On the other hand, speaking the language of otherness may also lead to a bitter truth that affects the experience of the journey and, therefore, its narration. Learning a foreign language, as Theroux does for many of his travels, is walking on solid ground; instead of experiencing that child-like state of blissful ignorance that springs from not knowing the other's language, the traveller listens first-hand to political disappointments or complaints about social injustice. In his introduction to *The Old Patagonian Express* (1979), the account of his train journey from Massachusetts to the southern tip of South America, Theroux admits that the gloomy mood of his narrative was due in part to the very fact that he knew Spanish and 'speaking to people in their own language, hearing their timid turns of phrase, or the violence of their anger, or the idioms of their hopelessness … could be distressing' (Theroux, 1997: xv).

In most cases, first contact experiences provoke mixed feelings: desire and anxiety, puzzlement and enlightenment, excitement and disappointment, hope and despair. For Pico Iyer, the intricate emotions of travelling to a foreign country are analogous to the hasty and perplexing excitements of a romance; as he explains in an article for the online magazine *Salon*:

every trip to a foreign country can be a love affair, where you're left puzzling over who you are and whom you've fallen in love with. All the great travel books are love stories, by some reckoning – from the *Odyssey* and the *Aeneid* to the *Divine Comedy* and the *New Testament* – and all good trips are, like love, about being carried out of yourself and deposited in the midst of terror and wonder. (Iyer, 2000)

To risk the unknown, then, is a real adventure of the spirit. Abroad is a blank page that travellers intentionally fill as they try to make sense of the strangeness that surrounds them. Yet, it is not only the linguistic barrier that makes the traveller aware of difference; there is a whole set of cultural mechanisms which equally well affect first encounters with otherness, and which become predominant in places completely different from the traveller's ideological and cultural backgrounds. In their first contact with a new territory, travellers have to negotiate between the little they carry with them and the many alien things that the foreign land has to offer. The self moves between two distinctive worlds: that microcosm of familiar boundaries to which the traveller is culturally attached, and that other strange world where she or he may feel a complete outsider. The two worlds are divided by an imaginary borderland that separates the familiar from the strange and whose crossing involves leaving behind the protection of old habits to become a foreigner. It is often stated as axiomatic that the experience of travel confuses the individual. In spite of the traveller's eagerness to adapt to anywhere, the feeling of being excluded from a specific circle may bring about emotional and psychological disruptions. A traveller like Theroux, who loves challenging trips and journeying among remote people, has no hesitation in comparing the foreigner's experience in a world of strangers with a kind of madness. As he asserts in *The Tao of Travel*:

> Otherness can be like an illness; being a stranger can be analogous to ex-periencing a form of madness – those same intimations of the unreal and the irrational, when everything that has been familiar is stripped away. It is hard to be a stranger. A traveler may have no power, no influence, no known identity. That is why a traveler needs optimism and heart, because without confidence travel is misery. Generally, the traveler is anonymous, ignorant, easy to deceive, at the mercy of the people he or she travels among. The traveler may be known as 'the American' or 'the Foreigner', and there is no power in that. (Theroux, 2011: 123)

To venture beyond the familiar makes travellers weak. As Theroux suggests, they must pack as much confidence into their bags as they can fill it with, set out on their journey in a hopeful mood, figure things out along the way, trust in the kindness of strangers, and convince themselves that the feverish unreality of first impressions is but a temporary state. Unfamiliar with foreign habits, currency or language, travellers can become pitiable individuals, wandering figures whom natives identify with oversimplistic labels. Throughout his numerous travels, Theroux makes a record of the variety of terms the natives from different lands apply to foreign-looking people. In his collection of travel essays *Fresh Air Fiend* (2000), Theroux explains that in the Arabic language the word for foreigner is *ajnabi*, and 'the root means something like "people to avoid"' (Theroux, 2000: 12). It is not in vain that Theroux explains the etymology of the word; in remote corners of the world, the visitor, the newcomer, is regarded with a degree of suspicion. But foreigners are not only distrusted; they are also mocked. In *Riding the Iron Rooster*, Theroux and his fellow travellers see a work-gang of smiling Mongolian painters. Theroux comments that these workers are not actually smiling, but simply dazzled by the sun; on second thoughts, however, the traveller recognises that their smiles may have denoted humour: 'they might well have been smiling in recognition at our exact match of the Chinese slang for foreigners: "big noses" (*da bidze*)' (Theroux, 1989: 56). In Ethiopia, a foreigner is a *faranji*. As Theroux recounts in *The Tao of Travel*, it is a term that conveys anti-foreign feelings; it symbolises the loneliness of a Western traveller in off-the-beaten-track black Africa. During the traveller's stay in Harar, a city in eastern Ethiopia, *faranji* becomes a constant refrain:

> I was followed by children chanting, '*Faranji*! *Faranji*! *Faranji*!' Sometimes older people bellowed at me, and now and then as I was driving slowly down the road a crazed-looking Harari would rush from his doorstep to the window of my car and stand, spitting and screaming the word into my face. (Theroux, 2011: 126)

Being constantly misunderstood in a world of strangers requires an enormous mental effort. Likewise, any relation of contact may become an arduous process. The traveller's vivid impressions produced by a foreign landscape are now and then peppered with worries, irritations, disappointments and self-doubts. There usually comes a time on the journey when the title of Bruce Chatwin's last memoir, *What Am I Doing Here?* (1988), seems just the right epithet for the traveller's troubled position. Lost and terribly foreign, it is at these moments that the self comes into question: 'Who am I among these people? Why am I here? What am I trying to prove to myself and others? Do I look too foreign? How does the other see me?' Moving among strangers, the traveller's identity is drawn into a process of analysis; the experience of culture shock is followed by a systematic exploration of the status of the self and the search for an interpretation of the real purpose of the journey. This process of self-discovery may destabilise the traveller's former perception of his or her own self, especially when the physical aspects of the journey do not meet the traveller's expectations.

Like many other travellers on foreign terrain, the Australian-born Larry Buttrose found that Chatwin's title expressed his own self-doubt. There is a passage in his collection of travel narratives, *The Blue Man* (1997), where he finds himself on a night bus to Bamako, feverish, dehydrated and on the verge of the break-up of a long-term romance with his partner Kathryn – a hardy woman who happens to be travelling with him. They have been moving across Mali for weeks and the traveller's mind and body have been altered by culture clash and physical illness. Buttrose signals his discomfort by expressing his uncertainties not only about his own self, but also about the essence of the act of travelling itself. As he explains, the journey reveals itself as a futile struggle, a meaningless effort to prove that the traveller is not on the verge of extinction:

> I found myself revisiting doubt. What was I doing here, on this bus, beyond enduring the lot of a hapless, stupid tourist? Was my body again trying to tell me something – that perhaps I was not cut out for this kind of thing? Was 'travel' just a romantic dream? And what was it anyway, travel? All the world was going the way of the theme-park, even, soon, Timbuktu. (Buttrose, 1999: 251–252)

Resorting to humour is a clever method of dealing with spatial and emotional dislocation. Facing otherness with jokes is a form of self-protection. It is a familiar ploy of the contemporary travel writer to turn his own misadventures abroad into amusing experiences for others. Of all travellers, the American Bill Bryson is probably the best example of this. Though his journeys follow the beaten track and can be seen to be fairly standard tourist itineraries, they constantly prove that cross-cultural anomalies may throw up funny scenes. Bryson's trademark humour is mainly directed at himself. His travel books are exemplary not only of his propensity to grumble and moan, but also of his notorious tendency to self-ridicule. 'Self-parody' – as Holland and Huggan (2003: 35) suggest – 'offers self-protection'. In this sense, Bryson's sense of humour is used as a shield to defend himself against harrowing cross-cultural interchanges. In *Notes from a Small Island* (1995), which recounts his engaging trip around Britain, Bryson remembers his first sight of England as a young, naïve backpacker. He arrives in Dover on a foggy midnight with the excitement of an American who sees Europe for the first time. All hotels and guest-houses appear to be shut up. The railway station is also shuttered, and so Bryson finds himself in the middle of a sleeping foreign town:

I was standing wondering what to do next when I noticed a grey light of television filling an upstairs window of a guesthouse across the road. Hooray, I thought, someone awake, and hastened across, planning humble apologies to the kindly owner for the lateness of my arrival and imagining a cheery conversation…. The front path was pitch dark and in my eagerness and unfamiliarity with British doorways, I tripped on a step, crashing face-first into the door and sending half a dozen empty milk bottles clattering. (Bryson, 1998: 11–12)

This is but one of many examples where Bryson stumbles upon and over British otherness. Throughout his stay in Dover, the traveller makes a poignant record of every anomaly that attracts the attention of an arriving stranger; the reader gets the impression that the more he tries to establish contact with a place, the more he becomes aware of his own foreignness. British cultural eccentricities, social habits and incidental civilities are the recurrent butt of Bryson's wry humour. As he recounts:

I was positively radiant with ignorance. The simplest transactions were a mystery to me. I saw a man in a newsagent's ask for 'twenty Number Six' and receive cigarettes, and presumed for a long time afterwards that everything was ordered by number in a newsagent's, like in a Chinese takeaway. I sat for half an hour in a pub before I realized that you had to fetch your own order, then tried the same thing in a tearoom and was told to sit down. The tearoom lady called me love. All the shop ladies called me love and most men called me mate. (Bryson, 1998: 19–20)

These are the naïve deductions of a young traveller who is just beginning to embark on a personal journey through an unfamiliar land. With the keen eye of the foreigner willing to merge into new surroundings, Bryson captures the difference conveyed by a strange atmosphere. But these are all first impressions. Travellers should go beyond the cultural stereotypes of the foreign land as they try to integrate all the alien elements into their own self and to adjust to the atmosphere of the place; they should become intimate with the unfamiliar, adopt the native's point of view, and minimise exoticism, or – as Dennis Porter indicates, quoting Malinowski and his *Argonauts of the Western Pacific* (1922) – 'de-exoticize' the experience (Porter, 1991: 275).

The process of feeling at home among the locals never runs smoothly. For a traveller like Paul Theroux, it is more an act of defiance than a wish for cultural attachment. As he admits in his book of travels through China, the Chinese proverb 'We can always fool a foreigner' is taken by him as 'a personal challenge' (Theroux, 1989: 1). Theroux spends a year traversing a country whose bigness, as he asserts, 'makes you wonder. It is more like a whole world than a mere country' (1989: 1). Crossing China from Manchuria to Inner Mongolia and Tibet, passing by the cities of Shanghai, Beijing and Canton, and never leaving the ground – as he always does in his train books – Theroux converses with all kinds of locals, trying to look closely at their lives. Along the way, he provides a careful record of his own experiences as a foreigner, including his inability to adjust to some types of Chinese cooking and to extreme weather conditions. In his restless desire to adopt foreign ways of living and aspects of the cultures from all over China, Theroux tries to reduce his level of otherness to the minimum. He follows the natives and learns about their daily routines and cultural mores, feeling somehow a pang of melancholy for a life he is just passing through. This is certainly an emotion that Theroux admits to experiencing throughout his many journeys. In another of his travel books, *The Pillars of Hercules* (1995), the traveller acknowledges that 'the worst part of travel ... is the sight of people leading ordinary lives, especially people at work or with their families; or ones in uniform, or laden with equipment, or shopping for food, or paying bills' (1995: 46). It is not enough for the traveller to dissolve boundaries between his own self and others; as Theroux makes clear in *The Tao of Travel*, he really wants to be part of what he calls 'the gone-native class', a category which he opposes to 'the cleaner class' (2011: 119). Exemplary members of this second group would be travellers who, rather than merging into the foreign surroundings, remain immune to the influence of the native people.

Like Theroux, a great number of contemporary travellers aspire to belong to 'the gone-native class'. They move around the globe undoing the ties that have bound them to a particular zone and culture, and trying to recreate an identity in line with the atmosphere and spirit of the place they are discovering. In their quests for integration, some travellers are more inclined than others to emulate local habits and native life. As the old saying goes: 'When in Rome, do as the Romans do'. And this is what the British travel writer Jonathan Raban tries to put into practice in the course of his travels around the USA. In one of the first episodes in *Hunting Mr Heartbreak* (1990), Raban disembarks in New York for a two-month stay in a sublet apartment. Dressed in all-American clothes, he melts into the city, aspiring to be 'a regular guy at last' (Raban, 1991: 67). Within a few weeks, he builds for himself a neighbourhood which holds, in his own words:

> everything necessary for survival – a Polish bistro, a Korean supermarket, a laundry, a cigar store that sold the *Nation* and *New Republic* as well as imported pipe tobacco, a good florist, two bars, a proper butcher, a

diner. I could address the doormen on my block by name, and I had two beggars to whom I regularly gave alms. At two in the morning, ditched from a shared cab on Seventh Avenue, I would march, sidewalk-craftily, along 18th Street until I gained the eastern side of Broadway, which was where Neighbourhood began. Here my shoulders would unhunch, my pace slow, and I'd start nodding at strangers. (Raban, 1991: 107)

Raban's wish-list items are indicators of his own willingness to fit into the new environment. His gradual impersonation as a New Yorker is based on finding his own place in a rectangular block that encloses a curious amalgam of elements. 'Neighbourhood', as he calls that self-contained area where he has settled, becomes familiar, a new home. The role he chooses to occupy, and the space that surrounds him, makes him feel safe and belonging. Within a few weeks, the traveller has become something of an insider, but such an accomplishment implies a clear departure from his former self. To be a New Yorker not only requires a change of attire, but also a new way of life, the construction of a new sense of place. Raban, as most travellers do, moves outward, towards the other. The longer he is in contact with the other, the more his identity is transformed.

In *Video Night in Kathmandu*, Iyer maintains that unfamiliar places 'to some extent remake us, recast us in their own images, and the selves they awaken may tell us as much about them as about ourselves' (Iyer, 1989: 26). Iyer has no hesitation in penetrating foreign environments by following a process of mimetic observation and learning: in Thailand, he spends most of his evenings in bars; in Tibet, though not a Buddhist, he dedicates most of his days to the silence of mountain monasteries; and in Japan, where intricate social codes are not easy to decipher and 'a foreigner seems always to be an outsider', the traveller finds himself 'turning slightly Japanese – aloof, efficient and lyrical' (1989: 26). For Iyer, as he explains later in the book, Japan is 'the world's great Significant Other' (1989: 331), so it is hardly surprising that he regards it as the 'ultimate compliment' to be called 'half Japanese' by the owner of a *minshuku* – a Japanese-style guest-house – after Iyer shows his appreciation for some national painters (1989: 341). This is an example of reciprocity, one in which the pattern reverses itself and the other, the local, is the one who gazes back. It may be noted that the owner of this guest-house in which Iyer stays looks at the traveller not as a mere object of curiosity, but as half-native, as someone who somehow resembles himself in his admiration of Japanese culture.

For those travellers who feel comfortable in a world of differences and who rebuild their own selves from their contacts with natives, setting off homewards can prove to be a mixed experience. The return home concludes the various stages of the traveller's long journey, but where home is turns out to be uncertain for some. When the journey is over, and abroad is no longer so foreign, the traveller seems to be exposed to a sense of personal anticlimax. On the final page of his book of travels to China, Paul Theroux writes: 'This Chinese trip was so long and it claimed so much of me that it stopped being a trip. It was another part of my life; and ending the travel was not a return but a kind of departure, which I regretted' (1989: 487). It is not Odysseus's return to Ithaca, his homeward goal, that Theroux describes, but the melancholy journey home of a traveller who has established lifelong ties to the places and the people he has met, and now must sever them. Because of the transformational quality travel itself provides, going beyond the limits of the known establishes a form of rebirth; it implies a willingness to identify with the other and a certain denial of one's former identity. Despite the initial confusion of first contact and the feeling of alienation that travellers may feel as foreigners moving among strangers, the border-crossing of the self does not generally have negative consequences. Quite the contrary. The movement among different cultural frameworks invites the traveller to entertain a wide range of possibilities: personal growth, the construction of a new sense of place, the resurgence of an identity more akin to the ideology and principles of the host country, and the possibility of a life perhaps more satisfying than the one lived previously. Most of all, this crossing over of frontiers between self and other conveys what many authors within the genre consider to be the greatest joy of travel: responding to the appeal of otherness.

References

Bryson, B. (1998) *Notes from a Small Island*. London: Doubleday (original work published 1995).

Butor, M. (1992) Travel and writing. In M. Kowalewski (ed.) *Temperamental Journeys: Essays on the Modern Literature of Travel* (pp. 53–70). Athens, GA: University of Georgia Press.

Buttrose, L. (1999) *The Blue Man: Tales of Travel Love and Coffee*. Victoria: Lonely Planet (original work published 1997).

Chatwin, B. (1998) *What Am I Doing Here?* London: Vintage Classics (original work published 1988).

Holland, P. and Huggan, G. (2003) *Tourists with Typewriters: Critical Reflections on Contemporary Travel Writing*. Ann Arbor, MI: University of Michigan Press (original work published 1998).

Iyer, P. (1989) *Video Night in Kathmandu: And Other Reports from the Not-So-Far-East*. New York: Vintage Departures (original work published 1988).

Iyer, P. (2000) Why we travel. *Salon*. At http://www.salon.com/2000/03/18/why (accessed 26 October 2013).

Porter, D. (1991) *Haunted Journeys: Desire and Transgression in European Travel Writing*. Princenton, NJ: Princeton University Press.

Raban, J. (1991) *Hunting Mr Heartbreak*. London: Picador (original work published 1990).

Theroux, P. (1989) *Riding the Iron Rooster: By Train through China*. London: Penguin (original work published 1988).

Theroux, P. (1995) *The Pillars of Hercules: A Grand Tour of the Mediterranean*. New York: Fawcett Books.

Theroux, P. (1997) *The Old Patagonian Express: By Train through the Americas*. New York: Houghton Mifflin Harcourt (original work published 1979).

Theroux, P. (2000) *Fresh Air Fiend: Travel Writings, 1985–2000*. New York: Houghton Mifflin Harcourt.

Theroux, P. (2011) *The Tao of Travel: Enlightenments from Life on the Road*. New York: Houghton Mifflin Harcourt.

7 Representations of Maramureş in Contemporary Female Travel Writing: Dervla Murphy, Caroline Juler and Bronwen Riley

Marius-Mircea Crişan

Many British travellers who visit Romania (since the anti-communist revolution of 1989) express an enthusiastic attitude combined with a vivid spirit of observation which can sometimes be critical both of the world observed and of the self. The derogatory tone which characterised most of the travel impressions written by their predecessors in the 19th century has been replaced by texts which often prefer question marks to exclamation marks. As Pia Brînzeu states, contemporary British and Irish writers who visit Romania describe their experiences as 'journeys of discovery and initiation', in which the authors 'highlight the moral fibre of the Romanians, their courage in facing political and economical hardships, their new tolerance for ethnic minorities, and their love for art – all of which make Otherness less a threat than a promise' (Brînzeu, 2010: 553). The curiosity is real and the traveller is ready to take his or her visit as a challenge, and sometimes the discovery of the other occurs at the same time as the discovery of the self.

'Romania is an extraordinary place, and few people who have not been there can appreciate its beauty and complexity' writes Caroline Juler (2003: 16), and this feeling permeates all the texts selected for analysis in the present chapter: *Transylvania and Beyond* by Dervla Murphy (1995), *Searching for Sarmizegetusa* by Caroline Juler (2003) and *Transylvania* by Bronwen Riley (2007, with photographs by Dan Dinescu). Even in the 19th-century travel literature which described the space of contemporary Romania, women travellers had, in my opinion, a deeper perception of life. If the gentlemen coming from the Great Britain would rely on what they were told by their aristocratic hosts, the ladies would prefer to construct a vision of the world based mostly on their own perceptions. If the gentlemen reduced their perceptions of the peasants to derogatory stereotypes, pointing to their backwardness and 'superstitious' ways of living, the ladies would often pay attention to the farmers' spiritual lives, to their traditions and folkloric culture (see the examples of Nina Elizabeth Mazuchelli and Emily Gerard discussed in Crișan (2009)). Although this distinction has become more muted when one speaks about 20th- or 21st-century travel literature about Romania, I think that the sensibility of the perceiver is still more touching in the travel impressions written by women. And one of the Romanian regions which has impressed contemporary British visitors most is Maramureș.

The Attraction of a Unique Place

For all three travellers discussed in this chapter, the journey to and around Maramureș is an adventure which sometimes can have quite deep implications. All these travel memoirs emphasise the special place of the region in the spiritual geography of Romania, because, as Caroline Juler writes, 'nowhere is the sense of deeply-embedded rural traditions more concentrated than in the north-western land called Maramureș' (Juler, 2003: 23). The authors consider that the geographical location of this 'isolated plateau of unbelievable beauty tucked away behind a barrage of mountains' (Juler, 2003: 23) determines its special character. They are aware that, because of its isolation, this region has occupied a particular position over the centuries and that folkloric traditions have been better preserved, a characteristic which has generated great anthropological interest in Maramureș. Bronwen Riley considers that 'it has one of the richest surviving peasant traditions in Europe' (Riley, 2007: 149).

A frequent tendency among contemporary travellers is to offer a response to the stereotype of Transylvania as the land of Dracula. Dervla Murphy is attracted by the romantic image of this region found in Walter Starkie's *Raggle-Taggle* (1933), a book which she read in her childhood. She is so enthusiastic about visiting the place that she found in her readings, that as soon as she hears about Ceaușescu's fall she prepares for the journey. She comes to Romania in the winter which succeeds the revolution of 1989 and finds a country confronted with political change, whose citizens are both enthusiastic about and confused by the signs of a new world.

Caroline Juler began her journeys in Romania the 1990s, in order to do research for *Blue Guide Romania* (a work she started in 1994). Before visiting the country, Juler does library research, and her reading in the British Library reminds her of Bram Stoker's investigations on the same topic, done a century before. But her direction of study is completely different: the library is 'somewhat drier than Bram Stoker's must have been' and the contemporary author wants 'to avoid sensationalising a country' that she barely knows. Her aim is, instead, 'to give a fair and balanced view but not to pull any punches' (Juler, 2003: 16).

Bronwen Riley also refers to Stoker's research on Transylvania and Wallachia, but her book offers again a different image from the stereotypical space imagined by the Irish author. In her case, the impact on the reader is even stronger, because the text is accompanied by many suggestive photographs by Dan Dinescu, so that the book *Transylvania* is both a travelogue and a photography book.

However, the authors are aware of the strength of this stereotype in Western representation. For instance, Caroline Juler presents the vision of life of two middle-aged sisters who live in Cluj-Napoca. They talk to Caroline about the disadvantages of the consumerist system and their discussion concludes with some solutions proposed for the moral crisis of contemporary capitalism. However, Juler is aware that their opinion does not matter for the globalising world and writes ironically: 'But who would listen to three middle-aged ladies commiserating over the state of the world in out-of-the-way Transylvania? There was more chance of Dracula becoming a universally recognized symbol of peace' (Juler, 2003: 29).

In their travelogues, the authors replace the negative stereotypes associated with Transylvania and Romania with representations which shed light on Romanian values. This country and its inhabitants have influenced the authors' spiritual perception of the world. Referring to the refection of Romania in British travel literature, Jessica Douglas-Home, in her foreword to Juler's book, writes:

> To many of these travellers, Romania has exerted the most powerful fascination. They have found that this country more than any other has illuminated their inner beliefs with the intensity of a magnifying glass. (Juler, 2003: 7)

For Caroline Juler Romania is a major point in her search for a reflective space, which can offer an alternative to the consumerist culture she lives in. The discovery of a complex world, full of contradictions but based on spiritual values, has a healing effect on the foreign visitor. One of the main features of the Romanians is their strong religious faith:

> I needed Romania: while its craziness could be stressful – and hilarious – in the extreme, its sufferings were so much greater than mine that it

offered a kind of healing. There was also the strength of its people's religious faith which, although certainly on the wane by comparison with what it had once been, was something that took me by surprise. (Juler, 2003: 16)

Her experience in Maramureş is both wonderful and confusing, and after her first journey she is sure that she has to come back to the region. When the inhabitants ask her if she enjoys their country, she is aware that they would not understand her enthusiasm: 'How could I explain how much I liked but could not understand Romania, that in far-off England we did things so differently, but not necessarily any better?' (Juler, 2003: 37). Later, Juler explains to her readers: 'what she [her guest] told me bore the imprint of her religious faith. I was more sceptical by nature, but there was something in this country that had taken hold of me and would not let go' (Juler, 2003: 61).

Bronwen Riley has also perceived the spiritual dimension of Maramureş, ever since her first visit to the region in December 1997. In the cold winter, she feels that the wooden churches observed on the horizon can offer her the warmth she needs:

In December 1997, on my first visit to Maramureş, the sight of these wooden churches soaring intermittently above the snowy landscape provided encouragement and a grateful diversion as the bus rattled precariously up and down a series of hairpin bends on a narrow, icy road surrounded by beech forests deep in snow. There was heating inside but all the windows frames were loose, and only the ice that had formed between the gaps provided insulation from the cold outside. (Riley, 2007: 151)

When she visits a Maramureş village for the first time, she cannot help entering its 18th-century wooden church: 'Someone was coming out of the door of the old church, and I could not resist a quick look inside' (Riley, 2007: 154).

There is a strong attraction to Romanian places in the three travel memoirs, and the travellers need to satisfy it by exploring human habitations and their surroundings. 'The romantic image of Transylvania attracted me as it has so many Britons in the past', admits Caroline Juler (2003: 16).

On her first journey in Maramureş, Dervla Murphy feels a similar attraction. In order to perceive the beauty of nature, she prefers to walk all the way to Sighetu Marmaţiei over the Gutâi Pass. But, after 12 miles of walking, when she arrives at a spot which was supposed to offer her a stunning panoramic view, a blizzard strikes suddenly. She hitchhikes on a beer-truck, but, as soon as the weather improves, she wants to get down and to continue her walk, as she feels again the irresistible call of nature. The scenery is tempting: 'To the north sharply peaked hills and long rough ridges overlooked narrow valleys – all brilliantly sparkling and beckoning' (Murphy, 1995: 117). However, the driver prevents her from undertaking such a risky adventure: he warns her that the mountain road is dangerous and a storm will start again. She realises that his advice was good, because a tempest will start again after a short interval.

The attraction to the open spaces of Maramureş has deeper implications. Juler confesses that 'the greenness of Maramureş, real and metaphorical was good for my soul', and even thinks of the possibility of living there in an archaic rural style: 'Looking across to the opposite hillside with its traces of terracing, I could imagine settling down in this green haven, buying a cow and some geese, maybe a pig' (Juler, 2003: 74). Bronwen Riley (2007: 151) is aware that other English people also feel this attraction to Maramureş. She tells us that an Englishman who was doing research in a village close to Ocna Şugatag has invited her to visit that rural community.

Besides the scenery and the rural architecture, the travellers are also impressed by people's attitude towards their guests. The hospitality of the inhabitants of Maramureş is a leitmotif in the travel memoirs dedicated to this region. Dervla Murphy considers that 'even by Romanian standards, Maramureş hospitality is extraordinary' (Murphy, 1995: 124), and recounts that during her stay at Sighetu Marmaţiei total strangers often insisted on paying for her meals or drinks, as a kind of reciprocation for Ireland's warm attitude towards the situation in Romania during the days of the revolution.

Caroline Juler, who states that 'Romanians are usually happy to talk, especially to foreigners' (Juler, 2003: 32), also emphasises the hospitality of the inhabitants of Maramureş. She is always welcomed by intellectuals, peasants or even by the monks on the mountain top. One of the scenes which impressed her most was listening to a class of nine-year-old pupils singing carols in a cold classroom in Breb, 'and the sense of coldness evaporated like breath on a frosty morning' (Juler, 2003: 26).

Bronwen Riley also remarks on the hospitality of the inhabitants. When she arrives at the house of the vet who knows where her compatriot is staying, the vet finds a woman to guide her to the destination. Her guide, 'with typical Romanian solicitude towards strangers' (Riley, 2007: 151), insists on sharing the weight of the foreigner's bag, even though she has to carry a large woollen sack slung over her shoulder.

The travellers frequently show their fascination for the landscape of Maramureş. Interest in the Romanian landscape is a constant theme in

British travel literature as well as in fictional representations. Since the 19th century, the mountainous part of it has been the subject of several British books, and even today Caroline Juler states that 'mountains enveloped in ancient, mixed forests cover a great part of the land and there are areas where you can walk for days and not see another human soul' (Juler, 2003: 17). The beauty of Maramureş' scenery is a leitmotif in the travel memoirs analysed in this chapter. Sometimes even the route to Maramureş seems to anticipate the approach of a special region, enveloped in a spiritual atmosphere. During Juler's train trip from Braşov to Cluj-Napoca and then on to Baia Mare, the sky has an impressive light: 'The light had an unearthly quietude, and like the atmosphere which lay over Romania itself, it was bewitching and bewildering by turns' (Juler, 2003: 29). During her stay in Maramureş, Caroline Juler often immerses herself in the beauty of the landscape. When an old woman sees her walking in the street of Deseşti, she wants to help her find what she is looking for. But the only aim of her stroll is to discover the beauty of the place, 'soaking up the extraordinary scenes that unfolded before me like a child's picture book' (Juler, 2003: 44).

The Maramureş village and its surrounding area are perceived as a space of self-discovery, and the traveller feels the harmony between herself and the world:

> Bordering the village, wild woodland linked fingers with the open meadows, the orchards and rectangular stands of maize and corn. Fences were there to keep animals out rather than in; nothing was parcelled off, nothing gave the impression 'that trespassers would be prosecuted'. It was an amazingly liberating sensation. And the prettiness had not been landscaped as though for a single, wealthy landowner; it was shared and had a purpose. I felt at one with the world. (Juler, 2003: 44)

The varied landscape of Maramureş often makes the visitor feel that she is living a dream and then is suddenly awakened. The haystacks are constant elements which enliven the scenery. Here is a sample of the Maramureş landscape again as observed by Caroline Juler:

> About 12 kms south from the Berbeşti turn lies the village of Călineşti. On the way the view changed. The outlines of the mountains changed, reinforcing the sensation that this was a real place not a dream. To the south and east I could see the Lăpuş and Ţibleş ranges. Gentler foothills rose in between; in Romanian they are called piemonţi as in Italian 'piedmonts', and their slopes were sprinkled with haystacks. These haystacks fascinated me: in Romania they can be as expressive as a

Rodin sculpture. I have seen them leaning together in family groups, marching down a pasture in soldierly rows, and standing alone as though in meditation. To keep the hay dry, it is occasionally stored on a low, square platform which has a movable roof. This gives the impression of a hat. In winter the haystacks give off heat and you can see steam curling out of them. (Juler, 2003: 67)

The Spiritual Dimension of the World

Admiration for the religious faith of the inhabitants of Maramureş is frequently professed in these travel memoirs. Spirituality is considered a defining feature of the Romanian people in general, and here Caroline Juler emphasises the role of the Orthodox Church. The discovery of her own spiritual dimension is influenced by her experience in Romania: 'With hindsight I realise that the healing I found in Romania came from a few individuals whose faith and courage exceeded mine by miles' (Juler, 2003: 16). Even the peasants who live in poverty experience the joy of life, because they are 'rich in spirit' (Juler, 2003: 61). Faith is part of the common life of the peasants she meets. While the women of Ieud are reverently listening to the words of the Bible, the children are playing in the churchyard, without disturbing the religious service. The following scene shows the familiar character of the spiritual manifestation:

Listening reverently to Bible readings in the afternoon sun, the women of Ieud looked like a row of exotic bees taking an unaccustomed rest. Used to the tension of city life, I expected a parental explosion, but none came. Nobody hushed the laughing, playing children or even frowned at them. There was no need, the church was more like an extension of their own homes – than a place where they went as a duty or to make a show of piety once a week. They looked after the church and in return it embraced them. (Juler, 2003: 92)

The travellers emphasise the role of women in the spiritual life of the community. Juler observes that they express their devotion to the church more frequently than men. Riley also notices that women form a devoted congregation, and are ready to obey the canons of the church:

At Easter, women were more likely to fast completely for three days, forgoing all food and water so that they could take communion. During this time, they continued to go about their many arduous daily chores, looking after the household and animals and preparing the Easter feast. (Riley, 2007: 154)

The most representative symbols of Maramureş' spirituality are the wooden churches; eight of them, dating from the 17th and 18th centuries, have been listed by UNESCO as World Heritage sites. The travellers often stress their fascination with the architecture of these buildings. Bronwen Riley considers that 'one of the chief delights of the landscape is the sight of its distinctive wooden churches, their spires, covered in oak shingles, soaring up to a height of 45 metres. They are such an elegant and harmonious element of the countryside that they seem to be part of it' (Riley, 2007: 149). Caroline Juler has carefully described these monuments of the region. Deseşti's wooden church, one of the UNESCO monuments, is depicted as 'a gem of a building'. The author's fondness for this historic monument is suggested by her impression that 'from a distance it looks as though you could hold it in the palm of your hand' (Juler, 2003: 47). Her description presents the main features of the church's architecture:

It is their steeply-pitched, softly curved and shingled roofs that give them their special character. In Maramureş a second layer continues the shape of the upper one. In Deseşti the tower is square and has a lookout platform at the top; above this the tower comes to a point with a smaller turret on each of its four sides. The turrets ... used to show that the village had the right to enact its own laws. Deseşti church is chunky and solid, but its lines, sweeping upwards to the sharp ridge and the point of the spire, give it great dignity. On the outside, the decoration is sparing: a raised ropework belt encircles the body of the church and frames the door at the west end. The squared-off logs which form the walls and brace the great weight of the roof are held together with interlocking joints. There is a long bench on one side of the building where the roof hangs wider and lower than the other.... (Juler, 2003: 47)

Height is the main characteristic of the wooden churches in Maramureş. In the case of Breb's church, the roof is at least three times higher than the walls, 'giving it a splendidly protected appearance rather like a hedgehog' covered with wood shingles instead of spines (Juler, 2003: 26).

The authors of the travelogues are also fascinated by the interiors of the wooden churches, which are decorated with impressive paintings. Riley considers that these images are the result of a mixture of Orthodox and

Catholic elements, but they are remarkable for the 'homely originality' of the artist, who 'depicts the immediate world of the Romanian painters – its landscape and architecture, horses and carts, flowers and trees' (Riley, 2007: 154). The author of *Transylvania* also refers to the functionality of these paintings, which have been designed to present the teachings of the Church to illiterate believers.

Some of the most common subjects of these paintings are heaven and hell, and scenes of the final judgement. Riley remarks on several paintings of the kind, such as the image of heaven on the walls of Budeşti's church, painted by Alexandru Ponehalski, or the 'particularly moving' *Creation of the World* at Deseşti, painted by Radu Munteanu (Riley, 2007: 154). Caroline Juler considers the frescoes of the latter church 'a positive wonderland of Neo-Byzantine folk', whose 'centrepiece is a superb tree of life set in a paradise garden; showing the intimate symbiosis between Christian stories and archaic folklore' (Juler, 2003: 46). She explains that Radu Munteanu was a local artist who was inspired by the medieval churches of Moldavia.

The architectonic structure of Deseşti's church is also described by Caroline Juler. She explains that although the layout is influenced by the Byzantine model, the outline is Gothic. The worshippers enter the church at the west end, and the outer chamber, called the *pronaos*, has a low and flat ceiling, and it is separated from the *naos* by a wooden partition. The ceiling of the *naos*, which occupies the largest space in the church, 'rises to a barrel vault which lies directly underneath the pointed roof' (Juler, 2003: 46). In Orthodox churches the altar is separated by a screen, which is painted in horizontal rows. Juler observes that the image of Christ is at the top and the most important saints are painted below him, while the patron saint, Christ and the Virgin Marry are represented on the bottom screen. The worshippers can see the altar only when the Imperial Doors are opened at certain moments of the liturgy, and then the cross and 'the embroideries bathed in radiant candlelight' (Juler, 2003: 47) are revealed to them.

Juler also describes some particularities of the religious service she observes in the church of Deseşti. She notices that the choir sings the songs unaccompanied by any musical instrument, and the choristers stand facing the screen, while the candles and candelabra provide an intimate light. The opening of the Imperial Doors is perceived as a climax in the service and the symbolism of light is significant: 'When the Imperial Doors were thrown open, we were momentarily dazzled by the blaze from the altar' (Juler, 2003: 47–48).

Another image representative of the Maramureş spirituality is the depiction of the Ladder of Virtue in the *pronaos* of Călineşti's wooden church. When Caroline Juler discovers it, she cannot help herself letting out a 'Wow!' (Juler, 2003: 68). The ladder symbolises Christians' efforts on their ascent to heaven, and climbing it corresponds to arduous advances in their spiritual condition. The ladder has 33 rungs, each of them representing a year of Jesus's life and the fulfilment of a particular virtue. Christ is represented at the top of the ladder, leaning out of the window of heaven, 'ready to embrace anyone who makes the grade' (Juler, 2003: 68).

It is not only between the walls of the church that the inhabitants of Maramureş manifest their spirituality. Riley observes that on some important feast days, the service is held outside. She is impressed by 'the elegant gazebos' (Riley, 2007: 151) in the grounds of the churches, used for liturgy on such occasions. Sometimes the service is held in front of the crosses placed at the end of the village. The wooden cross of Berbeşti impresses Caroline Juler with its rich symbolism: it contains anthropomorphic images of the sun and moon and Christian figures: 'St John and Mary Magdalene clustered protectively around a Virgin and Child'. The author sees this cross, made at the beginning of the 18th century by serfs tied to the land, as a symbol of the continuity of the old traditions: 'the mark of potent, ancient beliefs was still on it, as though some quirk of fate had failed to sweep it away, like Romania itself' (Juler, 2003: 65).

Religious symbols are also found in the everyday life of the inhabitants of Maramureş. Caroline Juler observes that the wooden houses of the village Sârbi are decorated in a similar manner to the church, and the gates and porches 'were enlivened by sun symbols, trees of life, birds and rope motifs, their outlines worn soft by the years' (Juler, 2003: 75).

The connection between man and nature is also a leitmotif in the texts which describe Maramureş. Riley has the impression that the wooden churches 'seem to spring up out of the surrounding landscape' (Riley, 2007: 151). The churchyards are seen as spaces of the self's reintegration in the universe. Riley perceives the cemeteries in Maramureş as 'living organisms and extensions of the sacred space'. The communion of the dead with nature is suggested by the scenery: 'Fruit trees shelter the lovingly tended graves, which are decorated with cut garden flowers, while wild flowers are left to grow between the graves' (Riley, 2007: 151). The same atmosphere characterises Juler's description of Deseşti's churchyard:

> The church stands on the top of a hill surrounded by a cemetery and scattered prunus trees. The cemetery was full of tombs bedecked with colourful flowers. Between them the grass grew long, and haughty cockerels with glossy plumages roosted on the graves without a by-your-leave. Some of the graves were marked with plain wooden crosses that had sunk into the ground. Others were made of black-painted metal

wrought into decorative arabesques. The crosses had semicircular hoods and the names of the dead were painted on the stems in white lettering done by hand. Someone had tied long, blue ribbons on them, and these were fluttering in the wind as though for a party whose guests were temporarily missing. (Juler, 2003: 46)

The harmony between man and nature is also expressed in the folkloric literature of Maramureş. Caroline Juler chooses one of the texts which express this relationship as a motto for her chapter on Maramureş:

The lives of people and wood are closely related. Both grow from a seed and reach for the sun. A tree which grows alone is like a child that is brought up on its own; it has a bad time. Life is much better when there are many of us together. A tree that is battered by the wind will always be sick. It is vulnerable to fire and the axe. (Juler, 2003: 21)

Juler finds one of the most often repeated sayings, 'the forest is the Romanian's friend', meaningful. Her host at Deseşti, Paşa, explains to her that besides the practical function of the wood, its use also has a symbolic meaning, because 'wood is a more human and intimate material than stone', and, at the same time, 'it is more fragile, like our lives'. Paşa believes that 'the memory of this special relationship with the forests lives on' and 'it is reborn every time someone makes a wooden tool or builds a timber house' (Juler, 2003: 44).

Juler finds this harmony between man and nature in the everyday life of the peasants of Maramureş. The structure of Petru Pop a Niţu's household and the relationship between his family's members suggest a harmonious way of living. This woodcarver of Breb lives with his wife, his grown-up son and his son's wife and children. During their discussion with the carpenter, the guests have to keep their voices low, because a baby is 'snoozing bliss-fully in a swinging wooden cot'. Instead of television, telephone or radio, the room is equipped with traditional objects, and the walls are decorated with embroidered cotton towels. The author is impressed by the sense of balance in life she finds in this traditional family: 'Everything had a sense of rhythm, space and proportion that made you feel good to be there' (Juler, 2003: 27). Juler is fascinated with the manner in which the household is organised:

This was the place of Petru Pop a Niţu. It was a fascinating place. As well as sturdy barns for sheltering animals and storing machinery, in one corner of the yard there was a narrow, rectangular container with basket work walls. It was about ten feet high by six feet long and no more than two feet wide, and it was covered with a pitched and shingled roof. In Romania, farmers feed their livestock on maize cobs, and this prehistoric-looking container was designed to keep the cobs fresh through the winter. To me it was not simply a piece of equipment, it had personality. It was the same with so many other tools and structures that I saw in Maramureş: made by hand and based on models which had been passed on through many generations, they had acquired a simple authority that I found enormously pleasing. It was not only that they looked right for the job they had to do, but that they also had an element of fancifulness. This was something that I was sure the Romanian sculptor, Brâncuşi, had picked up in his own work. (Juler, 2003: 26–27)

Not only does this particular house of Maramureş suggest an atmosphere of harmony. The whole rural community is perceived in an idyllic light. Here is a description of the village of Deseşti:

The farmhouses were clustered together in the village as they were in Breb, and as they had once done in England before the 17th century enclosures. Dogs barked. Cockerels crowed. Cattle and oxen lowed. There were no cars. God seemed to be in his Heaven. (Juler, 2003: 42)

And this peaceful atmosphere characterises the neighbouring region of the village too:

The trees and blackcurrant bushes were loaded with fruit. We were only a quarter of a mile from the dusty road, but there was an atmosphere of plenitude: everything seemed to be flowering or bearing fruit, taking its time without harassment. (Juler, 2003: 42)

For a lady who comes from an English urban milieu, picking mushrooms and wild fruit in the forest gives her a special satisfaction, and she has the impression that she finds herself in a landscape that is 'orchard, open heath and forest' (Juler, 2003: 50). Paşa explains to her the difference between the poisonous and edible mushrooms, and when they bring home the crop, the guest enjoys a delicious meal.

One of the main symbols of the Maramureş' identity is its distinctive gates. Dervla Murphy discovers their characteristics at the museum of Sighetu Marmaţiei, where the high farmyard roofed gateways are the most beautiful exhibits. The traveller explains that the dimensions and the exquisiteness of the carvings on the gates were also marks of the social position of the owner. Enthusiastic about discovering the world of Maramureş' art in woodwork, Dervla Murphy feels that she has had 'a blissful morning' (Murphy, 1995: 126). Caroline Juler is also an admirer of the gates of Maramureş. She notices that the wooden houses and their households are separated by wooden palisade fences and the entrance is marked by a tall timber gate, which can sometimes reach 12 or 15 feet high. In a detailed description of the gates in Breb, Juler catches their main features:

> The frame that supported them was constructed ingeniously to hold a side door and sometimes a seat as well, so that one side of the gateway was like a porch. Each gate had a narrow shingled roof which sheltered the whole ensemble. The vertical posts had raised patterns on them; some of them looked like ropes and had been curled into rudimentary stick figures or flower heads. Many of the gates were deeply weathered and leant heavily askew on their hinges; one or two were brand new and had been oiled to a bright orange colour. The gates were solidly functional, but also terrific pieces of sculpture. (Juler, 2003: 25–26)

Juler knows that each gate has its own story and often pays attention to the details of some of the older, ramshackle ones. She looks carefully at an old gate in the village Mara, dating from 1938, and reflects on the meaning of its carvings: rope-work figures, solar symbols and a representation of the tree of life. She observes the row of silhouettes in the shape of picks and axes on the ridge and explains that the peasants designed these elements in order to invoke good spirits to look after the household and frighten evil spirits away. Thus, this gate 'was part of the symbiosis between religious and pagan beliefs that made rural life here so potentially mysterious'. She has the feeling that this 'sturdy and dignified but not austere' gate sums up 'the character not only of the architecture of Maramureş but of its people as well' (Juler, 2003: 37).

The authors also entertain feelings of trepidation for Maramureş and are afraid that the marks of this traditional world will disappear under the influence of globalised modernisation. When Dervla Murphy visits the museum of Sighetu Marmaţiei, the guide ends his presentation on a pessimistic note: '"Soon," said Dumitru, "the status symbols will be tractors"' (Murphy, 1995: 127). Murphy enjoys the marks of the past she encounters during her journey in Maramureş. Instead of complaining about the old train she takes from Sighetu Marmaţiei to Salva, she is thrilled by having such a special experience. Murphy depicts the long and almost empty train as 'a specimen of nonagenarian machinery', a 'marvel' (Murphy, 1995: 129) which, although it goes at a modest speed, is still able to reach its destination. The frequent stops of the train are perceived as opportunities to enjoy the beauty of the landscape instead of reasons for complaining about the slow speed.

Caroline Juler is similarly concerned about the fragility of this traditional world. At the beginning of her book, Juler explains that her travelogue is 'also a gut reaction to a tragic circumstance: the loss of an ancient culture' (Juler, 2003: 17). She realises that the traditional values of Maramureş are preserved in a world which stands in need of economic progress. The village Breb is so picturesque because it is somehow isolated from the rest of the world, as its streets are not asphalted, and when it rains they are filled with mud. In Deseşti, Juler has the impression that the village has a medieval look. But she is fond of this atmosphere and is afraid that its traditions could disappear:

> There were moments of anxiety when I feared the beauty of Maramureş would vanish before my eyes. In these moments it was as fragile as a body that has been preserved in a vacuum; once someone punctures it, the body falls to dust. I knew there were people who felt like me, and for that reason they kept the place a secret. (Juler, 2003: 65)

Juler explains that she hopes that the well-being of the inhabitants of Maramureş will increase without losing the customs which make the region unique:

> Which was more important: my pleasure as a tourist or the well-being of thousands of people? Was it selfish of me to want Maramureş to stay where it was? But in fact I did not want it to stay where it was, only that it should go forward in a way that did not destroy what was already good – and what the West had lost. (Juler, 2003: 66)

Bronwen Riley also observes that the Maramureş of the new millennium was different from the Maramureş she saw in the 1990s, which also changed from the way it looked in the 1970s. She knows that intellectuals have long been concerned about the disappearance of the authentic folklore of the region. However, she is aware that, in spite of its conservative character, folk culture is not a static phenomenon, and it has often been influenced by certain exterior factors. Riley gives a suggestive example:

> An old woman whom Ion Minoiu recorded in Oaş, a remote region west of Maramureş, was acclaimed in her village for her ability to sing

long songs, yet she never sang the same one twice and would always improvise to suit her mood and audience. Maramureş is often talked about as a 'living museum' where traditions are preserved which have died out elsewhere, but this term, designed to captivate tourists, is a fallacious one. A living culture cannot be static, just like the old woman's songs. (Riley, 2007: 165)

The representation of Maramureş in these travel memoirs can therefore be read as the best invitation for foreign visitors to discover a unique region, and for us Romanians to reflect deeply on our cultural and spiritual values and the sorts of risk they are exposed to when those visitors do indeed come.

Acknowledgements

This work was supported by a grant of the Romanian National Authority for Scientific Research, CNCS – UEFISCDI, project number: PN-II-RU-PD-2011-3-0194.

References

Brînzeu, P. (2010) Journeys to the other half of the continent: British and Irish accounts of the Carpatho-Danubian region. In M. Cornis-Pope and J. Neubauer (eds) *History of the Literary Cultures of East-Central Europe: Junctures and Disjunctures in the 19th and 20th Centuries. Volume IV: Types and Stereotypes* (pp. 549–560). Amsterdam: Benjamin.

Crişan, M. (2009) Superstition and religion in Stoker's sources on Transylvania. In R.A. Henderson (ed.) *Perspectives on English Studies* (pp. 49–64). Turin: Trauben.

Juler, C. (2003) *Searching for Sarmizegetusa: Journeys to the Heart of Rural Romania*. Glanrhyldwilym: Starborn Books.

Murphy, D. (1995) *Transylvania and Beyond: A Travel Memoir*. Woodstock: Overlook Press.

Riley, B. and Dinescu, D. (2007) *Transylvania*. London: Frances Lincoln.

8 Tourist Experience in Narrative Fiction: E.M. Forster's *A Room with a View*

Fernanda Luísa Feneja

> *Sailing henceforth to every land, to every sea,*
> *We willing learners of all, teachers of all, and lovers of all.*
> Walt Whitman, *On Journeys Through the States*

E.M. Forster's *A Room with a View* (1908) opens with the arrival of Lucy Honeychurch and Miss Bartlett in Florence at the Pensione Bertolini. Lucy, the main character, is introduced in the second paragraph, expressing her great disappointment at the British atmosphere she encounters there and which seems to dominate the whole place. She voices this when she first hears the owner's accent: 'And a Cockney, besides! [...] It might be London.' A look around the room confirms her initial impression, as almost everything there resembles England – the guests, the drinks, the decoration. Even though this constitutes the diegetic departure point from which the whole plot will develop, it is worthwhile highlighting, in particular, the traveller's mindset that spurs Lucy's negative reaction: the search for the new, the unknown, the different that travel embodies. As Casey Blanton (2002: 18) states in her study of travel writing, travelling is 'a symbolic act, heavy with promises of new life, progress, and the thrill of escape'.

The idea and the spirit of travel constitute a common element in diverse literary genres. Within these conjoined genres, we can find both non-fiction narrative, such as travel writing or writings of place, and narrative fiction, for example novels and short stories, all dealing with the experience of journeying. Specialist studies of literature and tourism – the latter understood not only as a field of sociological study but also as an economic activity in its own right – have shed a great deal of light on recent and contemporary travel practices.

It is, then, the aim of this chapter to discuss how such diverse areas can merge in specific ways, suggesting new paths of interdisciplinary reflection.

This chapter will consider, for that purpose, *A Room with a View*, focusing on a number of aspects that will, it is hoped, illustrate the fruitfulness of this perspective – in other words, it will take a close look at certain narrative features, including space, character and time, as well as at other narrative traits in the novel which go to form representations of tourist experience. Finally, reflections will be offered on how such features reinforce the potential of the text for meaningful commentary.

E.M. Forster's trip to Florence in 1901 is thought to have inspired the creation of the novel, which was first published in earlier versions called, respectively, *Lucy* and *New Lucy*. While the former, written between 1902 and 1903, focuses mainly on the Pensione Bertolini's guests, who bear a strong resemblance to the characters he met, the latter, begun immediately after *Lucy* was concluded, was more wide-ranging. Being drafts or forerunners of *A Room with a View*, they both make a now invisible contribution, it must be acknowledged, to the latter's structure and its thematic issues, as we shall see.

Among Forster's major works like *Howards End* (1910) and *A Passage to India* (1924), *A Room with a View* was classified by the author himself (2011: 209) as 'the nicest', a judgement corroborated by critics in general; both Cavaliero (1979: 93, 105) and Colmer (1983: 43), for example, use the superlatives 'the sunniest' and the 'most well-liked' to express the same idea. These critical considerations emphasise the light tone of the story and its comic elements, while in no way undervaluing the moral standpoint which it assumes.

Even if the plot is a fairly conventional one, and the love story theme likewise, the book has long been acclaimed (Silva, 2001: 160, 163) for the sensitivity the author shows in dealing with the topic, as well as for the thorough organisation underlying its apparent simplicity. Indeed, this organisation has long fostered discussion of a number of major themes revealed in this lighthearted story, among which one might mention the polarity between convention and spontaneity, tradition and progress, reason and feeling. Many of these dichotomies rest on contrastive representations of the British and Italian characters, and have been given special attention in these terms in studies by John Martin (1977), John Colmer (1983) and Glen Cavaliero (1979), just to cite a few. A fictional treatment of this broad contrast is made possible in the novel through the main character's trip to Italy: Lucy travels to Florence on a planned vacation, accompanied by her older cousin, Charlotte Bartlett, a conservative spinster – a practice that is consistent with the social behaviour of 19th-century English middle-class families, who would promote travel to Europe as a way of complementing their children's education. Indeed, in part because of developments in transport, especially the railway, and of the increase in free time, mass tourism is believed, as Tim Youngs (2006: 6) states, to have originated in the early 19th century. More specifically, with Napoleon's defeat in 1815 Europe became once again accessible to the British. Florence, where the action takes place both in the first part of the story and in the final chapter, was a common tourist destination, alongside Rome and Venice, an itinerary that could be traced back to its origins in the Grand Tour.[1] It should be noticed that women already took part in such early expeditions.[2]

The point of the book's title is made clear as early as the opening chapter, when they find out that they have to stay in a room with no view over the Arno River. Lucy and Charlotte's disappointed comments are overheard by another guest, Mr Emerson, who kindly offers to swap rooms with them. Making the acquaintance of the Emersons constitutes a key event in the narrative, as Lucy eventually falls in love with George, Mr Emerson's son, and the development of their relationship sets up some of the most important questions explored by the text. According to Colmer (1983: 44), however minor the occurrence itself might be, it signals the first encounter between two opposing worlds: one faithful to convention, as Lucy's embarrassment and hesitation show, and that of practical reason and spontaneous behaviour, which the Emersons symbolise throughout the novel. Indeed, it is a generous outlook on life that their gesture clearly signals from the very beginning of the novel. Colmer (1983: 44) interestingly relates this starting incident to various connotations of the word 'view', so prominent in the novel's title. From his perspective, the idea of the need for a 'view' represents the second of the two opposing worlds depicted in the story and the need to embrace an attitude towards life that would go far beyond the limits of social propriety, which, at this initial stage, Lucy still finds hard to abandon. She is a product of Victorian/Edwardian upper-middle-class mainstream society and, as such, is faithful to its conventions. Douwe Fokkema (2000: 562, 565) maintains that these are, precisely, the basic units of her culture, the regularities in behaviour to which people adhere, even if to different degrees. A capacity for interpretation and adjustment, however, also belongs in one's understanding of how conventions work. Clearly, the opening episode involving Lucy and the Emersons suggests a rupture in terms of the conventional code underlying their social exchange, even if, as Colmer (1983: 44) also notes, Lucy's reaction might seem exaggerated.

Furthermore, the metaphorical meaning of 'view', the idea that underpins this episode, also draws on the distinction between the finite and the infinite, which need to be harmoniously related (Colmer, 1983: 44). Such concepts are of special relevance: they spring from a semantic field regarding space, in which a confined, finite space, a room at a guest-house, can be the springboard for a broader, further view over the surrounding landscape, an infinite space ahead. Obviously enough, they represent the two perspectives identified above, and also the two options the protagonist faces – the deeper implications of which she is not aware of at this point of the narrative.

Lucy's inner development goes on to illustrate the appropriateness of this metaphor, of the powerful potential of the word 'view', as the wider horizon provided by Mr Emerson's gesture will eventually change her fundamental outlook on life. From our perspective, too, the metaphor of the room with a view at Pensione Bertolini reinforces the idea of place as a core narrative category in the novel, as it not only frames but also highlights the foreigner's view over a new place in a new country. Such a view, be it in literal or in symbolic terms, implies the interaction of different cultural contexts, which, while central to any concept of travel involving a seer and a seen, also supports the plot construction in *A Room with a View*. The particular contact established between a traveller's background and identity and the newness he or she encounters will prove all the more important in shaping, transforming and broadening his or her worldview. Therefore, we can see that personal identity and Otherness belong in this process, a binary relationship that travel writing explores, be it, as Blanton (2002: 106) argues, because representations of place involve one's position *vis-à-vis* the Other, or because the portrayal of different manners and customs necessarily reproduces the Other textually.[3]

The importance of place in this and Forster's other books (different 'abroads' feature in most of his novels) derives primarily from the protagonist's passages away from and back home. Lucy makes her life-changing trip, returns to England and then makes her second journey back to Italy, transformed. Such a conceptual feature is crucial in any narrative text, interacting with all other thematic categories, and includes not only the physical elements where the action takes place (the setting), but also the movements of the characters across different geographical locations and, at a more restricted level, through interior places. The social atmosphere of a place further adds to possible sub-categories of space (Reis & Lopes, 2002: 135) – a theoretical frame of reference that can be clearly applied to *A Room with a View*. In this category, other writings of place include travel writing, which Blanton (2002: 106) defines as the representation of place and the subsequent fixing, in our minds, of 'the contours and colours of a particular region of the globe'.

A Room with a View is clearly good travel writing too. The novel's second chapter opens with a powerful description of Florence, expressed from a foreigner's perspective:

It was pleasant to wake up in Florence, to open the eyes upon a bright bare room, with a floor of red tiles which look clean though they are not; with a painted ceiling whereon pink griffins and blue *amorini* sport in a forest of yellow violins and bassoons. It was pleasant, too, to fling wide the windows, pinching the fingers in unfamiliar fastenings, to lean out into the sunshine with beautiful hills and trees and marble churches opposite, and, close below, the Arno, gurgling against the embankment of the road. (Forster, 2011: 13)

This excerpt captures the appeal of the Italian atmosphere, of the newness, the charm of the place, which will be further explored in Lucy's sightseeing trip to Santa Croce.

The Santa Croce episode trip is emblematic of the opposition between naturalness or spontaneity and convention, but it is especially significant for the purpose of this discussion because of the issues raised by the traveller's reactions to visited places. Although Lucy takes her *Baedeker*, she feels deprived of orientation when she loses sight of her guide, Miss Lavish, who was carrying it at that moment. Again, this trivial incident is very significant. Indeed, the *Baedeker* can be considered a metonym for the cultural dependency represented by popular travel guides (the book takes its name from its original editor, the German Karl Baedeker, who founded the company in 1827);[4] its common use in fiction creates the British tourist stereotype, dependent on the book's guidance and simultaneously limited by its clues and recommendations. Therefore, as Lucy enters Santa Croce church without her travel guide, she feels lost because she no longer knows what she is supposed to admire, and also because what she feels does not accord with what she suspects is 'the right thing to feel', an impression that, to a significant degree, all but blocks any aesthetic experience at all during her first trip.

At this stage of the novel, she represents, as Isabel Silva (2001: 166) has noted, 'her class and period', which brings her closer to the status of a character type. Forster himself, who theorised the novel in his critical work *Aspects of the Novel* (1927), mentions 'types' as a term for what he classifies as 'flat characters',[5] those who are 'easily remembered by the reader afterwards' because 'they are constructed round a single idea or quality' (1995: 68–69). However, as Forster (1995: 78) also notes, this is the original, pure form of such characters, while most often a number of other factors conspire in their creation and make them share characteristics with the other pole in his brief taxonomy, his 'round characters'. These are, in his view, able to surprise and convince us: this type 'has the incalculability of life about it – life within the pages of a book'. Clarifying such concepts here helps us to understand

Lucy's development throughout the novel, within a sociocultural context governed by convention and rupture. Hence, at the beginning of the novel, her uncontested acceptance of norms and standards, of common behaviour, brings to light her stereotypical character. The Santa Croce scene is a prime illustration of this. Entering the church, she thinks: 'Of course, it must be a wonderful building. But how like a barn! And how very cold! Of course, it contained frescoes by Giotto, in the presence of whose tactile values she was capable of feeling what was proper' (Forster, 2011: 18).

The reference to Giotto suggests that, some time before, she must already have heard or read about the painter; the conditioned response to art is unmistakably connected with the realm of orthodox, conventional, flawed learning, which is soon to be questioned by the views on art of Forster's own counterparts in the novel, the Emersons. As Lago (1995: 1) contends, he considered art the dimension in human life that makes it more elevated and enjoyable. Taking into account the cross-cultural encounters that pervade the novel, together with the impact they have on the protagonist's transformation, this perspective seems to converge with Bredella's idea that art frees us from 'rigid, stereotypical concepts of reality and from becoming insensitive to the claims of the other' (Bredella, 1996: 51).

In fact, a second encounter with the Emersons, which occurs in this very episode, spurs Lucy's initial, growing awareness of her inner doubt, as Mr Emerson ironically comments on her lack of the *Baedeker*: 'It's worth minding, the loss of a Baedecker. *That's* worth minding.' This intriguing comment causes Lucy some confusion: 'Lucy was puzzled. She was again conscious of some new idea, and was not sure whither it should lead her' (Forster, 2011: 20). In fact, the new idea disturbing her mind, though not explicitly revealed in the text, will become evident in her growing response to Mr Emerson, who becomes the main catalyst for her personal development. Throughout the visit to Santa Croce, his approach to life is constantly exposed to Lucy, covering issues such as religion, aesthetic fruition, truth and generosity. When he tells her bluntly 'I think you are repeating what you have heard older people say. You are pretending to be touchy; but you are not really' (Forster, 2011: 21), he means, as Silva (2001: 166) contends, that truth should always outweigh convention and manners, a life principle that should also apply to art. Earlier in the chapter, Miss Lavish, referred to in the text as 'the clever lady', had anticipated the same sort of consideration: 'I hope we shall emancipate you from Baedeker. He does but touch the surface of things. As to the true Italy – he does not even dream of it. The true Italy is only to be found by patient observation' (Forster, 2011: 14–15).

This idea of authenticity in life in general and as a way of understanding art mirrors Forster's views on culture and knowledge, as he defended a comprehensive concept of art, including diversity of expression, and of culture as an open model encompassing, for example, tradition, affection and delight. Hence, as Lago (1995: 3) states, he also rejects the idea that the artist should be confined to an ivory tower. Such empirical, questioning views lie beneath the protagonist's doubts as she stands before some of the great works of the Italian Renaissance, and soon initiate her self-learning and discovery as, when forced to enjoy Santa Croce church on her own, she frees herself from all guidance and recoils from the typical tourist behaviour she witnesses: 'Then the pernicious charm of Italy worked on her, and, instead of acquiring information, she began to be happy' (Forster, 2011: 19). Such a liberation process will empower her real aesthetic quest, when, as Silva (2001: 170) maintains, her search for beauty in art will be answered by life instead. What becomes significant here is the authenticity she learns to value in her own physical and intellectual responses, made possible by her spiritual journey. Thereafter, Lucy clearly abandons the features of a flat character and becomes a rounded one.

Learning is another component of this framework, relating to culture beyond the scope of formal education and involving necessarily the creative arts. The Forsterian rationale for learning is that it is a natural, life-committed phenomenon (Lago, 1995: 1). An early paragraph from the second chapter of *A Room with a View* demonstrates this idea. A thorough picture of everyday life in Florence is provided, the whole scene being captured from the window of Pensione Bertolini through Lucy's eyes:

> Over the river men were at work with spades and sieves on the sandy foreshore, and on the river was a boat, also diligently employed for a mysterious end. An electric tram came rushing underneath the window. No one was inside it, except one tourist; but its platforms were overflowing with Italians, who preferred to stand. Children tried to hang on behind, and the conductor, with no malice, spat in their faces to let them go. (Forster, 2011: 13)

Such 'patient observation', in Miss Lavish's words, seems so rewarding and enriching that the learning of art or history may be at risk in the face of it: 'the traveller who has gone to Italy to study the tactile values of Giotto, or the corruption of the Papacy, may return remembering nothing but the blue sky and the men and women who live under it' (Forster, 2011: 14).

The excerpt is relevant inasmuch as it underscores the authenticity, the naturalness, the identity of Italy against all formal, elitist culture. Again, it seems to celebrate the spirit of the place, something Lucy will later be able to fully perceive and absorb. Nevertheless, and considering the scope of the present discussion, we should reflect on whether Lucy's profile constitutes that of a tourist or rather the broader one of a traveller (and a learner). Following the critical judgement on mass tourism that can be inferred from Lucy's initial thoughts and attitudes, it could be argued that this is one of the central strands in the novel's overall meaning and one of the elements that guides its character construction.

The distinction between traveller and tourist has been clarified in tourism studies and has been addressed in literary discourse, usually in fairly pragmatic terms. The United Nations Conference on Tourism and International Travel, held in Rome in 1963, first classified travellers according to the length and purpose of their trips to a foreign country, which generally made the tourist a sub-type of the traveller. Nowadays, the definition provided by the World Tourism Organization (WTO) is much broader: the tourist is a visitor who spends at least one night in the visited place (actually, the term 'overnight visitor' is used), whether in his or her own or in another country (see http://media.unwto.org/en/content/understanding-tourism-basic-glossary). Also, according to Licínio Cunha's reference work on tourism studies (2001: 31–32), the WTO considers that tourism involves visitors' activities beyond the scope of their daily routine, usual atmosphere and social interaction, as well as travel, transportation and a destination, the latter being the place where a number of tourism facilities are to be found.

This simple framework, because it relies substantially on the inter-relation between travel and tourism, makes it clear that both plot and setting in *A Room with a View* combine these elements: Lucy Honeychurch corresponds to the given definitions of traveller, visitor and tourist. Considering the range of types of tourism,[6] her stay in Florence and the aims of her journey would fall into the category of cultural tourism, which, as Cunha (2001: 49) contends, relates to the aim of seeing new things, enlarging one's knowledge, getting to know what is specific about other people's traditions, different cultures, past and present, or spiritual needs. The concept of 'cultural tourist' is deeply rooted in travelling as a way of learning, and was very commonly practised in the 19th century, although the journey as an individual quest for knowledge and intellectual enrichment can be traced back beyond the 18th century (Leal, 2000: 234) to the custom of visiting European cultural centres, like those in Italy or France, and to as far back as in the 16th century, pursuing aims that included not only culture and education, but also youthful health and enjoyment, the principles indeed that underlay the Grand Tour (Towner, 2002: 227).

As far as *A Room with a View* is concerned, Lucy's cultural and educational journey bears a certain relation to these ideals: in fact, the plot seems to follow a structure based on concentric, interdependent circles, each of which paves the way for the next: the outer one represents the encounter with a new place (Italy), the intermediate one with new, significant people (like the Emersons, whom she meets in this new place) and the central one with herself, when she undertakes an inner journey of self-discovery, which entails risk, openness and the chance of happiness. Place, as a core narrative category, is central to the semantic construction of the novel,[7] which is a quest for self-realisation.

The idea of a link between self-knowledge and travelling is elaborated on by the Portuguese writer Teolinda Gersão in her novel about Lisbon, *A Cidade de Ulisses* (2011), in which she also draws a subjective distinction between tourists and travellers: from her perspective, while the former look for new places as a way of escaping from themselves, the latter look for themselves in new places and, by doing so, get to know such places more deeply (Gersão, 2011: 31). Therefore, in her view, one's discovery of a place is primarily driven by the search for self-knowledge.

This process illustrates Lucy's path of self-reflection and her resulting self-knowledge, which coincides, in terms of plot development, with the novel's happy ending; as she eventually manages to see past the conventions and accepted behaviour patterns that have shaped her Victorian upbringing and education, she restores her authentic capacity to feel and begins to subscribe to the Emersons' outlook on life, one that is based on truth above all things. In terms of character development, she gives clear evidence of the proleptic statement made by Miss Lavish ('the clever lady') on Florence in Chapter 2 of the novel: 'One doesn't come to Italy for niceness, one comes for life' (Forster, 2011: 15), and which, having become a famous quote, might have served as an advertising slogan for Italy.

It has also been mentioned (Silva, 2001: 180) that Lucy and George's marriage symbolises the merging of two distinct social groups in British society: the old world, represented by Lucy and her family circle, and the new world of progress and reason, symbolised by the Emersons. While this is noticeable and consistent with the emergence of a shared outlook on most life matters, what is more important in this analysis is Lucy's conversion to truth, authenticity and generosity, her lesson in humanity, through travel itself. While it could be argued that it is her relationship with the Emersons that spurs the whole action and with it the subsequent, overall outcome, none of this would have been possible without the central role of place and dislocation. It is the traveller's mind-set in Lucy that enables her to feel what both Silva (2001: 184) and Leal (2000: 239) call 'the spirit of the place', something that involves emotion, aesthetic discovery, intercultural learning and exchange. Ultimately, Lucy is illustrative of the idea that travelling implies change, and usually for the better.

In her study of learned tourists, Luisa Leal (2000: 234) states that they differ from common ones inasmuch as they choose their itineraries from a literary repertoire that provides them with previous knowledge of a place, thus creating a specific form of mediation, of contact with that place. In this sense, we can conclude that Lucy Honeychurch fails to qualify as a learned tourist, as her initial knowledge of the places to visit was almost totally restricted to the information provided in her *Baedeker*, but, conversely, her innate responses give life to Forster's belief in culture as something spontaneous and close to real life. Also, visiting sites and viewing art objects, the trait of modern mass tourism to which she generally conforms, can be, according to Cohen-Hattab and Kerber (2004: 58), very significant in the construction of cultural identity. Lucy's experiences as a character definitely contribute to *our* interaction with a sense of place in literature as readers, partly illustrating Leal's conclusion (2000: 238) that knowing a place is, after all, knowing the texts, which go far beyond the journey.[8]

Indeed, this serves to add the dialectics between reality and textuality, between place and its representation in literature, to our discussion, leading to a consideration of the role of literature in tourism instead of its converse (the role of tourism in literature), which we have been reflecting on in Forster's novel. Cohen-Hattab and Kerber (2004: 58, 68) maintain that creative literary representation helps to foster richer ways of getting to know places, more complex forms of interpreting what they call 'the character of a place' and its cultural identities, thereby going beyond the tendency, born out of present-day mass tourism, to stereotype certain destinations to a degree.

To conclude, *A Room with a View* can be regarded a hybrid genre where travel writing, fiction and narrative of place are interwoven and merge. In such cases, literary interpretations can be enriched by understandings derived from the field of tourism research. It can serve as a reference text, 'fixing in one's minds', as Blanton (2002: 106) puts it, the spirit of Florence. In other words, cultural knowledge about Italy and individual responses to it are generated in a richer and more open text than *Baedecker* or the Lonely Planet, and in this form can be communicated to future travellers.

In *A Room with a View*, turn-of-the-century Italy, as seen through a traveller's eyes, becomes a unique place of social transformation. Its representation in a literary text, in narrative fiction, makes it part of a corpus of literary travel texts which continue to offer possibilities for exploration, both by literary analysis, on the one hand, and by bringing to bear the perceptions of interdisciplinary studies on tourist experience, on the other.

Notes

(1) The Grand Tour was a standard European itinerary the British gentry would undertake from the 17th century on, as part of their education, and was considered a rite of passage.

(2) The Portuguese travel book *Viagens d'Altina* (*Altina's Travels*), for example, is illustrative of this trend: it consists of a long first-person travel narrative of a woman (Altina), in the late 18th century, on a journey through a number of European countries that lasted almost two decades (Luís Caetano Altina de Campos, *Viagens d'Altina nas Cidades Mais Cultas da Europa e nas Principaes Povoações dos Balinos, Povos Desconhecidos de Todo o Mundo*, Lisboa: Oficinas Simão Thaddeo Ferreira, 1798–1805) (Anastácio, 2006: 2–5).

(3) Blanton draws both on Dennis Porter (*Haunted Journeys: Desire and Transgression in European Travel writing*, 1991) and on Mary Louise Pratt (*Imperial Eyes: Travel Writing and Transculturation*, 1992), respectively. However, because she deals with colonisation and imperialism, Pratt analyses mainly the distance created between observer and observed.

(4) Interestingly enough, John Colmer (1983), when elaborating on Forster's former versions of *A Room with a View*, considers that the first one, *Lucy*, could be considered precisely a *Baedeker* novel, due to the emphasis placed on local and cultural aspects of Italy, such as its art, architecture or atmosphere.

(5) Flat characters reflect better notions of social space so as to give a more accurate, generally critical view of society (Reis & Lopes, 2002: 136).

(6) Tourism studies and the tourism business resort to different ways of classifying tourism according to the purpose of or reason for the trip. Such forms of categorising tourism can be exhaustive; the online *Travel Industry Dictionary* (http://www.travel-industry-dictionary.com), for example, lists 45 different types, ranging from 'accessible tourism' to 'weather tourism'. See also Online Reference Guide, 'Main types of tourism', at http://inf .newkerala.com/top-travel-destinations-of-the-world/main-types-of-tourism.html (accessed 15 September 2012).

(7) Reis and Lopes refer to the undeniable potential of semantic representation enabled by space as a narrative category (Reis & Lopes, 2002: 139).

(8) Leal (2000: 238) draws on Agustina Bessa Luís's *Breviário do Brasil* (Porto: Edições Asa, 1991) to state how texts can provide a more comprehensive and deeper representation of places.

References

Anastácio, V. (2006) Viajar com a Imaginação: Jonathan Swift e Luís Caetano Altina de Campos. *Convergência Lusíada* 22, 157–174. At http://www.vanda-anastacio.at/articles/1_Viagens imaginarias_locked.pdf (accessed 20 September 2012).

Blanton, C. (2002) *Travel Writing: The Self and the World*. New York: Routledge.

Bredella, L. (1996) Aesthetics and ethics: Incommensurable, identical or conflicting? In G. Hoffmann and A. Hornung (eds) *Ethics and Aesthetics: The Moral Turn of Postmodernism* (pp. 29–52). Heidelberg: C. Winter.

Cavaliero, G. (1979) *A Reading of E.M. Forster*. London: Macmillan.

Cohen-Hattab, K. and Kerber, J. (2004) Literature, cultural identity and the limits of authenticity: A composite approach. *International Journal of Tourism Research* 6, 57–73.

Colmer, J. (1983) *E.M. Forster: The Personal Voice*. London: Routledge and Kegan Paul.

Cunha, L. (2001) *Introdução ao Turismo*. Lisbon: Verbo.

Fokkema, D. (2000) The politics of multiculturalism and the art of code-switching. In I. Allegro Magalhães *et al.* (coord.) *Literatura e Pluralidade Cultural. Actas do 3º Congresso Nacional da Associação Portuguesa de Literatura Comparada* (pp. 561–571). Lisbon: Edições Colibri.

Forster, E.M. (1995) *Aspects of the Novel*. Orlando, FL: Harvest/Harcourt, Brace & World.

Forster, E.M. (2011) *A Room with a View*. London: Penguin Books.

Gersão, T. (2011) *A Cidade de Ulisses*. Lisbon: Sextante Editora.

Lago, M. (1995) *E.M. Forster: A Literary Life*. Houndmills: Macmillan.

Leal, M.L. (2000) Turistas cultas: Contacto, testemunho e mediação. In I. Allegro Magalhães *et al.* (coord.) *Literatura e Pluralidade Cultural. Actas do 3º Congresso Nacional da Associação Portuguesa de Literatura Comparada* (pp. 233–240). Lisbon: Edições Colibri.

Martin, J.S. (1977) *E.M. Forster: The Endless Journey*. Cambridge: Cambridge University Press.

Reis, C. and Lopes, A.C. (2002) *Dicionário de Narratologia*. Coimbra: Livraria Almedina.

Silva, I.M.F. (2001) *The British Abroad in E.M. Forster's Fiction*. Lisbon: UAL.

Towner, J. (2002) Literature, tourism and the Grand Tour. In M. Robinson and H. Christian Andersen (eds) *Literature and Tourism: Essays in the Reading and Writing of Tourism* (pp. 226–238). London: Thomson.

Youngs, T. (ed.) (2006) *Travel Writing in the Nineteenth Century: Filling the Blank Spaces*. London: Anthem Press.

9 Deaths in Venice: Dying for a Holiday

Anthony David Barker

There are a number of reasons for imagining that going on holiday is a risky business. People who otherwise hardly ever go near water find themselves close to or in large bodies of water for long periods of time. People who take very little exercise expose themselves to activities requiring considerable exertion. In addition, they tend to eat and drink too much on holiday, and to eat and drink things they are not used to. Individuals put off seeking medical attention they might need until after their holiday, or find it too complicated or troublesome to seek that help while away. A myth persists that suicide rates increase during the holiday period, although evidence for this is patchy. Emotional or relational problems can certainly come to a head though in holiday environments. Seasonal changes and the weather of a particular country are known to have an effect on mood. More recently, there has been an increased suicide rate in southern European countries where, due to recession, formerly lax authorities are now tigerishly pursuing their citizens for undeclared income and unpaid taxes. Anecdotal evidence about holiday mishaps is unreliable since the fact that more and more of us have been taking more and longer holidays makes it not merely likely but statistically inevitable that more bad things are going to happen to us on holiday. By that logic, more good things must happen too. But, having said that, a death or getting seriously ill on holiday trumps a stimulating or restful time in most people's estimation.

Death on holiday is a serious and difficult business for professionals as well. The websites of the British consular services, for example, contain a wealth of information and advice for the friends and relatives of those who die abroad, in respect of funeral and repatriation services, enough to suggest at any rate that this constitutes a significant part of their advisory duties. Take the case of British couple, Roger and Mathilde Lamb, holidaying with their four boys in Essaouira, Morocco, in late August 2011. Mathilde died falling from a holiday apartment window, following what appears to have been a family argument, and Roger died falling from a different apartment a few days later. In neither case was the word 'jump' used but it hovers unstated behind the phrases used in news reports: 'The exact circumstances of their deaths are still unknown' (Sky News UK, 2011). Whatever the causes of this domestic tragedy, it played out in front of four startled children in two strange apartments in a foreign country during a family holiday. Clearly, there can have been a negligible amount of premeditation in these events. But we do not need this example to understand that holiday periods can be a crucible for stresses and strains in intimate and family relations.

In this connection, many websites deal specifically with how to get through the holidays harmoniously. Sheri and Bob Stritof offer the following marital advice:

1. Talk with one another about your expectations of the holiday season.
2. Anticipate problem areas such as finances, time constraints, or in-laws.
3. Make some strategic plans for handling these potential hot spots.
4. Remember, you can always rent a hotel room. You don't have to stay with extended family.
5. Between the two of you, develop a secret code that means 'get me out of here!'
6. Make sure you only play non-competitive games.
7. Remind folks to not discuss religion or politics

('How to survive the holidays', at http://marriage.about.com/cs/holiday survival/ht/holidays.htm)

Strangely enough, the opposite is also supposed to be true: a good holiday is claimed to be able to save a shaky marriage. The *Daily Mail* in September 2009 reported the following initiative:

If you're experiencing marital strife, the thought of sharing your two-week holiday in the Maldives with a marriage guidance counsellor may not be conducive to patching things up.

But if one Indian travel firm's idea to use holidays to pull couples back from the brink of divorce catches on, the concept could be heading for Britain.

Mumbai-based KV Tours and Travels is offering 'divorce tourism' packages where couples are accompanied by a relationship counsellor to encourage them to give things another go.

(TravelMail Reporter, 2009)

Even when all such attempts at reconciliation prove fruitless, there are other holiday niche markets that can meet the needs of the broken-hearted. The *Daily Mail* for 31 July 2009 reported:

> It seems there is a cruise to suit everyone....
>
> But U.S. company Cruise.com is going a step further – with what it claims are the first cruises aimed at the divorcee market.
>
> Two separate divorce-themed cruises are on offer, the first with Norwegian Cruise Line's Norwegian Sky from Miami to the Bahamas on October 16, and one with Royal Caribbean's Radiance of the Seas....
>
> Anyone who has fallen foul of love has a unique opportunity to apply for a berth and begin their new life at sea.
>
> Anthony Hamawy, president of Cruise.com says: 'These cruise groups were designed for divorced individuals to meet, party and perhaps even connect with others who have shared similar relationship experiences.'
> (Clark, 2009)

With all these attendant risks, do we dare go on holiday? The purpose of this chapter is to explore whether, although foreign holidays have always been characterised by a certain degree of unpredictability, associated with the adventure of 'other places' and their different ways of doing things, the danger might also be identified as emanating from within. In short, the question is asked whether holidays have some special propensity to bring out fault lines in relationships and reveal inner frailties in individuals as well. The argument is that many great writers have long identified exactly this feature of the foreign holiday in their work; the Venetian holiday is here chosen as a striking example of the phenomenon.

'Vedi Napoli e poi Muori' is a phrase apocryphally coined by Goethe at the end of the 18th century. 'See Naples and die!' is the familiar English translation, which is generally taken to bear witness to the sense of repleteness visitors should feel at beholding the great panoramic bay of the third largest city in the world at that time (after London and Paris). As the 19th century wore on, however, the phrase began to take on another meaning, as cholera, spreading from the east, gripped the Mediterranean ports of Italy, southern France and the Maghreb. With the growth of manufactures putting money in the pockets of an ever-widening middle class and with the spread of the rail network throughout Europe, travel and tourism had been opened up to many by the late 19th century. Revenues from tourism had become so very important to Italy that when the last great outbreak of cholera occurred in Napoli in 1910/11, it was effectively hushed up by a conspiracy of official silence. The whole troubled relationship between Italian cities, their local administrations and their many visitors is dealt with in some depth in Frank M. Snowden's *Naples in the Time of Cholera 1884–1911* (1996) and Eugenia Tognotti's *Il Monstro Asiatico: Storia de Colera in Italia* (2000).

Our own contemporary formulation of satiated expiry is the bucket list: '10 [or 20 or 50] things to do before you die'; '10 [or 20 or 50] places to see before you die'. This formula is also a publisher's ploy and an irresistible temptation for the alarmingly large number of people whose passion is the compilation of lists on the web. To become one of those places that people must see before they die is, incidentally, the devout wish of every promoter of tourist venues. In general, there is a high degree of congruence between such lists. In lists of 10, 7 often recur; in lists of 50, some 35 might be the same. Indeed, as of 2010, Italy leads the list of countries with World Heritage sites, with 44 sites, 42 of which are cultural and only 2 natural.

One of these magnificent must-visit places seems to have created and preserved a strong association with death itself, and that is Venice, the jewel of the Adriatic. So how did Venice acquire this unlikely association? One suspects that it derives from the myth of Venice itself being in the throes of dying. For most of my adult life, a vigorous 'Save Venice' campaign has been in permanent operation. Following disastrous floods which threatened the survival of the city in 1966, UNESCO has been campaigning for funds to restore Venice. We have become accustomed to being told that Venice is decaying and falling into the sea.

Jan Morris devotes a considerable part of her best-selling book *Venice* to the Venetian mode of dying. She writes.

> Everybody dies in Venice. The Venetians die in the normal course of events, and the visitors die as a matter of convention. In the Middle Ages, the population was periodically decimated by the plague ... a single fifteenth-century epidemic reduced the population by two-thirds; nearly 50,000 people died in the city, it is said, and another 94,000 in the lagoon settlements.... When Titian died of the plague, in 1576, only he amongst the 70,000 victims of that particular epidemic was allowed burial in a church. Nor is this all very ancient history. A silver lamp in the Salute was placed there as recently as 1836, to mark the end of a cholera plague: and there were ghastly scenes of suffering – corpses lowered from windows into barges, mass burials in the lagoon – when cholera attacked Venice during the 1848 revolution. (Morris, 1993: 141–142)

After further observations on malaria and the city's harsh winter climate, she reviews Venice's claims that it has healthy and stable atmospheric pressure and that the water is bacteriologically self-purifying:

> It is odd, all the same, how often foreign consuls and ministers have died in Venice in the course of their duties.... Wagner died in the palace that is now the winter casino. Browning died in the Ca' Rezzonico ... Diaghilev died here, and Baron Corvo, and so did Shelley's little daughter, Clara.... Even Dante died of a fever contracted during a journey to Venice. The angry Venetian modernists like to say that this has become a city 'where people come to expire'. (Morris: 142–143)

Two extraordinary rituals follow on from this. The first is the funeral cortège which proceeds in state up the Grand Canal, in a livery uniquely its own. The second is burial on the cemetery island decreed by Napoleon for all Venetian burials, San Michele, and a place run with military precision. Traditionally, after a decent interval of 10 years, the bones of the humble dead were harvested to make landfill; now more reclaimed land is made available decently to accommodate the deceased. That last journey of Venetians and unlucky visitors to the city seems of necessity to imitate the mythical trip across the Styx by boatman Charon to the Underworld, and it is therefore no surprise that Venetians have developed their own particular cult of the dead. San Michele is a sight frequently coming into view as you move around Venice, being little more than 500 metres off the Fondamente Nove to the north of the city.

The purpose of this chapter, however, is to look at the way that Venice's reputation for unnatural death has been perpetuated in the 20th century. This has mostly been achieved in works of literature, but in many cases those works have been supported by equally famous films. So I propose to discuss four film and book combinations. For most people, the foundational text for this is Thomas Mann's *Der Tod in Venedig* (*Death in Venice*), published in 1912, but it was in many ways preceded by Henry James's *The Wings of the Dove* (1902). I should say that a secondary focus of this chapter is on the way cinema must necessarily realise a sense of place differently from a novel; it does so more immediately, more vividly and (I would argue) more promotionally.

Venice was Henry James's favourite place on earth. He engineered reasons throughout his life for being in Venice. His story *The Aspern Papers* (1888) transfers its source action from Florence to Venice just so its narrator can hang around in Venice waiting for the papers of the title to pass into his hands. In order for this to happen, the death of their owner must first take place. Waiting in Venice therefore becomes an ancillary benefit for James's unnamed collector. For James, Venice was the ideal place to make a good death. His heiress in *The Wings of the Dove*, Milly Teale, comes there to pass her last few months of life. She takes charge of a Venetian palace but, once installed, seems to take very little interest in Venetian street life or its artistic treasures. The palace comes to seem a kind of bastion against messy mortality. This is how Milly senses it is to be in Venice:

> The charm turned on them a face that was cold in its beauty, that was full of a poetry never to be theirs, that spoke, with an ironic smile, of a possible but forbidden life. It all rolled afresh over Milly: 'oh, the impossible romance – !' The romance for her, yet once more, would be to sit there forever, through all her time, as in a fortress; and the idea became an image of never going down, of remaining aloft in the divine, dustless air, where she would hear but the plash of water against stone. The great floor on which they moved was at an altitude, and this promoted the rueful fantasy. 'Ah, not to go down – never, never to go down!' she strangely sighed... (James, 1974: 292)

The Palazzo Leporelli (based on the Palazzo Barbaro on the Grand Canal in Venice, where James actually completed writing *The Aspern Papers*) becomes her world and, as James says, 'she turned her face to the wall'. Other characters, however, must pursue her to execute their stratagems. These figures, although far from being conventional tourists, are seen out and about in Venice. But, as with many of late James's characters, their engagements are largely mental, the short joustings of pairs of characters. A late arrival is Milly's doctor, Sir Luke Strett, and an unusual ritual takes place where the novel deflects attention surrounding the details of Milly's decline onto the doctor's sight-seeing in the company of Milly's suitor, Merton Densher. Strett avoids revelations about Milly's health and Densher scrupulously avoids asking, so we witness a strange suspension of the drama in touring around Venice. The overall effect, however, is calming on the pent-up Densher.

> They walked together and they talked, looked up pictures again and recovered impressions – Sir Luke knew just what he wanted; haunted a little the dealers in old wares; sat down at Florian's for rest and mild drinks; blessed, above all, the grand weather, a bath of warm air, a pageant of autumn light. (James, 1974: 392)

Indeed, it would be fair to say that a lot of what does not happen in terms of narrative is displaced onto Venice as a kind of temporal luxuriance. It serves as, according to Pigott (2013: 9), 'a "green space" … away from the scheming, cold world of "society" London, in which genuine love and affection and beauty may grow'. The gravity of Milly's situation is thus suspended in beauty, and then finally passed over altogether as the other principals depart and Milly is allowed to die offstage, and the social aftermath of her death transfers back to corrupt London.

The Iain Softley film of 1997 cannot be so forbearing about the delights of Venice. It must display them and it must absorb Milly into them. Milly is at the heart of all the trips to San Marco and elsewhere; she embraces the bustle of the crowded backstreet canals and becomes distressed when certain sights are not available to her because (implicitly) her time is limited. Venice must seduce Milly every bit as much as Merton Densher. Consequently, the film of *The Wings of the Dove* is a costume drama/neo-noir hybrid. Lovers Kate Croy and Densher conspire to bilk Milly of her fortune, while carrying on behind her back. A masked Venice street festival, such as we find celebrated in Byron's Venetian poem *Beppo* (written 1817, published 1818), is the site of both seduction and duplicity. Softley's Milly is a more innocent victim of her friends' schemes than James's, although she does finally come to understand the nature of her situation. Interiors are filmed on location inside the Palazzo Barbaro (among other famous venues). Densher remains in Venice to be an integral part of her good death, and is present at her funeral, which partakes of the full glory of Venetian ritual, the special barge and burial on San Michele. The Milly Theale who had 'turned to the wall' in the novel, who had immolated herself in her fortress, turns to the open air, the streets and the waters of Venice in the film. The change of artistic medium dictates this.

Thomas Mann's writer character Gustav Aschenbach is unused to taking holidays in *Der Tod in Venedig* (citations are from David Luke's 1998 translation *Death in Venice*). Aschenbach first gets the idea of going on holiday when he sees a somewhat grotesque figure hiking in the hills above Munich. The locale is near a cemetery and some businesses dealing in headstones are not far off. As Mann writes:

> He now became conscious, to his complete surprise, of an extraordinary expansion of his inner self, a kind of roving restlessness, a youthful craving for far-off places, a feeling so new or at least so long unaccustomed and forgotten that he stood as if rooted … trying to ascertain the nature and purport of his emotion.
>
> It was simply the desire to travel, but it had presented itself as nothing less than a seizure, with intensely passionate and indeed hallucinatory force, turning his craving into vision. (Mann, 1998: 199)

Under this compulsion, he resolves to head south by train to Trieste and then down through Croatia to the coastal resort of Pula. From Pula he decamps to an island in the Adriatic, which he promptly takes a dislike to because of the plethora of Austrian tourists there. Retreating back to Pula, the fastidious Aschenbach discovers quite by chance that there is a ferry direct to Venice. For a man who has, as his sole purpose as a writer, 'the ascent to dignity' (Mann, 1998: 206), and who has planned and controlled his every impulse, his journey to Venice is strangely haphazard and his time spent there oddly accompanied by grotesques and mountebanks. The man who sells him the boat ticket regales him thus:

> 'A very happily chosen destination!' he chattered … 'Ah Venice! A splendid city! A city irresistibly attractive to the man of culture, by its history no less than its present charm!' There was something hypnotic and distracting about the smooth facility of his movements and the glib empty talk with which he accompanied them, almost as if he were anxious that the traveller might have second thoughts about his decision to go to Venice. (Mann, 1998: 210)

Even the practised insincerity of the tourism professional does not blight what Aschenbach discovers to be the perfect way to approach the city for the first time, by water. The arrival at his hotel is attended by a number of inconveniences, and the appearance of more grotesques, an epicene old man on the boat and a Charonesque boatman whom he finds to be operating illegally. The holiday is thus heavy with ill auguries. Aschenbach seems febrile throughout the stay and quite unable to relax – there is clearly some intimation of professional blockage or crisis. Into this disturbed scenario comes the Polish boy Tadzio, and Aschensbach begins to fixate on him as an incarnation of the principle of beauty which is at the core of his ideals as a writer and which seems to this point to have become clouded and prob-lematic. After a lifetime of prim self-discipline, he begins to surrender to this passionate obsession, revelling in his lack of proportion and perspective. Venice is therefore the part-chosen, part-random venue for Aschenbach's discovery of abandon.

He briefly appears to come to his senses and prepares to leave but an accident with his luggage provides him with the excuse to return to his hotel and the Lido. Luggage is a major factor in *Death in Venice* – it creates trans-portation problems on arrival and is the reason for Aschenbach's failure to flee the cholera. It does not feature in *The Wings of the Dove* because James's all-female travelling parties have hired Italian couriers and escorts who take care of practical, physical and linguistic difficulties. Later 20th-century stories give up the massive trunks that characterise travel in the mid and late 19th century but concern themselves much more with the logistics of journeying and accommodation, and particularly with dealings with local people, which are often glossed over in earlier fiction. Aschenbach finds himself quite isolated on his holiday and obtains help (and candour) only from the English travel agency he consults (based upon Thomas Cook's), a clerk of which tells him about the official cover-up of an outbreak of cholera. He had suspected this was the case because Venice had 'a sweetish, medicinal smell that suggested squalor and wounds and suspect cleanliness.... Even on the *vaporetto* taking him back to the Lido he now noticed the smell of the bactericide' (Mann, 1998: 245–246).

As Aschenbach's Dionysian abandon gathers pace, he becomes himself one of the grotesques he has sighted, going to the barber, having his hair styled and dyed and having make-up applied in the (forlorn) hope of disguising his advancing years. The reward for submitting to this affectation is a kind of clownish humiliation, but the overall result of his obsession is lingering too long into an outbreak of cholera. It is clear from this summary that a combination of holiday accident, fate and compulsive behaviour brings Aschenbach to his end. He dies on the beach sitting in a deck chair with a rug over his knees, slumped sideways and remaining like that for several minutes before anyone notices.

What does the city of Venice have to do with this highly charged narrative? Well, Mann's text, like Joseph Conrad's *Heart of Darkness* (1899), is often sparing of specific reference but the topography of the city is unique and unmistakable. Venice seems to be part of a vortex of feelings and ideas about beauty, proportion, passion and art, which come to a head in Aschenbach's personal crisis. At an obvious level, this is a willed suicide, played out against a backcloth of Venetian splendour. The Visconti film of 1971 gives colour and flesh to Aschenbach's infatuation. It also gives music. Mahler had died in Venice in May 1911, and although this fact had influenced Mann, the character of Aschenbach is not based on Mahler. Visconti's protagonist, however, clearly is. Mann's writer becomes Visconti's composer. Debates about writing become concerns about music and, of course, images of Venice itself are bathed in Mahler's luxuriant music. Music, as it usually does, carries a heavy emotional charge in film art. Mann's story, which is spare in dialogue because of Aschenbach's solitary state, becomes a visual and musical extravaganza, celebrating both *eros* and *thanatos* in equal measure. But whereas Milly makes a good (and unavoidable) death in Venice, Aschenbach's is touched with excess and folly. Mann equivocates more on this than does Visconti, inasmuch as the latter's music trumps the film's narrative. Mann seems more alive to Venice as a freakish human construction, Dionysian in its decay and failures as well as in its celebration of sybaritic pleasure. Visconti's and Mahler's music generalises the protagonist's death as metonymic of all mortality and so dignifies it. The story's homosexual and pederastic content, which was such a triumphantly bold gesture in the written story, made it problematic for the conservative film industry and for Warner Brothers in particular, which worried about the possibility of prosecution for obscenity in the USA. The company was calmed, however, by a command performance of the film in London on 1 March 1971 before Queen Elizabeth II, to raise funds to save the city of Venice. Once again, the uniqueness of Venice, and the urgency of the cause, seemed to make palatable what might otherwise have been awkward for the film's backers.

About the same time this film was released, Daphne Du Maurier's short story 'Don't Look Now' (1971) was published. It does not have the weight of either of the works just discussed, but it did provide the source for a magnificent film of the same name directed by Nicolas Roeg in 1973, and it is the first pairing to have no significant time lag between the publication of the story and the making of the film. Du Maurier gives us modern tourism as we can easily recognise it. English couple John and Laura are holidaying in Venice 18 months after the death of their young daughter, Christine, from meningitis. They meet by chance a pair of sisters also on holiday, one of whom is blind and clairvoyant. They claim to be able to see Christine sitting with her parents. The still grief-stricken Laura responds to this; the sceptical John resents and resists it. John's efforts therefore go into preventing his wife from meeting up with the sisters but the popular tourist venues and organised tours conspire against him and keep throwing them together. The sister's message is now that there is danger and that they should leave Venice. Fate takes a hand when a phone call from England tells John and Laura that their surviving son is sick with appendicitis. Laura hastens to his side, flying out, but John must remain to collect his car in Padua and go home overland. During this hiatus, he catches a glimpse of his departed wife on a *vaporetto* with the two sisters and comes to the conclusion that she has been kidnapped.

Now a more modern take on Venice is given prominence: Venice as a disorientating labyrinth. John has to find his way around Venice alone; he has a crisis that needs an official response; he experiences language difficulties and cultural misunderstandings. Hoteliers and the police are less than convinced by his story. The sisters are later found and arrested, but a phone call from Laura in England reveals that John has imagined the sighting. Leaving the scene of his embarrassment, having delivered the sisters back to their *pensione*, John spots what looks like Christine, follows and corners her, only to be turned upon and killed by a murderous female dwarf. Despite his scepticism, John has been the possessor of second sight all along but has ignored all the warnings of danger to him, even those emanating from his own ghost-daughter, courtesy of the medium.

The Roeg film is an amplification and subtilisation of the story. It makes three radical changes. Firstly, it makes Christine's death one by drowning, to connect her loss with the presence of water in Venice. Secondly, it gives John a job as a church restorer working in Venice, thus removing the holiday motif. And lastly, it transposes the action to late autumn, refusing Venice in its summer finery and instead giving it a shadowy, putrescent air. Made just a few years after Visconti's film, *Don't Look Now* takes up the *eros* and *thanatos* motif as well. There are clearly strains in the marriage, caused by blame over the loss of the child (both parents had been nearby at the drowning but distracted by other things) and reflected in their differing reactions to the sisters. In extending John's clairvoyance to the moment of his daughter's drowning during the opening sequence of the film (one of the greatest pieces of editing in British cinema), the film ties John's and his daughter's death to his own stubborn resistance to his psychic gift. It is an incredulity he does not scruple to show his wife, causing her much distress. Their discord over second sight and the loss of their daughter is counter-balanced by the film's celebrated love-making scenes. *Don't Look Now*'s best feature, however, is its use of Venice and Italians. Without being deliberately xenophobic or cartoonish, never have foreigners and foreignness looked more forbidding. The hotelier, the police chief and even John's employer, a Catholic potentate, might in their suggestion of dark deviousness have strayed in from the exactly contemporary film *The Exorcist*. The film's subtle expressionism makes Venetians come across as shifty and sinister; a series of murders of women have been taking place unobtrusively in the narrative and, once again, they have been played down by the authorities. Venice is just in the process of completing the season and then shutting down. The alleys and street and back canals become places where violent spirits can lurk. Following John's murder, the imagined sighting burgeons dramatically into his splendidly realised Venetian funeral. Laura, flanked by the two sisters and in widow's weeds, accompanying his coffin to San Michele for winter burial, becomes the movie's last image. A holiday venue out of season always carries a note of sadness; *Don't Look Now*'s Venice delivers the apotheosis of this sensation.

The last book/film combination is Ian McEwan's novel *The Comfort of Strangers* (1981) and the Paul Shrader film (1990) of the Harold Pinter screenplay made from that book. Venice was clearly a loaded place for Pinter too, as in his own play *Betrayal* (1978), a wife's infidelity is revealed in a tense scene while on a family holiday in Venice with her husband and children. Pinter's biographer Michael Billington makes explicit his attraction to Venice as a place of revelations. Listing the many films set there, he writes: 'What all these works have in common is the notion that Venice forces outsiders to confront the reality of their lives and that this Borgesian labyrinth of a city is an agent of change and transformation' (Billington, 1997: 317).

McEwan's story is also about a couple on holiday and, again, the book tends to centre on questions of intimacy and passion. Colin and Mary are not married but they have been together for a while, and a lot of the time together is spent talking about Mary's children and their relationship with Colin. There are multiple occasions for disagreeing and getting lost on their Venetian holiday and they all seem to bring Colin and Mary back to their equivocations about their relationship. This is McEwan's commentary on their holidaying together:

> Alone, perhaps, they each could have explored the city with pleasure, followed whims, dispensed with destinations and so enjoyed or ignored being lost. There was much to wonder at here, one needed only to be alert and to attend. But they knew one another much as they knew themselves, and their intimacy, rather like too many suitcases, was a matter of perpetual concern; together they moved slowly, clumsily, effecting lugubrious compromises, attending to delicate shifts of mood, repairing breaches. As individuals, they did not easily take offence; but together they managed to offend each other in surprising, unexpected, ways; then the offender – it had happened twice since their arrival – became irritated by the cloying susceptibilities of the other, and they would continue to explore the twisting alleyways and sudden squares in silence, and with each step the city would recede as they locked tighter into each other's presence. (McEwan, 1982: 14–15)

This is one of the key perceptions of the literature of holidays: that strange locations throw one more and more back upon the resources of one's intimate relationships, and that if they are importantly wanting, this will be found out. Hence the city recedes and the couple become locked into each other. And in not paying heed to the city, they become insensible of its menace and the fact that they are being observed.

McEwan perceptively strikes many notes about modern holiday-making, both good and bad. He observes the baroque variety of Venetian maps, the cheapest useless and in the service of commercial interest, the biggest unmanageable and the most informative fragmented across five non-overlapping maps and thus guaranteed to help one get and stay lost. He observes the nature of service in the high season, and the frustration of trying to find basic repose or refreshment when these things are in general demand. He shows our curiosity about and distaste for others when they too are at their pleasures. Mostly he shows how disturbances of routine and ritual can lead to a wider disorientation.

Mary is a professed feminist, Colin her liberal companion; they argue over the strength of Mary's convictions but not over their rightness. On holiday, they casually meet local bar owner Robert, an anglicised Venetian, and his Canadian wife, Caroline. If Mary and Colin represent the gender accommodations of liberal culture, Robert and Caroline are the return of the biologically repressed. Robert is the last in a line of Italian patriarchs, obsessed with the authority his father levied over his mainly female family. The metonymic core of the novel is Robert's account of an incident from his childhood and its brutalising effect on him, leaving him to revere and emulate his father and to reproduce his outmoded and authoritarian domestic arrangements, including a sadomasochistic sex life with his wife. Colin and Mary at first experience their new friends passively and with wry amusement. Later on, after it becomes clear that they have been stalked, and that various forms of coercive behaviour are applied by their hosts, they escape Robert's home with relief. Colin has promised to return but this promise is lost in the transformation that their own relationship undergoes. They shut out Venice and remain in their hotel for four days, rekindling their intimacy and rediscovering each other erotically. On the fifth day, they go to the Lido for a conventional beach day. Compulsively, they return via the boat that will take them within sight of Robert's house. Caroline duly spots them and they are welcomed back in. Mary is drugged and Colin is assaulted and murdered by Robert as a substitute for the crippled, beaten but willing Caroline. The 'comfort of strangers' consists philosophically of an erotic encounter with death, as an ultimate carnal knowledge of the Other, in this case found casually on holiday.

The story finishes not splendidly on a barge to San Michele but in a Venetian hospital morgue, with Mary alone with Colin's corpse. The nature of intimacy, the novel's general theme (because it is equally a feature of the macabre Robert and Caroline's marriage), is seen as a dangerous and fragile thing, a vulnerability most tested in the unfamiliar surroundings of the holiday. Like John before her, Mary finds herself in the hands of polite Venetian officialdom, not sinister but matter-of-fact. Indeed, the roles are somewhat reversed from *Don't Look Now*, since the officials seem conventional figures and Mary and Colin seem darkly implicated in what has befallen them. The crime is surprisingly common, committed with a mixture of carefulness and clumsiness, ritualistic and indifferent to detection. The Venice finally evoked is reminiscent of Kafka:

> It had become apparent that the packed, chaotic city concealed a thriving, intricate bureaucracy, a hidden order of government departments with separate but overlapping functions, distinct procedures and hierarchies; unpretentious doors, in streets she had passed down many times before, led not to private homes but to empty waiting-rooms with railway-station clocks, and the sound of incessant typing, and to cramped offices with brown linoleum floors. (McEwan, 1982: 122)

Those 'brown linoleum floors' are like the return of normality suspended by the exoticism of foreign travel, especially in somewhere as different as Venice. Perhaps it is as a marker of distance from the normative, rather than for its artistic and architectural splendours, that writers seek out Venice for their confrontations with ultimate knowledge, which is finally of our own mortality. Mary had, after all, walked past those ordinary offices many times, not noticing that Venice was a city like any other.

Pinter's screenplay does not depart too far from the novel. It makes explicit the fact that Colin and Mary's second Venetian holiday is to recapture the spirit of the first, three years earlier, and they are on the point of deciding to get married and move in together. Robert's *machismo* is also accentuated, as he pays tribute to the imposition of social rules in Britain, a direct reference to Margaret Thatcher's government. It also deliberately locates Robert's house opposite Cemetery Island, where he says both his father and grandfather are buried. No attempt is made to flee justice at the end either, for Robert relishes the opportunity to tell his story again, to the police this time. As with *The Wings of the Dove*, the production is aestheticised with a heavy overlay of Italian style (lush Venetian interiors, Giorgio Armani outfits and Angelo Baldalamenti's music). Rupert Everett's Colin emerges as the universal object of desire, something reinforced from the novel by the superabundance of still photos taken of him. The police's scepticism at the end accentuates what is implicit in the novel, that there has been some collusion between the two couples in working towards this outcome, something Mary weakly denies. But McEwan puts it best in the mortuary scene.

> She was in the mood for explanation, she was going to speak to Colin … tell him her theory, tentative at this stage, of course, which explained how the imagination, the sexual imagination, men's ancient dreams of hurting, and women's of being hurt, embodied and declared a powerful

single organising principle, which distorted all relations, all truth. But she explained nothing, for a stranger had arranged Colin's hair the wrong way. She combed it with her fingers and said nothing at all. (McEwan, 1982: 125)

This touch of tenderness is almost the final gesture of both book and film.

Colin's last utterance, the one before the conspiracy overtakes him, is 'The thing about a successful holiday is that it makes you want to go home.' It is the concluding thought to a chain of reflections in which he understands all he has to do is to walk away from Robert. Good manners keep him where he is. He had earlier declined to leave Venice, as Mary had wished, because their departing flight was five days away and had been pre-paid. A similar humdrum attention to economics keeps John in Venice when his wife jets out to the bedside of their sick son.

Each one of the books discussed here makes some recognition of the renewed desire to go home consistent with a successful stay. Milly Theale's entourage are waiting out her end, to then return to their normal lives. Aschenbach makes a number of futile efforts to break away from his unfamiliar and unwanted compulsions. Mere logistics involving his car trap John in northern Italy. So four characters stay on in Venice to die. Other, luckier holiday-makers do manage to get home because, although Venice may be Europe's great stage of death, mere contingency also has a key part to play in all human outcomes.

References

Billington, M. (1997) *The Life and Work of Harold Pinter*. London: Faber and Faber.

Clark, T. (2009) Cruise.com to offer divorcee trips for the recently split. *Mail Online*, 21 July, at http://www.dailymail.co.uk/travel/article-1203270/Cruise-com-offer-divorcee-trips-recently-split.html#ixzz2jCrqgmcG (accessed 29 October 2013).

Du Maurier, D. (1973) Don't Look Now. In *Don't Look Now and Other Stories*. Harmondsworth: Penguin Books.

James, H. (1974) *The Wings of the Dove*. Harmondsworth: Penguin Books.

Mann, T. (1998) Death in Venice. In D. Luke (trans. and introduction) *Death in Venice and Other Stories*. London: Vintage.

McEwan, I. (1982 [1981]) *The Comfort of Strangers*. London: Picador.

Morris, J. (1993) *Venice*. London: Faber and Faber (revised edition; first published 1960).

Pigott, M. (2013) *World Film Locations: Venice*. Bristol: Intellect.

Sky News UK (2011) Morocco deaths: Couple were not arguing. Posted 29 August at http://news.sky.com/story/876871/morocco-deaths-couple-were-not-arguing (accessed 29 October 2013).

Snowden, F.M. (1996) *Naples in the Time of Cholera 1884–1911*. Cambridge: Cambridge University Press.

Tognotti, E. (2000) *Il Monstro Asiatico: Storia de Colera in Italia*. Rome: Editori Laterza.

TravelMail Reporter (2009) Marriage counselling in the Maldives? Travel firm launches 'divorce tourism' packages. *MailOnline*, posted 3 September, at http://www.dailymail.co.uk/travel/article-1210892/Marriage-counselling-Maldives-KV-Tours--Travels-launches-divorce-tourism-packages.html (accessed 29 October 2013).

Films

Death in Venice (1971) Directed by Luchino Visconti. Produced by Luchino Visconti. Alfa Cinematografica.
Don't Look Now (1973) Directed by Nicolas Roeg. Produced by Peter Katz. British Lion Films.
The Comfort of Strangers (1990) Directed by Paul Schrader. Produced by Angelo Rizzoli Jr. Sovereign Pictures.
The Wings of the Dove (1997) Directed by Iain Softley. Produced by Stephen Evans and David Parfitt. Miramax Films.

10 Peregrinating Objects: Consumptive Capacities of the Traveller's Personal Items in Robert Byron's *The Road to Oxiana* and Jason Elliot's *Unexpected Light*

Monika Kowalczyk-Piaseczna

Internal–External Relation

Travel, irrespective of its purpose or character, often involves an encounter with a reality divergent from the one known to the traveller thus far. Hence, every contact with another system of values and cultural norms may be expected to impel travellers to reconsider their inherited image of the world. Yet the travellers' roots and cultural conditioning, fostered by their own culture, seem to substantially shape their perception of a foreign land, its inhabitants and their own *self*. Employing critical stances that address identity and cultural exchange in the context of travel, this chapter aims to show that the explorer's luggage, camera or journal, representing pieces of his or her habitat, constitute physical extensions of the traveller's body and thus enable him or her to sustain the integrity of his or her own *self* in the course of a journey. Furthermore, offering an analysis of two pieces of travel reportage – Robert Byron's *The Road to Oxiana* (1937) and Jason Elliot's *Unexpected Light* (1999) – the chapter attempts to show that, in spite of the revision to which a traveller is compelled in the face of a new reality, the cultural heritage that he or she carries along the meandering routes of an unknown world to a large extent influences the choice and form of objects, photographs or descriptions with which the explorer determines to expand the bulk of his or her personal possessions.

Byron's and Elliot's everyday accounts of their journeys draw the reader's attention to somatic aspects of travelling. It seems that purely physical experiences, almost imposing themselves on the explorers during their itinerary, threaten the barrier the travellers had created around themselves in order to sustain the artificial distance between them and the *Others*. The Hungarian sociologist Elemèr Hankiss perceives the process of establishing such barriers as the main incentive for creating civilisations. As he claims:

> human beings have succeeded in developing ways and means – belief systems, behavioural patterns and institutions – which have protected them, with more or less success, against their anxieties and fears ... they have tamed raw and destructive fear and transformed it into a positive energy, a force that has played a major role in building human civilizations. (Hankiss, 2001: 7)

The barrier, established as a natural product of Western civilisation, and aimed at protecting one's *self* from the external influences that might be suspected of menacing its cohesion, allowed travellers to depart on a journey of exploration without the anxiety, or even the slightest supposition, that they themselves would be explored. Although Bakhtinian philosophy has seemingly led Western consciousness out of its conviction about bodily wholeness and inviolability (Bakhtin, 1984: 317), the corporeal 'shield' still appears to give an apparent feeling of safety to the person travelling through unknown territories. Yet whenever this virtual barrier is infringed by the external world breaking through it, be it because of a minor bodily injury or a severe illness, the illusion of being protected against the external threats ceases to exist.

The most elementary instance of the infringement of the traveller's body is the act of consumption, which is necessary for survival. One needs to derive nourishment from the land's body in order to satisfy the basic needs of one's own organism and thus to facilitate one's endurance of the often fatiguing route of one's journey. Yet the hardships of travel, especially those experienced corporeally, require a specific type of resistance that must operate during the necessary act of consumption. It is evident that once the traveller's organism rejects the nutrition provided by the land as unassimilable, the explorer's survival may be at risk. Hence, the absorbed nourishment needs to be digested in order to become admissible to the interior of the traveller's body. Digestion, in turn, is inevitably connected with an excretive act; therefore, some elements of the internalised and processed food supplied by the land need to be eliminated from the explorer's organism.

A similar process of exchange concerns the particular items reportage writers determine to take with them on an expedition. The physical dimension of travel involves the use of objects which, having certain functions in the traveller's own habitat, are expected to play the same roles in the reality unknown to them. Carried by them along their itineraries and thus continuously attached to their body, luggage, camera and journal function as extensions of their corporeality. Undergoing expansion and decline in contact with an unknown reality, in turn, the objects seem to confirm the Bakhtinian theory that regards the human body as an open structure.

Luggage, essential especially at moments when items from the traveller's homeland are required in an unfamiliar area, appears to be an extension of the traveller's habitat, and thus functions as a link between the journalist's home country and the examined reality. The memoir, in turn, collecting situations and events from the past which have shaped the explorer's personality, manifests its consumptive capacities with its blank pages, which are to be filled with new experiences from the explored space. A similar characteristic applies to the camera, which, containing parts of external reality, performs the role of the traveller's visual memory. Hence, either empty or already filled with some prizes from the traveller's past experiences, it displays its potential for subsequent fulfilment with depictions of the explored area and, thus, for mingling various realities in its single memory card.

All the objects that apparently remind travellers of the heritage they carry within enable them to sustain the wholeness of their *self*, and allow them to remain within their own framework of meanings at the moment of the encounter with a reality which, compelling the explorers to face unfamiliar, often incomprehensible experiences, evidently threatens this carefully woven structure with fragmentation or disintegration.

Luggage's flexible interior

If the imagined picture of the country one proposes to visit presents its inhabitants as aggressive and the atmosphere in the country as seditious, one may want to include in one's luggage appliances that are able to protect one's life. One's bag will also tend to contain certain medicines expected to relieve pain or any of the 'exotic' ailments that the unadjusted body of a foreign traveller may be exposed to at a destination. Anxiety over losing one's way among the convoluted paths of the unknown space, in turn, usually inclines one towards taking a map or any of the modern navigational devices that determine one's location reliably. Allowing the traveller access to a vast range within the Western European system of signs and symbols, those objects bring a sense of safety and a feeling of control, regardless of the illusory character of these sensations. According to Benedict Anderson, the use of a map or other forms of semiotic representation such as census or archaeological catalogues has served the European aims of creating 'a total-izing classificatory grid' (Anderson, 2006: 188) since colonial times:

> [The grid] could be applied with endless flexibility to anything under the state's real or contemplated control: peoples, regions, religions, languages, products, monuments, and so forth. The effect of the grid was always to be able to say of anything that it was this, not that; it belonged here, not there. It was bounded, determinate, and therefore in principle – countable. (The comic classificatory and subclassificatory census boxes entitled 'Other' concealed all real-life anomalies by a splendid bureaucratic *trompe l'oeil*.) (Anderson, 2006: 188)

Although Anderson's description concerns colonial ways of exercising power and control with the use of various forms of semiotic classification, it seems that both figurative and literal attachment to a map or any type of indicatory representation has remained one of the principal needs of a Western traveller. And though, as Jason Elliot claims, looking at the map of Afghanistan, 'in many places the road no longer existed' (Elliot, 1999: 16), the map still constitutes a trusted reference point for the traveller on a journey in a foreign land.

A cartographic image of the explored area, however, is not the only item which may be found in luggage, and which, in actual confrontations with an unknown land, may turn out to be incommensurate with reality. As elements 'borrowed' from the traveller's everyday reality, some of the luggage's contents often need to be adjusted to unexpected circumstances. That is the reason why some possessions, mainly those which seem of no avail in the situation encountered in the explored space, have to be eliminated or exchanged for ones that do respond to the different circumstances and thus become useful to the traveller. This is how Robert Byron describes the necessary clothing and weaponry he and his companions were compelled to procure in the face of severe weather and possible danger:

> we noticed that the north face of the mountains was still damp. Half a mile down the car stuck.... As dark fell, two white-cloaked shepherds came by with their flock. We begged them to wait and help us. They said they dared not, owing to the wolves. But one of them ... lent us a rifle and two remaining bullets to see us through the night.... we stayed

in the car.... Quilts and sheep-skins replaced our mud-soaked clothes.... I listened for a while to the wind soughing in the junipers and an owl hooting in the distance; then I too slept. (Byron, 2007: 224–225)

Since the emergent circumstances force one to replenish one's stock, a corporeal exchange between the land and the traveller's body extensions is bound to take place. Not only does this enable travellers to engage with the land's physicality, but, more importantly, it allows them to continue their existence within the overwhelming interior of the explored body. However, disposing of particular elements of the examined territory, which in their estimation are redundant or even detrimental to their objectives, travellers perform an often unwitting act of rejection, preceded by a scrupulous selection process.

The camera's mnemonic functions

An analogous exchange may be observed in case of another object that often accompanies a traveller. A camera, a device seemingly capable of immobilising and retaining a landscape and its inhabitants, has considerable capacity for expansion. Collecting ever new depictions of the surrounding area, the camera's memory card becomes filled with elements of an explored land. Simultaneously, it becomes involved in the act of translation from the somatic experience of absorption of sights and sounds into a semiotic representation of these particular experiences. A photograph is expected to constitute an iconic testimony to the somatic experience, as the tendency of human memory is to single out certain events and erase others. This phenomenon is often alluded to by various travel writers (e.g. Lamb, 2004: 145; Stasiuk, 2008: 59). Yet, it is the interpretation of a visual image of the 'perpetuated' sensations that allows a photographer, and subsequently the audience, to comprehend the 'ineffable'. Internalising the external elements in the form of signs, the camera seems to 'consume' the targeted reality. Afterwards, however, the captured image ceases to be exclusively a reflection of this reality, and the photographed objects and individuals become subjected to subsequent reinterpretations.

This peculiar feature of photography is given much consideration by Sarah Bassnett *et al.*, members of the Photography Research Group (see the website http://publish.uwo.ca/~sbassnet/Photo.html). The authors base their conclusions on the research done by a British 'photography theorist John Tagg' (quotes here and below from the website) (see Tagg, 1993). As can be read in these deliberations, 'photography is a discursive system, rather than a coherent object or a unified medium or technology, ... [therefore] the meaning and status of a photograph are considered as an event'. Thus, even in the moment of framing and taking a photograph, the photographed objects and people cannot be regarded as motionless figures, since they are ceaselessly involved in a reciprocal relation. Hence, the illusory character of the 'mnemonic' function a camera is expected to perform is exposed. The process of immobilisation of the landscape, photographed person or object is only seeming.

A picture constitutes only a momentary depiction of a transient reality and, after being developed or printed, it no longer functions as a reflection of the interrelation of objects represented in the image. Moreover, in time and with acquired experiences, the traveller's perception of the photographed image also alters, revealing the purposelessness of any endeavour to retain reality. This interdependence is aptly described by a Polish reportage writer, Andrzej Stasiuk, in *On the Road to Babadag* (2008). This author captures the fallibility of memory thus:

> During travel, history is being constantly transformed into a legend.... Noone will be able to put it all together, and to create the whole story.... Over and over again, history, events, consequence, thought and a plan dissolve in this landscape.... Time triumphs over memory. (Stasiuk, 2008: 59)

The above notwithstanding, Western writers are inclined to perpetuate selected elements of the local inhabitants' customs and traditions, which overtly jeopardises Eastern people's right to privacy. Discerning a threat to their integrity, the residents of the examined area erect, in either a literal or a figurative sense, a wall protecting them from external glances, and preventing the travellers from the West from expropriating or rejecting from their photographs the selected elements of the Eastern space. An official confirmation of the locals' reluctant approach is illustrated in *The Road to Oxiana* by a letter from the 'Persepolis Shiraz Oriental Institute Persian Expedition', in response to Byron's request for permission to take and publish photographs of Persia:

> Dear Mr. Byron, ... The situation is this: ... in Persia, the only way of preventing everybody to come, to take photos and to sell and publish them, is not to allow photographing.... I have had the most unpleasant correspondence with the Government on this account. Hence, we have made the arrangement, that people, interested in the publication of photos, might get them from the Oriental Institute ... and publish them acknowledging the provenance. (Byron, 2007: 159)

The inhabitants of Persia solve the problem of Western tourists' rapacious manner of taking photographs of their country in quite a definitive way. Not only does it allow them to protect themselves from the foreigners' eyes but it also gives them control over the picture of Persia they want to present to Western European *Others*. In consequence, the objects that are to be 'consumed' by the traveller's camera are not selected by the travellers themselves, but are already chosen and prepared for Western eyes. This deprives travellers of power over meanings, which is the Persian government's primary concern – the power of choice and interpretation of given elements of Persian reality, which could create an inadequate or undesirable picture of their country in the West.

The consumptive capacities of a journal

The third item 'participating' in a journey, which appears to be capable of the figurative act of consumption, is a journal (diary or memoir). Expanded with descriptions of an examined area, its inhabitants and one's personal attitude towards them, a journal becomes a narrative testimony to the intercultural encounter that often takes place during travel. As an instrument textualising the private sensations of the author, it captures them in a linguistic form. Stephen Greenblatt remarks in *Marvellous Possessions* (1988) that 'the form of the journal entry characteristically registers first the material sighting and then its significance; the space between the two … is the place of discovery where the explanatory power of writing repeatedly tames the opacity of the eye's objects by rendering them transparent signs' (Greenblatt, 1988: 88).

Subsequently, the semiotic figures corresponding to the traveller's experiences are subjected to interpretations and the journal undergoes certain modifications, which time and distance exert on the explorer's perception of the encounter with another reality. In accordance with this rule, Elliot (1999) takes his time to deal with his incomprehensible experience, which he does with the use of certain rhetorical manipulations. Creating a peculiarly hazy picture of Afghan reality, he endeavours to extenuate the appalling impact of the *uncanny*. Whatever seems to exceed the traveller's idea of the real is blurred and made vague. He makes the border between the reality of his somatic experience and the obstinate feeling of unreality that accompanies him during his journey indistinct, and he shrouds his whole account of his time in Afghanistan in a dreamlike vision:

From the beginning we became captives of an unexpected light. Even as we stepped into its unaccustomed brightness that first morning, it seemed probable we had entered a world in some way enchanted, for which we lacked the proper measure.... For an hour or more we had been wandering a grid of broad streets flanked by slender pine and plane trees, hoping for a remembered landmark.... we ... felt the thrill of strangeness at every step. The light was as delicate as crystal.... It stripped far-off shapes and colours of the usual vagaries of distance and played havoc with space, luring the mountains from beyond the city to within arm's reach and catapulting forward the expressions on faces two hundred yards away. Under its spell the landscape seemed to dance on the very edge of materiality ... the ordinary rule of things seemed less likely to apply. (Elliot, 1999: 289–290)

The depiction of the country within this dreamy shroud, however, seems to have yet another underpinning. Disillusioned with the divergences between his own experience and the alleged true stories which reportage authors frequently claim rights to, the writer seems to suggest to his readers that a journalist is capable of presenting only a semi-factual account of travel. As a subjective report, often biased by one's pre-existing concept of the *unknown*, a travelogue derives from the traveller's individual perception of a different reality and the recipient's readerly competence. Thus the created image of the *Other*, additionally distorted by the linguistic translation of the explorer's somatic experience, usually confirms readers' preconceived ideas about the distant realms and consolidates their convictions about the world existing beyond their own civilisation. In *Unexpected Light*, Elliot exposes the manipulative qualities concealed in the rhetorical measures used in reportage. Himself confused and overwhelmed by the all-embracing sense of unintelligibility that he experiences within the unfamiliar territory, the writer defines the genre of travel literature with an evident undertone of sceptical irony:

What, after all, was a travel book? ... a man or a woman sets off for foreign parts ignorant of both the language and geography of the place, with an out-of-date map and borrowed phrase book, preys shamelessly for as long as the family trust fund will allow on the hospitality of the native people, and returns home to hastily record his or her first impressions in a semi-fictional collection of descriptions that affirm the prejudices of the day. Then, reminded of the mediocrity of the experiences described and to ease the risk of any intellectual burden on the microscopic attention span of the reader, he or she retrospectively invents a fashionable 'quest' around which the narrative can be twisted in every direction except towards the truth, fits it tidily with invented dialogues, speculative history, sweeping inaccuracies, mistranslations, verbose accounts of having braved hazards endured daily by ordinary local people without complaint, portrays as revelation long lists of trivial facts known to every local schoolchild and bludgeons the original spirit of the endeavour in an attempt to appear erudite with the academic verbiage of out-of-print encyclopaedias, disguising all the while the discomfort of being at sea in an alien culture by resorting to the quirky, condescending humour that its couch-bound audience will think of as funny. (Elliot, 1999: 15)

Although such an idea of travel writing could discourage prospective reportage readers from choosing the genre as a source of information about a foreign land, simultaneously, with this overtly sincere description of rhetorical manipulations that can be found in a travel book, Elliot makes his readers aware of the processes of selection journalists perform during their travels. Regarding only some elements of the *unknown* as real, they decide which aspects of the *Other*'s world are to be 'consumed' and subsequently 'digested' by consecutive readings of their reportage.

Exploring the theme of corporeality further, and acknowledging not only the journal, but also the luggage and the camera as tangible extensions of the traveller's body, the acts of 'consumption' and 'excretion' taking place with the use of those items may be regarded as the most rudimentary ways of producing bodily *abjects*. Endowed with absorptive capacities, these objects appear to be able to devour those elements of the examined space and the morsels of its corporeality the traveller selects. The selection, certainly involved in the literal consumption of food and beverages available to the traveller throughout a trip, more significantly concerns the individuals and parts of the landscape that the travel writer deems worthy of perpetuating. Thus, already the selection process is burdened with the traveller's interpretative proclivities and is entirely dependent on his or her individual volition.

The Significance of Roots

Since journal writers practise a specific form of travelling, as they are usually obliged to do so by the type of commission they are operating under, the supply of the peregrinating objects accompanying them on their journey with the proper things for 'consumption' constitutes a promise of future benefits. Yet, even then, the process is not independent of the traveller's individual preferences concerning the choice of elements of the explored reality which, according to him or her, would suit the assigned task. These preferences, in turn, seem to be conditioned by the traveller's roots, social and cultural background, and the whole inventory of experiences owing to which he or she has managed to develop ideas about the surrounding reality.

It seems clear, then, that the traveller starts a journey already imbued with what Stephen Greenblatt calls 'the stories that a culture tells itself, its conceptions of personal boundary and liability, its whole collective system of rules' (Greenblatt, 1988: 64). These ideas provide an individual with a sense of stability and safety. To preserve these values, travellers withdraw their attention from any particular situation or phenomenon which may disturb or distort their image of the surrounding world. Creation of a system of meanings which enables one to perceive the world within certain frames of understanding not only allows one to recognise one's like, but, more importantly, to identify any aberrations from the norm. It also makes one realise that everything and everyone who does not fulfil the requirements of a particular category must be eliminated from it and regarded as a dispensable element of reality (Hankiss, 2001: 7). Therefore all the objects of perception which travellers select either fit the categories shaped by their culture, or become classified as 'Other', 'different', 'exotic' – apparent aberrations from cultural standards.

After the acts of categorisation and selection and the process of 'consumption' which follows them are complete, the subsequent 'digestion' phase may be expected to occur. Encasing the somatic encounter with the *Other*, the explorer's camera and journal transform the experience into a system of signs recognisable to the traveler and a prospective audience. The reality captured in those objects, consciously or not, may be misinterpreted and misrepresented again, as the strangers' eyes will translate it into their own language and cultural categories. These particular transitions may be perceived precisely as the acts of 'digestion' of the previously selected nutrition. After choosing an object to photograph or to describe, travellers need to make the nourishment with which they decide to expand their corporeal extensions more digestible to their body, which is poorly adjusted to the new flavours. Thereupon, their recipients appear to perform the same act to facilitate their own 'digestive' process.

It is not therefore surprising that the inhabitants of the land, exceedingly conscious of their position as 'products for consumption' and wanting neither to be 'consumed' nor 'digested', frequently discourage the traveller from exploring their reality. Their suspicions are undoubtedly triggered by the capacity for absorption and retention of external reality that the objects derived from the traveller's original environment have. Byron describes the peculiar reaction a Western traveller evokes in the inhabitants of Middle Eastern countries. As he claims, 'here, [a tourist] is still an aberration', not much welcomed and treated mostly as a complementary source of profit (Byron, 2007: 42). He admits that although travellers may appear to be useful to the local economy, any close relations with them are always considered suspicious.

This is how Byron presents the negative attitudes of Persians evoked simply by the proximity of a foreigner:

> the anti-foreign feeling … has come to a head. The disgrace of the Bakhtiaris is partly ascribed to their friendship with the English; visitors, anxious to see the more civilised side of Persian life, always travelled through their country. In consequence, all Persians, except those officially instructed to associate with foreigners, shudder away as though one were a mad dog. (Byron, 2007: 125)

It appears that, regardless of the number of Western travellers visiting their country every year, Persians still manifest their hostility towards the foreign tourist, which remains deeply rooted in their consciousness. Analogously to the inhabitants of the East, however, the Western explorer appears to have similar difficulties in overcoming convictions about *Otherness*. Quite notably, the writer seems to be incensed by the fact that, instead of being warmly received as a researcher looking for a 'more civilised side' (Byron, 2007: 125) of the country he intended to examine, he, like any other foreigner from the West, is regarded as a possible fount of danger and misery. Hence it seems evident that, just like the objects, preconceived ideas may also undergo only minor modifications and a subsequent reorganisation after the sojourn with the *unknown*.

Object-Dependent *Self* Reconstruction

Unable as they are to accept the lack of affinity of the Western world order to Eastern reality, travel writers attempt to overcome their fears by the use of rhetorical techniques; either, like Jason Elliot, by blurring their reportage descriptions and elucidating certain inaccuracies of the account with examples of the delusiveness of personal memory (Elliot, 1999: 3) or, like Robert Byron, searching for signs of Englishness within the explored land (Byron, 2007: 136).

In spite of a certain awareness of the inappropriateness of their own standards, both travel writers are rarely able or willing to break the language-constructed paradigms which allow them to express their experience by means of linguistic signs. New experiences, in turn, tend to go beyond the social and cultural norms which have thus far constituted the basis of their perception. Corporeally highlighting their existence, the somatic experiences of an unknown reality undermine the legitimacy of creating such norms and disprove the universality of their use. Elliot describes one such circumstance thus:

> Always there is this kind of suspense on a journey where you are both isolated and robbed of your language. Under such conditions the means by which you make sense of things begins to be transformed; you can no longer rely on familiar signals but a cryptic sequence of tiny events, the pattern of which you sense more keenly as your isolation grows. It leads to a kind of parting of the ways; you either let go of your worries and put your faith in the natural unfolding of events or are plagued with anxieties, which multiply as darkness falls. (Elliot, 1999: 191)

In situations when language categories no longer apply, it often appears that the objects which explorers take with them on an expedition begin to perform the role of reference points. Irrespective of the circumstances, which may turn out to be either perilous or simply incomprehensible, peregrinating items 'borrowed' from the recognisable context remain intelligible to the traveller, thus creating an illusory sense of safety. Owing to their storing capacity, in turn, the objects provide the traveller with the apparent ability to retain experiences and, by these means, to prevent his or her identity from disintegrating, especially when the experience of Eastern reality turns out to be untranslatable and inexpressible by means of the linguistically based categories created by the traveller's culture. Western travellers become aware of the inadequacy of their cultural norms within Eastern reality each time they experience the surrounding land corporeally. Their bodily sensations, though to a certain extent describable by means of language and thus consolidated in the pages of a book, often go beyond most of the linguistic means the writer is familiar with and able to employ.

Byron and Elliot have apparently found a way of dealing with such circumstances. The rhetorical measures they apply to compensate for lacking appropriate and sufficient words to capture their individual experience is one possible way of taming the new reality and coping with its threatening features. However, the travellers are aware that, in the face of physical sensations, the discursive methods they use may fail, and only the body and its 'extensions' may turn out to be compatible with the physical character of their experience. Even if the objects that the travellers carry with them appear to be poorly adjusted to the explored reality, they are still the familiar factors, invariably remaining the elements out of which the travellers' *selves* may be reconstructed. For, in the face of an apparently inexpressible experience, the body often turns out to be the only tool which travel reporters are able to resort to. Thus, in the cultural exchange which most often takes place during an expeditions, literally attached to their bodies and reducing or increasing their bulk in contact with the external, peregrinating objects allow explorers to sustain the integrity of their *selves*, whenever they face the challenge of restructuring their ideas about reality.

References

Anderson, B. (2006) *Imagined Communities: Reflections on the Origin and Spread of Nationalism.* London: Verso.

Bakhtin, M. (1984) *Rabelais and His World*. Bloomington, IN: Indiana University Press.

Byron, R. (2007) *The Road to Oxiana*. Oxford: Oxford University Press.

Elliot, J. (1999) *An Unexpected Light: Travels in Afghanistan*. New York: Picador USA.

Greenblatt, S. (1988) *Marvelous Possessions: The Wonder of the New World*. Oxford: Clarendon Press.

Hankiss, E. (2001) *Fears and Symbols: An Introduction to the Study of Western Civilization.* New York: Central European University Press.

Lamb, C. (2004) *The Sewing Circles of Herat: A Personal Voyage Through Afghanistan*. New York: Perennial.

Stasiuk, A. (2008) *On the Road to Babadag (Jadac do Babadag,* trans. M. Kowalczyk-Piaseczna). Wołowiec: Czarne Publishing House.

Tagg, J. (1993) *Grounds of Dispute: Art History, Cultural Politics and the Discursive Field*. Minneapolis, MN: University of Minnesota Press.

11 Travelling in/to Africa: Narratives of Postcolonial Encounters

Ana Luísa Pires

Postcolonial theory (also known as postcolonialism) can briefly be described as a critical Western discourse whose main objective is the deconstruction of Western structures of knowledge and power by questioning the duality between coloniser and colonised upon which those structures have been based, and by giving voice to marginalised groups. Postcolonial theories have been explored since the 1950s in various creative and academic fields, but with a greater impact in literature, sociology, philosophy, anthropology and political science.

As the travel and tourism industries are rapidly advancing into territories that were once European colonies, tourism researchers have begun stressing the need for a postcolonial approach to tourism, especially in such highly sensitive tourist spaces as those found on the African continent, where several former colonies are facing the multiple challenges of recent independence. For many developing nations in Africa the tourism industry plays a crucial role as a lever for social and economic development, given that it constitutes a major source of job creation and foreign exchange. The movement of affluent Western tourists in search of exotic and unexplored holiday destinations in economically underprivileged African countries exposes an unbalanced relation between tourists and hosts that seems to replicate colonial travel patterns.

Despite tourism's entangled power relationships at work in postcolonial locations, not a lot of attention has been given to the conjunctions between postcolonialism and tourism theory, with most research on tourism still focusing on more traditional sociological and/or economic disciplines. Postcolonial theories can provide tourism research with new insights into the examination of the complex networks of assumptions and expectations that characterise tourism encounters in postcolonial locations. The introduction of critical perspectives in tourism research has the potential to open important spaces in which to reinterpret and even question Western constructions of travel and tourism, commonly based on images of colonially influenced exoticism. However, it is of extreme importance that these critical perspectives, the majority of which still originate in Western academia, focus on the often neglected and/or misinterpreted character- istics and aspirations of the host societies. As Iyunolu Osagie and Christine Buzinde note:

> tourism scholarship has been pertinent, relevant, necessary and sym- pathetic to the oppressed; it has nonetheless been framed from the perspective of the, often removed, Western researcher and thus does not take into account the local issues as articulated, lived, and dealt with by the locals. As a result, although such research has brought much needed awareness to (post)colonial issues, it has sometimes done so without meaningfully involving the Other *as voiced*. (Osagie & Buzinde, 2011: 211, original emphasis)

One way to give voice to the 'Other' regarding tourism issues is through the analysis of cultural texts such as plays, films and novels produced in these complex, postcolonial locations, as they constitute important discourses on social relations, considering local questions from the perspective of the local population. This chapter looks at some of the most pertinent concerns and proposals regarding a postcolonial approach to travel and tourism as expressed by both tourism researchers and by three contemporary African postcolonial writers – Mia Couto, João Paulo Borges Coelho and Zakes Mda – who have dealt with issues raised by travel and tourism in/to the African continent in their literary works.

These days, the vast majority of Western tourists still travel to post- colonial locations in search of some form of exoticism, which may be found in natural elements of landscape, fauna and flora, or among the cultural products of the local peoples regarded as traditional, such as rituals, artefacts and costumes. Frequently overlooked in this situation, however, is the fact that much in the same manner that colonising powers attempted to categorise colonised peoples in order to better impose their colonial policies, such exotic facets are commonly manipulated (by tourists and hosts alike, as will be seen) so that tourists can easily recognise them. This means that both colonial-era narratives and contemporary tourist narratives have been complicit with the production of misconceptions about destinations and peoples found in colonial locations, with some of the most recurrent tourist representations regarding those destinations and peoples relying heavily on cultural perceptions that have been developed in the West.

The subjugation of African regions and peoples occurred mainly through military action, but it was supported and justified by the circulation of varying types of texts. Penetrating into spaces previously unknown to the Western world, Europeans travelling and exploring the African continent from the 15th century recorded through writing the strangeness occasioned by the uncharted territories they came across. Manifest in these early writings on Africa is a compulsive effort to catalogue the unfamiliar natural and human features encountered, in what is an attempt to interpret those features according to Western conventions, thereby producing a sense of control over them. Examining the connections between early Portuguese writings on Africa and the Portuguese expansionist project, Josiah Blackmore discerns this kind of interpretative, yet controlling potential as extremely common in early texts:

> writers on Africa make observations on geography, the customs and skin color of natives, and the new natural and human worlds that nautical travel reveals. These observations seek to taxonomize – and therefore contain and control – the spaces and peoples of Africa. The Western observer shapes the world and its inhabitants and infixes them into a schema of observation and knowledge. (Blackmore, 2009: 73)

Presumptuously assuming the new African lands as *terra incognita*, this obsession with the description, classification and naming of unfamiliar features so common in official European records limits the recognition of any existent historical, social and/or cultural contexts in those foreign territories. This European enterprise of mapping and naming foreign territories was not restricted to geographical contexts, but encompassed already central political and cultural aspects of the colonialist project as well. A powerful means of asserting European superiority, these written records constitute for many critics one of the earliest exercises of colonial power. European (textual) authority over African territories evidenced by these accounts opened the way and was used as justification for the ensuing physical conquest of those territories, as Andrew Smith outlines:

> it was *in and through* travel writings and other forms of literature that Europeans learned to think of themselves as fundamentally different from the rest of the world. Of course, many of the accounts that Europeans gave of Africa, Asia, and the Americas were made in the prelude to or in the context of colonial rule. Descriptions of local practices and beliefs often sanctioned European governance as a moral force, or what is now called a 'humanitarian intervention'. (Smith, 2004: 243, original emphasis).

The European colonisation of African territories has left multiple, long-lasting impacts on both the colonised and the colonisers, extending far beyond the colonising period. A manifest repercussion of the colonising process is the way African cultures and identities are still often misunderstood and misrepresented by the West, which insists on perpetuating an image of authenticity and/or exoticism. In contemporary post-independence times, much Western travel to postcolonial Africa is still heavily influenced, whether directly or indirectly, by colonial-era narratives and representations of Africa and Africans. For most Western travellers to Africa, there is an understanding of the continent and its inhabitants (commonly referred to as an 'African imaginary') that precedes any actual contact and which discursively constructs, and at times even commodifies, Africa and Africans. It might be argued that in their attempts to comprehend the new realities they are observing, contemporary Western tourists replicate the manipulation of cultural identities undertaken by colonialism. According to Noel B. Salazar, such (mis)representations (which are part of what he terms 'tourism imaginaries') are not accidental, but strongly influenced by relations of political and social power:

> Whatever the form of tourism indulged in, people always travel with a set of expectations derived from various sources. Much of this prior information removes uncertainty and reduces risk on the one hand, yet on the other can also be seen as a form of control that channels tourist experiences into pre-determined forms.... A series of social practices, ideologies, and behaviors derived from tourism imaginaries subtly influence how people engage with the 'Other'. (Salazar, 2011: 876–877)

Western tourists' desire to travel to particular destinations located in former colonised territories is intimately connected to their imaginary constructions of those territories and their inhabitants as immune to modernisation, thus corresponding to the fantasy of an Edenic and authentic past, which they have seen reproduced in colonial narratives and modern versions of those fantasies.

In Mia Couto's *O Outro Pé da Sereia* (*The Other Foot of the Mermaid*), a novel in which different voyages and times are juxtaposed, the contemporary narrative follows the journey of an African-American couple to Mozambique in search of their African origins. It will be the presence of these foreign characters that will raise important questions related to Mozambican identities among the inhabitants of a remote village, Vila Longe. The introduction of this African-American couple is also a clear sign of Mia Couto's attention to the complicated networks of identification that exist in this area, given that there is currently a strong trend among success-ful African-Americans to trace and travel back to their African origins. Rosie and Benjamin Southman travel to Vila Longe as members of an NGO that aims to reduce poverty in Africa, but their journey also has personal motiva-tions: Rosie wants to study what she terms 'the African imaginary' and Benjamin is resolved to find his ancestors in the Mozambican village. It might be argued that in Couto's narrative Vila Longe is transformed by its inhabitants into a tourist destination that corresponds to Western interests, following a very common trend among tourism destinations and attractions in developing countries to be planned and developed in order to respond to the interests of Western tourists. As Anne-Marie d'Hauteserre puts it:

> Tourism in developing countries is eagerly organized for the Western traveler even as it becomes a locus of contradictions, juxtapositions, and intersections, and even as the new global cultural economy is increas-ingly a complex, disjunctive order, which cannot be understood in terms of a simple center–periphery model. Furthermore, deterritorialization has engendered movements of money and persons such that many travel agencies thrive on the need of diasporas for contact with their homelands. In this highly structuralist view, the tourist is not a free subject of thought or action, and nor is the host. (d'Hauteserre, 2004: 238)

Fully aware of these circumstances, the community of Vila Longe plans to put on a play in order to convince the Americans that Vila Longe is the perfect place for the NGO's funds to be allocated: 'Nós vamos contar uma história aos americanos. Vamos vender-lhes uma grande história' (Couto, 2006: 154).[1] The story includes passages of suffering related to slavery and colonialism, as well as a woman with spiritual powers who makes the connection between present and past by contacting Benjamin's ancestors. At the same time, dark passages in the history of Vila Longe, like the in-volvement of some of the villagers' ancestors in the slave trade, and signs of modernisation, such as the use of mobile phones, are strategically hidden from the Americans. These carefully chosen ingredients correspond to some of the most common representations associated with Africa, produced both inside and outside the African continent, deftly deconstructed here by Mia Couto. The plan set up by the villagers is not, as the narrator ironically explains, meant to deceive the African-Americans by presenting them with a distorted picture of Mozambican history and culture, but to please them by giving them exactly what they expect to find, so that Vila Longe, its inhabit-ants and their stories match the foreigners' preconceptions about Africa:

Estava dada a incumbência: ao estudar os papéis de Benjamin Southman descobririam aquilo que ele aspirava encontrar em África. Depois, encenariam em Vila Longe a África com que o estrangeiro sempre havia sonhado. Mentir não passa de uma benevolência: revelar aquilo que os outros querem acreditar. (Couto, 2006: 175)[2]

The exchanges between the Mozambican villagers and the foreign visitors disclose globalised, postcolonial Mozambique as a site in which former simplistic oppositions between the colonised (regarded as mere 'objects') and the colonisers (seen as 'agents') have been replaced by a complex game of projected desires and interests on both sides, that nonetheless assigns some kind of agency to the former, as Luís Madureira explains: 'The form of subaltern agency that Couto's account seeks to instantiate would thus have survived as the negated term in a dialectic of historical progress that has endured beyond the transition from colony to nation' (Madureira, 2008: 216). What this subaltern agency therefore seems to imply is that exploitation and misunderstandings between the African continent and Western countries are maintained in the postcolonial period, even though under new circumstances and a different designation, still marked by a reductive and patronising view of Africa by the West.

The inhabitants of Vila Longe are not portrayed as mere victims of misrepresentation by the Western tourists, but as actually being complicit in the creation of a distorted picture of their identity and culture in contemporary Mozambique, in order to profit from the foreign tourists. The inhabitants of Vila Longe are aware that the more primitive an image they present of themselves to the foreigners, the more chance they have of moving socially upward and, paradoxically, of becoming modern. Resorting to this attitude of acting primitive for others by staging their cultures as they try to adapt to modernity, the inhabitants of Vila Longe portrayed in Mia Couto's novel seem to correspond to the category of the 'ex-primitive' or 'performative primitive', described by Dean MacCannell in *Empty Meeting Grounds*:

Enacted or staged savagery is already well established as a small but stable part of the world system of social and economic exchanges. Many formerly primitive groups earn their living by charging visitors to their sacred shrines, ritual performances, and displays of more less 'ethnologized' everyday life. The commercialization of ethnological performance and display co-developed by formerly primitive peoples and the international tourism and entertainment industries, is potentially a long-term economic adaptation. (MacCannell, 1992: 18–19)

The foreign tourists, for their part, become immersed and unquestioningly engage in the authenticity play staged by the villagers, eager as they are to experience their fantasy of an African continent clear of any signs of modernity. Under the pretense of being tolerant towards and respectful of other cultures, the way the Americans visiting Vila Longe come to terms with the village and its inhabitants in the 21st century does not differ much, however, from the patronising attitudes displayed by previous generations of colonisers:

> Os americanos a tudo iam achando graça, tudo para eles era motivo de interesse antropológico. Benjamin limpou os olhos como se invisíveis poeiras atrapalhassem o foco da sua máquina fotográfica. Incessantemente, repetia:
> Oh, Africa, tão interessante!
> (Couto, 2006: 167)[3]

In the burlesque novella *Hinyambaan*, Mozambican writer João Paulo Borges Coelho describes the road trip undertaken by a South African white family – the Odendaals – from Johannesburg to Inhambane. As we follow the adventures of the Odendaals from the big South African city to the rural heart of Mozambique, it becomes clear how, even within the African continent, constructed perceptions of the 'Other' remain much alive. The white South African couple travel to Mozambique with a preconceived image of the country and its inhabitants as inferior and uncivilised, and therefore subservient to countries and peoples perceived as more developed (such as South Africa). Throughout the novella Coelho shatters these stereotypes by resorting to humorous situations, as in the following frontier scene:

> 'Se eu quisesse podia bem passar pela portagem com o acelerador a fundo que ninguém me apanhava', diz Hermann Odendaal.... 'Aposto que o funcionário está a dormir, além de que duvido que saiba ler a matrícula.'
> ...
> Abrandam e entram suavemente na portagem. Hermann Odendaal paga à inexpressiva funcionária que os olha do *guichet*. Enquanto espera pelo troco, repara em dois polícias fardados encarando o *Corolla* com despreocupação. Ao lado deles está estacionado um possante BMW, pronto a perseguir pequenos *Corollas* ... Hermann Odendaal sorri-lhes, percorrido por um calafrio.
> (Coelho, 2008: 12, original emphasis)[4]

The maintenance of an exotic portrayal of Africa by Westerners and Africans alike is an issue that concerns not just contemporary African writers but tourism researchers as well. Stephen Wearing and Simon Darcy underline the need for 'Commodified images and their discursive constructions ... [to] be disrupted and dissociated so that the host and tourist move toward a re-inscription of place with a different sense of self and identity' (Wearing & Darcy, 2011: 22).

In the novel *The Heart of Redness*, Zakes Mda depicts some of the most pertinent questions faced by past and present South African society by devising an intricate alignment between two distinct narrative strands set in the seaside village of Qolorha in two crucial historical moments for South Africa. The contemporary narrative takes place during the early post-apartheid period and the historical narrative discloses the early encounters between the Xhosa people and British colonisers in the 19th century. In the contemporary narrative, the inhabitants of Qolorha adopt opposing viewpoints regarding the proposal for a luxury tourist resort for the village: while those who defend the project see it as a classic introducer of modernis-ation, with potential to generate great economic returns, those who oppose it claim the resort will drive them further into poverty by excluding the majority of the local population from actually benefiting from it, while overexploiting their natural resources.

The answer to tourism development in Qolorha is presented by Camagu, a black South African intellectual disillusioned with post-apartheid politics and a newcomer to the village, who is able to transcend this duality by combining the positive aspects of both perspectives and adding his own academic and work experience, as well as his particular vision of the relevance of involving the local population in the development projects. Camagu's project, a cooperative-based ecological tourist development (initially a back-packers' hostel, which develops into a holiday camp), relies on and aims to protect the potential generated at local level by the historical, cultural and natural identities and resources found in Qolorha, but it depends on the forces of economic globalisation which make it possible for tourists from inside and outside South Africa to become aware of and take full advantage of this type of project. The *raison d'être* of Camagu's ecotourist project is in-trinsically tied to the economic and psychological well-being of both the local community and its potential tourists. Through his small-scale ecotourist project he transcends the binaries of tradition and modernity, of local and global interests, as he takes advantage of globalised processes already under way in order to benefit the local community. Camagu somehow manages to transfer his views on African culture as varied, complex and dynamic to the ecotourism concept he devises by getting the local population to become engaged with the development of Qolorha: 'I am interested in the culture of the amaXhosa as they live it today, not yesterday. The amaXhosa people are not a museum piece. Like all cultures, their culture is dynamic' (Mda, 2000: 248). In his discussions about tourism with both believers and unbelievers, Camagu defends the idea that a people's culture should not be looked at as being connected to a past that does not exist as such anymore, but rather as a dynamic element of that people's present life. He is critical of the kind of staged authenticity put on display in cultural villages throughout South Africa, and also found in Qolorha, which attempt to excavate a pre-colonial authenticity that is lost:

> That's dishonest. It is just a museum that pretends that is how people live. Real people in today's South Africa don't lead the life that is seen in cultural villages. Some aspects of that life perhaps are true. But the bulk of what tourists see is the past ... a lot of it an imaginary past. They must be honest and say that they are attempting to show how people used to live. They must not pretend that's how people live now. (Mda, 2000: 248)

In their reading of the text, Mike Kissack and Michael Titlestad claim that, though mindful of the complex history of Qolorha, Camagu's eco-tourist project is attuned to the present circumstances, thereby creating the potential to help the inhabitants of the village redefine their identities in the challenging context of post-apartheid South Africa:

> For Camagu, and the project of ecological tourism, the past is to be re-membered, not ossified and revered, while the present must be redefined and reinvented to provide people with the dignity of self-determination, forged within the confines and prospects of their present situation. (Kissack & Titlestad, 2009: 163)

Tourism scholars attentive to the complex questions raised by tourism in former colonised settings are stressing the need for more balanced tourism projects, such as the one outlined in Mda's novel, to be put forward in developing countries, as they require the involvement of the local community and, very importantly, because their small scale allows the preservation of the local culture, creating nevertheless important spaces for host–tourist interactions to take place:

> There is the need for a more equitable distribution of power between Western and host cultures where interaction occurs in a 'third tourist

space', where decision-making responsibility involves the hosts and where they receive economic returns. Within this conceptualisation tourism is not exploitative of local populations and benefits flow to local residents. The culture of the host community is respected and the tourist is open to experiencing aspects of the 'other' culture with a view to learning and expanding the self. The shift in the relationships of power between tourist and host culture enables both to interact and to learn from each other with an eventual hybridisation of cultures. (van der Duim *et al.*, 2005: 291)

The literary works by Mia Couto, João Paulo Borges Coelho and Zakes Mda analysed in this chapter stress the pertinence of applying a critical theoretical approach to tourism in developing countries in general, and in Africa in particular, given that many Western tourists still travel to post-colonial Africa with a heavy colonial 'luggage', which not only affects their perceptions of the continent and its inhabitants, but also influences Africans' self-perception as well, thereby disturbing possible fruitful interactions between tourists and hosts. Critical tourism research can contribute to a greater understanding of the postcolonial experience by focusing on cultural artefacts, including literary texts, produced in postcolonial locations, as these offer the perspective of the local population on the issues that concern them, including the advances of tourism.

Notes

(1) 'We'll tell a story to the Americans. We will sell them a great story.' (My translation)
(2) 'The task was given: by studying the documents that belonged to Benjamin Southman they would discover what he aspired to find in Africa. Then they would stage in Vila Longe the Africa the foreigner had always dreamed of. Lying is just a benevolence: to reveal what others want to believe in.' (My translation)
(3) 'The Americans found everything amusing, everything was a source of anthropological interest to them. Benjamin wiped his eyes as if invisible dust intruded the focus of his camera. He repeated endlessly:
Oh, Africa, so interesting!' (My translation)
(4) '"If I wanted I could well go through the toll at full speed so that nobody would catch me", says Hermann Odendaal.... "I bet the employee is sleeping, and I doubt he can read the licence plate."...
They slowed down and gently entered the toll. Hermann Odendaal paid the ex-pressionless employee who looks at them through the *guichet*. While waiting for the change, he notices two uniformed police officers facing the *Corolla* with nonchalance. Beside them is parked a powerful BMW, ready to chase small *Corollas* ... Hermann Odendaal smiles at them, crossed by a chill.' (My translation)

References

Blackmore, J. (2009) *Moorings: Portuguese Expansion and the Writing of Africa*. Minneapolis, MN: University of Minnesota Press.

Coelho, J.P.B. (2008) *Hinyambaan*. Lisbon: Editorial Caminho.

Couto, M.D. (2006) *O Outro Pé da Sereia*. Lisbon: Editorial Caminho.

d'Hauteserre, A-M. (2004) Postcolonialism, colonialism, and tourism. In A.A. Hall *et al.* (eds) *A Companion to Tourism* (pp. 235–245). Oxford: Blackwell.

Kissack, M. and Titlestad, M. (2009) Invidious interpreters: The post-colonial intellectual in *The Heart of Redness*. In D. Bell and J.U. Jacobs (eds) *Ways of Writing: Critical Essays on Zakes Mda* (pp. 149–167). Pietermaritzburg: University of Kwa-Zulu Natal Press.

MacCannell, D. (1992) *Empty Meeting Grounds: The Tourist Papers*. London: Routledge.

Madureira, L. (2008) Nation, identity and loss of footing: Mia Couto's *O Outro Pé da Sereia* and the question of Lusophone postcolonialism. *Novel* (spring/summer), 200–228.

Mda, Z. (2000) *The Heart of Redness*. New York: Picador.

Osagie, I. and Buzinde, C.N. (2011) Culture and resistance: Antigua in Kincaid's *A Small Place*. *Annals of Tourism Research* 38 (1), 210–230.

Salazar, N.B. (2011) Tourism imaginaries: A conceptual approach. *Annals of Tourism Research* 39 (2), 863–882.

Smith, A. (2004) Migrancy, hybridity, and postcolonial literary studies. In N. Lazarus (ed.) *The Cambridge Companion to Postcolonial Literary Studies* (pp. 241–261). Cambridge: Cambridge University Press.

van der Duim, R., Peters, K. and Wearing, S. (2005) Planning host and guest interactions: Moving beyond the empty meeting ground in African encounters. *Current Issues in Tourism* 8 (4), 286–305.

Wearing, S. and Darcy, S. (2011) Inclusion of the *Othered* in tourism. *Cosmopolitan Civil Societies Journal* 2 (3), 18–34.

Part 3
The Case of Portugal

12 Mythical Moors: Constructing a Cultural Tourist Itinerary Around Valpaços

Jenny Campos, Maria Manuel Baptista and Larissa Latif

Cultural Tourism and Identity

In the 1970s, cultural tourism was defined as the type of tourism that included picturesque vestiges of traditional peasant lifestyles (typically textiles, pottery and buildings); it was associated with attempts to approximate or otherwise recreate past cultures themselves. By the 1980s, the World Tourism Organization (WTO) was stating that cultural tourism was an increasingly widespread movement, driven essentially by cultural motives, which included such activities as study tours, cultural tours, festival attendance, visits to historic monuments and pilgrimages (WTO, 1985).

However, as Jenks (1993) argues, this type of definition can be seen as redundant, the concept of culture being equated with that of civilisation. In this sense, the author affirms, a definition which states that cultural tourism is merely tourism involving culture (the latter being understood as tradition, fine arts and heritage) does not really clarify the matter. Jenks goes on to say that several authors have contributed other definitions of culture, making this concept much wider than the one considered by the WTO. The International Council on Monuments and Sites (ICOMOS), for example, defines cultural tourism as an activity concerned with the discovery of places and monuments, but exercising a considerable positive effect on them, as it aims to guarantee their protection and preservation (ICOMOS, 1976). Cunha (2007), on the other hand, points out that it is impossible to separate history from culture. One must include in the definition of cultural tourism the travelling involved in the desire to see new things, to increase one's knowledge, to understand the particularities and the habits of other people, to get to know different past or present cultures and civilisations, or even to satisfy spiritual needs. Finally, Barreto (2004) states that cultural tourism is based on the seeking out of cultural heritage, where this is understood as both tangible and intangible heritage.

Thus, the most recent theoretical contributions seem to agree with the need (indeed the urgent need) to value 'place' through the preservation of its assets and the recovery of its local culture, but also by avoiding the repetition of themes and motifs that might tend to its trivialisation. This can easily happen, especially with mass tourism, and can compromise the complex historical character of a given heritage. The intimate relationship that is created with the history and the heritage of a particular location, especially when it really interacts with people and with their immaterial realities, is what allows us to find value in it. This relationship of reciprocity with our heritage gives legitimacy to initiatives that address the legacy our predecessors have left us.

Many studies agree about the growing global importance of this type of cultural tourism. This importance stems not only from the fact that the demand for this type of tourism is one of the fastest growing, but also because cultural heritage is related to the identity of a people. Awareness of the importance of valuing a heritage that embodies the intangible values of a culture has increased with every passing decade and tourism with a cultural focus is one way to maintain and raise awareness of the heritage and identity of a locality. Cultural tourism is therefore currently a very practical concern for many municipalities aiming for sustainable development and seeking ways to add value to their territory. By enhancing the cultural visibility of a city or municipality, cultural tourism can also contribute to raising the self-esteem of local people. However, in attracting visitors, cultural tourism should involve the whole community in its objectives, not just with the intention of developing the local economy, but principally by viewing the exploitation of cultural tourism as an engine of community spirit which can and should improve the quality of life of the population.

What we set out to do in this chapter is to construct a cultural tourist itinerary which would allow people to appreciate and draw value from the intangible heritage of the district of Valpaços in northern Portugal. This is a place associated with Moorish legends, as well as containing material assets related to these legends. This is one possible way of preserving the culture memories of this community. The constructions of which these legends speak are not merely inert objects and buildings: they seem to bring with them such a distinct aura of legend that each of these places is provided with a unique atmosphere. Much of this charm emanates from the mythological corpus that the community associates with these constructions.

The concept of 'intangible heritage' was first used in UNESCO's documents from the Mexico Conference of 1982 on cultural policies, at which the so-called Declaration of Mexico originated. After a long process of reflection, the Convention for the Safeguarding of Intangible Cultural Heritage was drawn up in Paris in 2003. Since then, the designation 'intangible heritage' has included oral expressions and traditions in addition to languages, performing arts, social practices, rituals and festive events, knowledge and practices concerning nature and the universe, and traditional craft-related skills, among many other things.

It is reasonable to affirm that the valorisation of the intangible cultural heritage from a given location can contribute to the strengthening of that location's identity and that, when combined with tourist activity, it can promote the conservation of festivals and traditions, as well as the improvement of the population's living conditions. Caponero and Leite (2010) state that the safeguarding of intangible assets is needed to support the continuation of communities and an important part of improving a people's social conditions. The transmission and reproduction of intangible assets allow for their continued existence.

Despite all the difficulties that have stood, or still stand, in the way of including intangible heritage as a fundamental element in attracting tourist activity, there are several cities that have managed to overcome these obstacles and have gained a profile in the market for cultural tourism. Many of them have been recognised by the European Commission not for their monuments or other infrastructure, but for their traditions. According to the Commission, this intangible living heritage can bring people together, giving them a sense of identity and continuity; it features culinary arts, handicraft traditions, legends, local arts and rural life. An example of this kind of city is Belogradchik in northern Bulgaria, which received the title of European Destination of Excellence in Local Intangible Heritage (2008), as it has based its whole cultural tourism strategy on the various myths surrounding the city. There is also a tourist route between Düsseldorf and Mainz based on visits (usually by hiking or cycling) to sites of local legends, involving elves and Lorelei, among others. The award for European Destination of Excellence in Local Intangible Heritage (2008) was also assigned to the town of Corinaldo in Italy, where, in addition to displays of traditional craftsmanship, the visitor can see several monuments and gardens.

All these destinations have in common the fact that they understand cultural tourism as being predicated on local personality and rooted in an authenticity that comes only when local people understand who they are and where they have come from. The personality of a place, its unique productivity, is what gives that place its atmosphere and special flavour. It is the local culture, given substance in the built heritage, urban morphology, local rites, rhythms and the popular imagination, that makes such places unique. As Ortiz writes:

> when you think of the memory of a people, the social movements of historical heritage maintenance are considered fundamental, where the entire population joins in the pursuit of a single goal, seeking to save the past in order to offer it to those who come after. For this to occur, the collective memory can only exist as part of living experience, as a practice that is manifested in the everyday life of the people. (Ortiz, 1994: 133, our translation)

Myths of the Moors in Valpaços

When we think of tangible or intangible cultural heritage, we immediately associate it with another concept: collective memory. Memory and perception of the collective are inherent in both aspects of cultural heritage. In this regard, Halbwachs (2004) differentiates individual memory (related to one's psychological development), memories relating to the individual, (recollection of how he or she has lived) and collective memory (related to joint action). For Duby (1976), the collective memory is a continuous stream of accomplishments and thoughts that we learned about, having no beginning and no end. In this sense, intangible heritage is presented both as living heritage and as an important instrument of identity. Intangible heritage, revealed in festivals, rites and traditional knowledge, is indisputably composed of inseparable cultural references from physical heritage, of monuments, streets and public spaces.

A good example of this connection is the municipality of Valpaços, which was founded in 1836. Its history includes the histories of the smaller municipalities that gave origin to it. In its territory there are prehistoric, Celtic and Roman remains, among others. Although there are no records to show that Muslim invasions were part of its history, the collective memory has preserved a rich mythological corpus associated with enchanted Moors that the population believes to be connected with the Muslim community which once inhabited the region.

In territorial terms, Valpaços is located in the interior part of northern Portugal and integrated in the region of Trás-os-Montes. In administrative terms, the 553 km^2 of land are distributed into 31 parishes, where around 17,000 inhabitants reside (this information is from 2011). According to the website of the municipality (http://valpacos.no.sapo.pt), the climate of Valpaços is characterised by severe winters and hot and dry summers.

The municipality has a rich and varied material heritage, mostly featuring civil and military architecture. The main gastronomic delicacies are: world-renowned and international award-winning olive oil, sausages, *cozido* and *feijoada à transmontana* (two kinds of stew with meat and vegetables), honey, almonds, chestnut soup and wine. The most distinctive and widely regarded handicrafts are those of blacksmithing, basketry, the manufacture of spirits and embroidery.

The way the local population interprets history (this being a fundamental process in the construction of their identity) has a special interest for us. According to Jodelet (1989) and Moscovici (2001), social representations are a form of socially established and shared knowledge, contributing to the perception of a reality shared by a certain group. These social representations constitute, therefore, the way in which individuals appropriate the world around them, helping them to understand and to act within their society. They can be seen as symbolic elements that individuals express through the use of words and gestures, in conjunction with local contexts, that is, the conditions under which individuals are seen to fit in and belong to a community. Understanding identity (or identities) as a process that emerges from cultural attributes is crucial for conceiving the role that representations play in building up the meanings of said identities. One might say that only from these representations is it possible to conceptualise identities, to explain their importance in contemporary society and in cultural and social domains.

The mythical Moors to whom we refer 'fit in the mythology of the enchanted, which from a legendary/historical perspective transforms these ancient peoples into marginal and clandestine archetypes, thus hidden and magical' (Lopes, 2007: 3, our translation). According to Lopes, these beings are 'legendary medieval reminiscences of the time of the Moors, this being an era of prosperity, whose remains are buried or hidden in remote and mysterious places' (Lopes, 2007: 8, our translation). Their relevance in the context of Trás-os-Montes is explained by the opposition between Moors and Christians, underlining the antagonism between the 'Other' and 'I/we' and highlighting that, in terms of the imaginary and the symbolic, the Moors in Trás-os-Montes are associated with the 'Other', independently of historical chronology, and conflating enchanted Moors with the ethnic group which occupied part of area from the 8th century on (Frazão & Morais, 2009). Martins Sarmento (1902) argued that the term 'Moors' became used to designate 'pagans' and that such traditions existed many centuries before the Arab invasion. According to this author, the Moors of the legends are actually the pagans of the local hill forts, tumuli and fountains, in fact all and any pagan beings.

The mythological corpus associated with the Moors of Valpaços places great emphasis on enchanted female Moors; however, it is still possible to trace the profile of the mythical male Moor. He is seen as the warrior, the attacker and sometimes the keeper of treasures. These characters are traditionally associated with such places as bridges, stairs, sinks and fountains. On the other hand, enchanted female Moors are characters of rare beauty. They usually have long black hair and they live in hidden underground palaces. There are several legends that report romantic relationships between Moors and Christians; there is even a legend that says a Moor was the king's mistress. The female Moors are sometimes described as hybrid characters (half woman, half goat or snake) who are longing for someone to break the spell that keeps them in this state. Such legends are explanations for the unexplainable and establish the difference between the sacred and the profane. They are an attempt to explain the origin of parts of the world, of objects, characters and phenomena, without seeking recourse to historical fact. Eliade (1989) notes that these myths relate to events that took place in a primordial time.

They can also be narratives of the exploits of supernatural characters that feed and give meaning to the culture and life of certain social groups, becoming a constitutive part of their reality. They are like a vertical dimension that stands against the horizontal dimension of human chronology and fact. In this sense, these myths make us understand everyday time and space through the prism of sacred time and space. These myths are stories told from generation to generation; they reportedly occurred at a time of yore. They seek to give meaning to human experience, contributing to the understanding of country and community. It is precisely the belief in a common imagined past that guides individuals in the history of their community and gives meaning to their sense of identity, leading to the idea of imagined communities, just as Benedict Anderson (2008) conceived them.

In the next section, we propose a cultural itinerary that reveals something of this link between the people of Valpaços and their legends of the Moors, via visits to the places with which these legends are associated. The following would be an actual tourist route.

A Cultural Tourist Itinerary

We tried to be methodical in designing this itinerary. We sought to conceptualise the best way to address the subject, so we first analysed the places to visit individually, seeking both geographical and thematic cohesion, but splitting the journey in order to facilitate the visitors' reading of the elements, allowing them at each staging point to absorb the experience that the route provides. The criterion of geographical proximity proved to be important in the drawing up of much of the itinerary, for distance between the sites is obviously an important factor in the journey of a tourist. Total travelling time was another important factor in the construction of the route we propose, since this itinerary should be implemented in harmony with other existing tourist offers and cultural assets of the district.

The constituent parts of the itinerary are classified according to the means of transport (car or on foot), the duration (one day), the destination (Valpaços), the market segment (inhabitants and visitors to the municipality), the number of participants (groups of up to five people), the geographical base (the municipality of Valpaços) and the cultural and artistic value of each part. In short, this itinerary is composed of various stops, all related in some way to the mythical Moors of Valpaços, and is an attempt to make the intangible tangible, and in so doing to give some idea of the identity of Valpaços. This theme allows visitors to encounter such different cultural values as the historical, the ethnographic, the geographical, the architectural, along with traditional and artistic activities, all constitutive of the identity of the place.

Starting the route, we propose a stop in the parish of Sonim, where, after a 10-minute walk, you can visit the Perna do Mouro ('Leg of the Moor' – place names in this context are extremely evocative). According to the local community, the carved images found at this rock serve to remind you that within the rock lived (and maybe continues to live) a mythical Moor (represented by the leg) who kept a great treasure (represented by a chalice), both inscribed in the stone (as a kind of drawing or engraving). The little slit on the left side of the rock is the place where the mythical Moor entered and exited. The website Valpaços Online (http://valpacos.no.sapo. pt/sonim.html) states that the rock has a prehistoric anthropomorphic engraving, discovered in 1879 by Marcelino S. de Sautuola. For its part, the study PNTA/2000 – Rupestrian Art Sites in Valpaços, made by IGESPAR (Instituto de Gestão do Património Arquitectónico e Arqueológico – the institute that manages Portuguese heritage), points out that:

> the front surface was intentionally prepared. One can observe in the remains of this preparation a clear intentional delimiting of the panel surface … its meaning is impossible to be determined. The panel is composed by 9 figures, among which the figure of a leg stands out, as well as circular motifs and an anthropomorph. (http://arqueologia. igespar.pt, our translation)

The itinerary continues on to the parish of Lebução. Legend has it that:

> under Ponte da Pulga (Flea Bridge) ... is a golden enchanted lamp concealed for centuries, which was left by the Moors. And that the spell can only be broken by a farmer who has a cow, which would give birth to two calves on a night with a full moon and they would suck all the milk she had.... the farmer cannot take advantage of the milk for any purpose, and for an entire year. (Parafita, 2006: 147, our translation here and below)

According to local authority, the River Calvo, which starts in the municipality of Chaves, acquires the designation of Ribeiro da Pulga (Flea Creek) after passing under Ponte da Pulga. The same source states that 'this bridge was destroyed by a violent thunderstorm that occurred on 17 June 1939'. In following this creek one can also visit the Arquinho (small arch) Roman bridge, a watermill and several windmills in the area. This creek, Ribeiro da Pulga, is also associated with legends that state that the rivers of Valpaços have their origin in the tears wept by enchanted female Moors.

Leaving Ribeiro da Pulga behind, it is a short journey to the parish of Alvarelhos, where we suggest a visit to the Fortim da Coroa (Fort of the Crown). The legend associated with this place says:

> near the village of Alvarelhos there is a ruined fort called A Coroa (the Crown). It is said that in it lived a Moorish king. And there is another site, between Alvarelhos and Orcides, called Vale da Batalha (Valley of the Battle), where it is said there were many battles against Moors who were always defeated because S. Tiago, mounted on a white horse, helped Christians, killing Moors without pity or mercy. (Parafita, 2006: 141)

Fortim da Coroa (a designation assigned by locals) is also known in the district as Castro (hill fort) da Lama de Ouriço or Cabeço da Muralha, this being a prehistoric fortified settlement surrounded by rows of walls (Martins, 1978; Montalvão, 1971). Traces of circular and rectangular constructions are preserved. Another outer wall has element of buildings which have so far not been identified.

Outside the village an image of a wine press has been carved into the rock.

Still in Lebução, and based on the same legend, we move on to Vale da Batalha. According to the monograph on Valpaços by Veloso Martins (1978), this place, located between Alvarelhos and Oucidres, has its name because locals say that there were several battles between Christians and

Moors (or Saracens), the latter being vanquished by Christians with the help of an unknown knight, presumed to be Santiago. For this reason, and in accordance with Cunha (2007), it is probable that this is the same apostle who is referred to as 'Santiago Mata-Mouros' ('Moor Killer'). It is said that Santiago retreated after the battles into the valley, where there was later built a chapel in his memory. In 1873 there were still the ruins of the chapel, but today the chapel does not exist, the closest chapel dedicated to Santiago being located in Mairos/Chaves (approximately 20 km away). Vale da Batalha is now a place where you can admire the broad and open landscape, as well as the varied fauna and flora.

Next on the route we visit the parish of Algeriz to see the Pia dos Mouros (the Moors' Sink). Legend has it that:

> near Argeriz, in the municipality of Valpaços, there is a place where you see two sinks, which the ancients called Pia dos Mouros (the Moors' Sink). There are also some very deteriorated stairs which give access to underground tunnels where the Moors lived. The elders say that the location is enchanted. (Parafita, 2006: 149–150)

According to the IGESPAR website (http://arqueologia.igespar.pt), this place was classified as a national heritage site in 1984. It is known as the rock art shrine of Algeriz but it is also known by the local population as Pia dos Mouros (Moor's Sink) or as Altar dos Sacrifícios (Altar of Sacrifices) (the name that appears on official signs). It was probably built in the Roman period. It consists of two parallel rectangular cavities and some small stairs. One can also identify slots that must have supported the foundations of a structure which has collapsed. Another website (Sigillum Militum Christi, 2010) reports that the finds from this site included 'two copper axes, a copper pin, a brass band, indigenous and Roman ceramic pottery'. These remains show that those who lived here were Romans and not Moors, despite legends to the contrary.

Several authors state that, on sunny days, you can see the Panóias Sanctuary (located in Vila Real), a national monument also built by the Romans, and where demonic cults held their initiation rites. Although experts have not yet identified the purpose of the Pia dos Mouros (the Moor's Sink), the structural similarities with the Panóias sanctuary are undeniable.

The next stop is Fonte da Urze (Fountain of the Heather) in the parish of Carrazeda de Montenegro. The legend says:

> there is a fountain hidden in the bushes which is known as Fonte das Urzes. The elders say that in it there is a treasure and a snake. And that the snake is a female enchanted Moor. This snake usually appears at

midnight to whoever passes by. And if the person who passes does not fear it, the snake takes them to the treasure. They say that many went there and found the snake, but they were always frightened and fled immediately. Therefore no one has ever found the treasure. (Parafita, 2006: 148)

Very little is known about this fountain except that it has a rectangular tank covered by a roof. We were unable to gather any information about this site, beyond Correia's recording of the myth, but even so we believe it is an interesting stopover because of the magic and mysticism that the community associates with this place and the eerie idea of a treasure which no human has ever had the opportunity to see (a rare feature in the mythological corpus we reviewed) but which in theory any fearless prospective visitor might.

Conclusions

It is clear from this research that heritage, tourism and identity are complex, interconnected concepts. The literature and fieldwork review we conducted revealed that the identity of Valpaços, associated at many points with the mythical Moors, has been conserved as a set of beliefs and practices anchored not only in material history but also in the continuous imaginary, symbolic construction of cultural dynamics. So, as a community's intangible assets are constantly being reprocessed and are renewing themselves, the collective notion of identity also undergoes transformations as the future is built by rediscovering and recreating the past.

In this sense, the collective imagination in rural communities is constituted by mental representations generated by social interactions in all their complexity. One can see that, through these forms, the population holds symbolic capital, which is characterised by the effort to achieve distinction from other social groups, and the converting of certain spaces into places of conviviality. People find meaning in the quest for territorial distinctiveness if it is perceived and accepted by the whole community.

According to Eliade (1965), the whole region has one (or several) centre(s), meaning a sacred place or places *par excellence*. It is in this place, here understood as associated with legends, that the sacred fully manifests itself. As this is a sacred space, which is given by a hierophany, we are confronted with a sacred and mythical location and not an unholy land. The religious man has then need to consecrate the space or build it ritually, revealing that the world can become sacred to him, even though suffering profane influences. What defines the place as sacred is the perception of the group involved, the belief system differentiating one group from another. The question of the authenticity and the uniqueness of each region is of crucial importance, since this is what will allow the visitor to select what specific region to visit. We believe, however, that for a set of legends to be part of an attractive and sustainable tourist product, the existing resources (material and immaterial) must be properly preserved. Tourism can benefit from the informed cultural appreciation of a locale, encouraging the recognition and prestige of cultural forms and ways of being without threatening them or the lifestyle or the interests of the community. To maintain the cultural identity derived from components of local culture is to keep safe the elements that constitute rich intangible heritage (transmitted from generation to generation). This heritage is constantly recreated in accordance with its environment, its interaction with nature and its history, generating a sense of identity and continuity. These practices of preservation promote respect for cultural diversity and human creativity.

The intangible heritage of Valpaços is thus more than just a tourist attraction; it is an element capable of highlighting, preserving and offering assistance to understanding and appreciating the cultural identity of the community. The development of tourism in the district should at every level be reconcilable with the preservation of heritage, the everyday use of cultural assets and the enhancement of local cultural identities. One of the main difficulties in pursuing this research was the physical degradation of some of the places discussed, which is an indication of the neglect the authorities have shown these important sites.

However, there is a growing awareness of the importance of protecting local cultural heritage; happily, some recent timely interventions have been made in this respect. There has been some safeguarding of places with special value, as in the case of the studies conducted on Pia dos Mouros. However, there remains a clear absence of sign-posting, for example. Access to the various sites on our proposed route is, in most cases, acceptable, but there are serious problems in how to find your way to these places (the exception being Pia dos Mouros). As well as the lack of information signs along the roads, they are also absent from the monuments themselves. There are no placards, pamphlets or other texts available where tourists can gather information about what they are seeing. Visitors would, therefore, need to engage a guide to provide the necessary contextualisation. The guide would also be responsible for relating not only the legends associated with these places, but those versions which find some confirmation in recorded history as well.

In the further development of tourist routes, it would be necessary to identify which roads or trails should be used, as well as bringing together information about the hostels, restaurants and bars that can be frequented along these itineraries. The cultural elements which are inevitably the highlights of these itineraries should be integrated in a package of activities that are pleasurable and relaxing as well as instructive. It is also essential that any future itineraries seek feedback from users and visitors, to test their appeal and in order to understand what their strong points of interest are.

References

Anderson, B. (2008) *Comunidades Imaginadas*. São Paulo: Companhia das Letras.
Barreto, M. (2004) *Turismo e Legado Cultural*. Campinas: Papirus.
Caponero, M. and Leite, E. (2010) Inter-relações entre festas populares, políticas públicas, património imaterial e turismo. *Lazer and Turismo* 7 (10), 99–113. Available at http://www.unisantos.br/pos/revistapatrimonio/pdf/Ensaio1_v7_n10_abr_mai_jun2010_Patrimonio_UniSantos_%28PLT_21%29.pdf (accessed 24 May 2012).
Cunha, L. (2007) *Introdução ao Turismo*. Lisbon: Verbo.
Duby, G. (1976) História social e ideologia das sociedades. In J. Le Goff and P. Nora (eds) *História: Novos Problemas* (pp. 130–145). Rio de Janeiro: Francisco Alves.
Eliade, M. (1965) *Le Sacré et le Profane*. Paris: Gallimard.
Eliade, M. (1989) *Aspectos do Mito*. Lisbon: Edições 70.
Frazão, F. and Morais, G. (2009) *Portugal, Mundo dos Mortos e das Mouras Encantadas* (3 vols). Lisbon: Apenas Livros Lda.
Halbwachs, M. (2004) *A Memória Coletiva*. São Paulo: Ed. Centauro.
ICOMOS (1976) Carta de Turismo Cultural. At http://revistas.ulusofona.pt/index.php/cadernosociomuseologia/article/view/338/247 (accessed 24 May 2012).
Jenks, C. (1993) *Culture*. London: Routledge.
Jodelet, D. (1989) Les représentations sociales: Un domaine em expansion. In D. Jodelet (ed.) *Les Représentations Sociales* (pp. 31–61). Paris: PUF.
Lopes, A. (2007) *B.I. das Mouras Encantadas*. Lisbon: Apenas Livros Lda.
Martins, A.V. (1978) *Monografia de Valpaços*. Available at http://www.santiagoanaunia.it/pdf/RELAZIONE%20DE%20MALHAES.pdf (accessed 3 May 2012).
Montalvão, A. (1971) *Visitas a Castros Nos Arredores de Chaves*. Chaves: Edição Policopiada.
Moscovici, S. (2001) Why a theory of social representations? In K. Deaux and G. Philogène (eds) *Representations of the Social: Bridging Theoretical Traditions* (pp. 8–35). Oxford: Blackwell.
Ortiz, R. (1994) *Cultura Brasileira e Identidade Nacional*. São Paulo: Brasiliense.
Parafita, A.J. (2006) *Mouros Míticos em Trás-os-Montes – contributos para um estudo dos mouros no imaginário rural a partir de textos da literatura popular de tradição oral. Vols I, II*. Tese de Doutoramento: Universidade de Trás-os-Montes. (Texto policopiado.)
Sarmento, F.M. (1902) Materiais para a arqueologia do concelho de Guimarães. *Revista Guimarães* 19 (3), 109–119. Available at http://www.csarmento.uminho.pt/docs/ndat/rg/RG019_02.pdf (accessed June 2014).
Sigillum Militum Christi (2010) Castro de Ribas, Santuário Rupestre de Argeriz – Pias dos Mouros. At http://sigillum-militum-christi2.blogspot.pt/2010/12/castro-de-ribas-santuario-rupestre-de.html (accessed 24 May 2012).
World Tourism Organization (1985) *The State's Role in Protecting and Promoting Culture as a Factor of Tourism Development*. Madrid: WTO.

13 (O)Porto: A Wine, a Place, a Route and a Meeting Point

Joana Ferraz Ribeiro and Gillian Moreira

Recent rapid changes in society, including a widening interest in marketing and consuming cultural activities and heritage, have encouraged the recovery and development of tourism in urban areas. This process is exemplified in the district of Ribeira, Vila Nova de Gaia, Portugal, renowned for its port wine cellars. No longer just a place of work and production of a wine, these cellars have become the biggest tourist attraction in the Oporto area. Similarly, the creation, in 2011, of the Urban Wine Route in the same city (the first of its kind in Portugal) reveals the changing relationship between tourism and culture, and the important contribution of port wine to the international development of the region. So Oporto ('Porto' in Portuguese), the city that provided a name for both a nation and a world-famous wine, has become a point of contact and exchange at the heart of a revitalised and reinvented tourism product. In this chapter, we look at the port wine experience from different angles, and consider the role of the wine itself, the place or places where it is produced, and its position within a carefully conceived wine route, in the marketing and consumption of this product.

A Wine...

When visitors to the port wine cellars in Vila Nova de Gaia are invited to taste the wine for which the city and the country are famous, they are encouraged to drink in the whole experience – the warmth of the wine, its rich flavours, the mixed aromas of the various types of wine, the dank air of the cellars. And they are invited to imagine the journey of the wine, from the simple grape grown in one of the many *Quintas*, or estates, of the Upper Douro Valley in north-eastern Portugal, one of the world's most beautiful wine regions, down the majestic Douro river in the characteristic *Rabelo* boats, up to the traditional wine lodges, each with its own family name, and onto the barrel-like tables for tasting (and buying) at the end of the visit. The tourist is offered a wine with a history and a view, as if given the opportunity to drink in the landscape of a region with unique weather and soil conditions, where grape growing dates back to prehistoric times. This may be a prelude to an actual journey to a *Quinta* and to the physical experience and technical insight provided by the guided tours of the vineyards.

The Douro valley

In 1756, the Marquis of Pombal, Prime Minister to King José I, created the world's first regulated and demarcated wine region, in the Douro Valley, with a view to preventing fraud and speculation but above all to defending the reputation of port wine. Today, port is one of the most controlled wines in the world, located firmly in the Douro valley region, which was classified by UNESCO as a World Heritage site in 2001.

The climate of this region is conditioned by its relief and topography (Figure 13.1). With mountain ranges to the west and south, and a plateau to the north and east, the upper Douro valley is protected from the influence and humidity of the Atlantic winds. Rainfall is consequently low and the

Figure 13.1 Slopes of the upper Douro valley, in the region of Pinhão

daily and annual temperature ranges are very high; winter temperatures frequently fall below freezing and summer temperatures rise to an unbearable 50°C in the deep valley of the upper Douro. It is this diversity of contrasts and these particular conditions, as Castelo affirms, which favour the cultivation of the grapes:

> The wealth of the Douro lies in the rich diversity of its contrasts. Valleys, deep gorges, countless and Dantesque precipices, chasms, rocks, slopes, mountains, cliffs, plateaus, dams, villages, etc.... From the giant rocks that huddle along the river as if to drink the precious liquid and then to transform it into sublime nectar ... to the mountains that plunge steeply into gorges and deep valleys; the petrified silence – that same silence that contrasts incredibly with the long centuries of human work on miles and miles of walls and wires, thousands and thousands of terraces and millions and millions of twisted, beautiful, unique vines.... Nobody is indifferent to all this grandeur, the entire living cultural landscape, which combines the work of nature and man and transforms the Douro relentlessly into a tourist magnet. (Castelo, 2002: 181–182, our translation)

While walking through the vineyards, the tourist's attention is drawn to the topography and harshness of the landscape. Because the region is mountainous (with hillside inclinations reaching from 35% to 70%), the topography dramatically determines the planting of the vines. For centuries, the slopes of the valley have been carved into terraces supported by stone walls, up to eight feet high. Whereas the surrounding regions are granitic, the soil of the Douro valley is stony, largely composed of the slate-like schist, further limiting the type of crops that can be planted there. Only the grape vines and olive and almond trees can resist the conditions. The soil is rich in nutrients but is free draining, obliging the vine to push its roots 15–20 metres down into the soil, through fissures in the bedrock, in search of water. The stone keeps the roots of the vines at roughly constant temperature and humidity throughout the year, due to the ability of the soil to reflect heat on the surface and to retain water at great depth. So although the hot dry climate and the rocky soil mean that yields are very low, translating into a low productivity per hectare, perhaps the lowest in the world of wine (the average is around 2.8 kg per hectare), the result is the rich and concentrated liquid we know as port wine.

The Douro is a clear example of the importance and strength of the people. There are still drops of sweat, perhaps tears of sacrifice, salting the trimmed lands, made beautiful by human hand. When we calmly look at the terraces, we can identify the struggle of man against the mountain in the construction of the immense vineyards mirrored in the river.... The Douro is divine hand and human hand. The Douro is a picture of sweat, berets wet with dew and shirts soiled with must; it is a long adventure.... And tourists who attend the treading of the grapes certainly cannot imagine the hard work that preceded that moment. (Borges, 2006: 13–14, our translation)

The tourist at the making of the wine

Some tourists buy package holidays that include the experience of wine and vineyards in addition to sun, sea and sand. These tourists are packed onto a bus or a boat and transported up the Douro to the upper reaches of the valley and offered the 'once in a lifetime' experience of being part of the age-old tradition and culture of the making of port wine. This usually takes place mid-September to October, during the harvest, when the tourists carefully handpick the grapes, side by side with the villagers, under the heat of the sun. Thomas Woodman, one of the pioneer travellers to the Douro during the early 1700s, wrote of the experience: 'The heat is so great that breathing is difficult' (quoted by Mayson, 2013: 10). Some 300 years later, modern-day travellers feel drops of sweat trickling down their foreheads as they too, for a short while, become one with the men and women who work from sunrise till sunset, several days in a row, to harvest the grapes.

Although in tourist guides the picture of a man carrying a large basket full of grapes on his back persists, these baskets are no longer in use, having been replaced by smaller plastic containers, which are easier to clean and easier to pile. Both grapes and tourists are carried down the hills and taken to the winery, where the grapes are crushed and the tourists find themselves facing a small group of men and women walking back and forth inside a wide granite tank called a *lagar*, treading the grapes and singing folk songs while others play musical instruments and invite the tourists to sing along.

The mood is one of celebration and of sincere enjoyment, and although tourists know that the authentic foot treading has been replaced by mechanical methods, they are happy to play along and agree to take their shoes off and step into the *lagar* to tread the grapes and sing and dance along with the villagers. This is a moment of imagined 'authenticity', a moment to record in photographs, to post on Facebook or send to family and friends, of themselves bare-foot, trousers rolled up, side by side with local men and women, treading the grapes, feeling the seeds and the skins beneath their feet.

While the wine will be stored locally until the end of the first winter to allow the cold temperatures to encourage its natural clarification, the tourists' trip to the vineyards, the route that took them to the source of port, brings them straight back down the river to the mouth of the Douro, where the wine will age. Since the Douro region is very hot in summer, it is in the cool, dark cellars close to the Atlantic Ocean that the wines evolve best because the average annual temperature is lower and the humidity higher, allowing the wine to age slowly and harmoniously.

Vila Nova de Gaia proved to be an ideal warehouse, served by a river that communicates with the producing region and that acts as a shipping port for the wine. Originally the wine was transported down this same route in traditional *Rabelo* boats, but nowadays the transportation is effected mainly by road in stainless-steel tankers. Several port wine houses have a replica of these boats which participate in a regatta on the Douro from the mouth of the river to the port wine cellars once a year, on 24 June, St John's day. A modern version of the *Rabelo* boat is used nowadays, no longer to carry port down the river, but to take people on daily boat trips up and down the river, recreating the route the barrels took for centuries.

A Place...

Port wine is probably the best known of Portuguese wines. Its roots are, as we have seen, in the upper Douro valley, and it is brought over 100 km down-river to the mouth of the Douro, to the city which gave it its name. So it is a wine which incorporates two places and two realities – the demarcated region of the upper Douro and the lodges of the urban Ribeira – connected to each other by the unifying axis that is the River Douro.

The wine cellars

The port wine cellars are a key place for the marketing of Portugal as a holiday destination and, although the history of tourism associated with these cellars used to be one of elite travel, nowadays a great variety of national and international tourists visit the cellars, transforming them into a vibrant space of social and cultural interaction and exchange.

The visit to the cellars starts in the foyer, where the tourist is met with brochures in several languages, pictures of the Douro valley and award certificates hanging on the walls that speak of the cellars' past, as well as many tools and objects associated with port wine production.

Most port houses were once family owned, so the tours usually start by focusing on the symbolic representation of the life, hard work and history

Figure 13.2 Tawny port ageing in old oak casks

of the family. If they visit several port cellars, tourists will realise that, apart from the different family names, there is a common story to the wine, expressed through the familiar bottles and barrels (the same in all port wine companies), the souvenirs and artefacts on offer, and through the wine terminology inherited from an English past (white, ruby, tawny, vintage, Offley, Taylor's, for example).

Tours lead the tourists through the world of wood-aged Ports that lie for decades in quiet, dark cellars full of barrels of various sizes and shapes (Figure 13.2). Contrary to table wine, which benefits from ageing in young oak barrels, port wine must age in the oldest wood possible. Some barrels are over 100 years old, and the oldest casks are designed to age the older wines. The guided tour continues into a darker and danker cellar, where the finest and rarest of all ports age. The *vintage* is a selection of the very best wine from a single exceptional year and its elite status makes it a wine sought after by wine lovers, collectors and investors. Tourists are impressed by the sheer number of bottles and by the fact that some wine is over 100 years old.

Drinking a piece of history...

At the end of the tour, the visitors are served a glass of red port. Although tourists are interested in the history and technique of making port, the information they value most has to do with the culture of drinking port. This dictates that fruity, red-coloured and full-bodied *rubies* are better drunk with cheese, cheesecake or chocolate, while the amber-coloured, mellower *tawnies* make excellent dessert wines. *White* ports are served cool as an aperitif with roasted almonds or olives. Despite the attachment to tradition, in the last couple of decades port has been adapting to new consumers and new possibilities, and aged tawnies are frequently presented no longer just as dessert wines but are also served slightly cool as an aperitif. There has also been a recent resurgence of a 1970s trend, the so-called port and tonic, a refreshing drink that combines port, tonic water, ice and a mint leaf, served in a long glass. The last decade saw the launch of the rosé port – a pink-coloured *ruby* port that breaks with tradition, both as a red port which is not red and as a red port that should be served chilled.

Collecting and belonging

Both the tours to the upper Douro and the visits to the cellars highlight the history and tradition associated with the marketing of port, selling an authentic experience which can be taken home along with the wine, one's photographs and other souvenirs, in line with what Jack and Phipps argue:

> Part of the labour of tourism is ... that of the future oriented work of preparing memories and of responding to the claims made by a place, and by people and materials encountered.... the taking of photographs and the buying of souvenirs give material, sustainable form to what is ephemeral. It is a way of symbolically distilling present-tense experience into fragments and forms that have a durability beyond tourist time.... Souvenirs represent the objects where stories and emotions could find focus and possession, not simply as a form of commodified relations but as objects that had a wider symbolic claim and wider narrative potential. (Jack & Phipps, 2005: 114)

The bottle of port acquired in the souvenir shop is a symbol of acquired experience and local knowledge, packed and ready to take home for the purpose of remembering and recreating the feelings, smells and tastes of the wine cellars and the Douro landscapes. This packing and taking home of experience involves the ritual purchase of artefacts, objects produced by touristic 'hosts' for tourists' consumption, which aim to transmit the essence of the hosts' traditional social rituals and which are marketed specifically within a tourist economy to cater to tourists' tastes:

> The great majority of touristic images tend not to be paintings or other objects of 'high art' but ephemeral relics of advertising, commercial exchange or personal souvenir making.... tourists travel to collect images, and these images are both objective and material (postcards, snapshots, videos) as well as subjective and immaterial (hopes, dreams, vision). (Crouch & Lübbren, 2003: 5)

The images and objects collected by tourists, in this case, the bottle of port, the photos and postcards of the places visited, and so on, are the proof of the lived experience of local culture, the wine tasted and the knowledge gained. Traditional port wine bottles, reproducing on each label the history, culture and gastronomic delights of that particular blend, recall an imagined authenticity when people lived more closely with nature and a simpler, cleaner way of life.

The Ribeira

The port wine cellars were established in Ribeira, in Vila Nova de Gaia, on the other side of the river from Oporto, for two main reasons: firstly, the temperature ranges and the relative humidity were more favourable; secondly, Gaia did not pay taxes to the Bishop of Oporto, and so, despite the wine being issued through the customs of Oporto, the storage costs were lower in Gaia. Thus, although Vila Nova de Gaia is the city that nurtures the wine into maturity, it is Oporto which gave it its name. Besides the wine, the region of Oporto is known worldwide for its architecture, its historic city centre (a UNESCO World Heritage site since 1996) and its football club.

Following the port route down the river or arriving by car or plane, tourists are brought sooner or later to the Ribeira (Figure 13.3). If one ignores the cable car, motor transportation and the modern clothing, the Ribeira looks like an 18th-century picture brought to life. And this is exactly the feeling and experience that the port wine companies wish to create. These companies were well ahead of local government initiatives when they opened the cellars to tourism in 1913 as a means of promoting their heritage, wine and brands. And today the port wine cellars are the main tourist attractions in the two neighbouring cities, divided and united by the River Douro. Not merely locations for the storage and export of port, the cellars have become the main element in the economic structuring of the historic centre and its cultural heritage:

Figure 13.3 *Rabelo* boats, the River Douro and the Ribeira

In medieval times, the riverfront of the municipality began to stand out as an important shipyard and trading post, reaching great prosperity in the 18th century, when Portuguese and foreigners, craftsmen, merchants and businessmen, settled in houses and warehouses in this area. Port wine or *vinho fino* (fine wine), as it is popularly called, is the emblem and the greatest wealth of the region, nestled in the cellars of the old town, where it acquires new taste, quality and long life..... (Ferreira, 2000: 121, our translation)

Despite its many benefits, the tourism associated with port wine has also had some negative impacts on the surrounding community, most notably the increase in volume of inner-city traffic. Moreover, in contrast to the regeneration of the historic centre and the restoration of the buildings and spaces directly connected with port wine, the private buildings in this district remain old and in a degraded state. Ferreira lists some of the social difficulties faced in the historic centre of Vila Nova de Gaia since the 1980s:

> urban social problems motivated by environmental and landscape degradation of the buildings, sociodemographic problems caused by the decrease in population in the historic centre, the consequent aging of the population boosted by social exclusion and by the low level of education and qualification. (Ferreira, 2011: 58, our translation)

On the other hand, the tourism generated by the port wine trade has clearly had a positive influence on the city as a whole and to some extent on its people: the urban renewal of the historic centre has created new areas for recreation, commerce and cultural expression and a heightened awareness on the part not only of visitors but also of the local population of the value of their cultural heritage and its preservation. According to Ferreira:

> This is justified because, at present, the cultural heritage begins to be taken into account in tourism strategies (given the increase in the number of tourists whose main or secondary motivation is the heritage), in such a way that their protection has become important to the promotion of tourism. (Ferreira, 2000: 117–118, our translation)

Indeed, the increased number of tourists has revitalised traditional economic activities (for example, in respect of local crafts), at the same time as new investments in the local economy (in restaurants and hotels, for example) have led to job creation. Existing infrastructure and services have been renovated, and new business opportunities associated with port wine tourism have emerged. For example, the *Rabelo* river cruises include a free tour and wine-tasting in a specific port house, as do the mini-train and mini-bus circuits around the city centre. As the wine-making process is staggered over the year, the port wine cellars are open all year round, helping to overcome issues of seasonality. Warehouses and stores have also been modernised and museums have been opened in various wine cellars, with greater importance attributed to the quality of the information and the guided tours provided. Thus, port wine tourism has contributed to the development of a unique tourist destination, as one website declares:

Go way down to the riverfront, a highly atmospheric and charismatic medieval quarter with colourful houses facing the river and its picturesque boats. This is the soul of the city that should be the starting point of a visit – and the place to return at night for the liveliest restaurants and bars…. With photogenic traditional boats floating at the quayside overlooked by colourful ancient houses, this is the most picturesque spot in the city and the place everyone loves…. The views from Cais de Gaia are perhaps the longest-lasting images of Oporto for visitors. It's impossible not to stand in awe at the city's stunning skyline, whose impact is further enhanced by the picturesque boats that stand in front, and the soaring double-decker Dom Luís Bridge. (GoOporto, 2013)

Such tourism has been a motor for the dynamic transformation of the tourist space of the Ribeira. Port wine continues to be the 'leading advocate' for the city and 'a very important factor in the cohesion of the territory' (Câmara Municipal do Porto, 2011). If, on the one hand, the development of wine tourism has permanently changed the reality of this region, on the other it has proved to be a key factor in preserving the city and its historic buildings.

A Route…

The tourist's…

Originally tourism associated with port wine was mainly limited to the cellars and the city centre. Nowadays, most tourists plan their visit in advance and know, when visiting Oporto, that they can also visit the valley and enjoy a wide range of facilities, restaurants and places to spend the night. The valley is no longer just the region where port is produced, nor is port wine the only reason to visit the upper Douro. It is just one among several experiences, including the spectacular boat trip and the scenery, which the valley, the region and the route have to offer.

Due to the establishment of Oporto as a hub for low-cost airlines (it is for example Ryanair's hub for south-western Europe), it has been promoted as a cheap destination for short breaks, and so a large number of tourists can get there relatively inexpensively from all over Europe. Still inside the airport, on both floors and walls, new arrivals are bombarded with attractive images and slogans associated with the north of Portugal, its culture, traditions and heritage. These images give tourists a first glimpse of landscapes and cityscapes that are just a short distance away. Images of the vineyards in the upper Douro valley line the passageways as if vines were growing on the airport walls, and ageing bottles of port are among the images which decorate the floor. Even without a glass in hand, the tourist is already *consuming* port.

The tourist's route continues from there either to the city centre or straight to the Douro valley, a route organised by the tourists themselves, or by tour managers, to pack a few short days with all the emotions, experiences, smells and flavours promised by guidebooks or websites.

Whether in Oporto, the upper Douro valley, or the wine cellars of Gaia, the tourist is led, by the guidebook or the guided tour, around places of interest and towards remarkable sites and buildings, and invited to participate in the rituals of port wine production and consumption.

The journey through Oporto comes to an end once again back at the airport, where departing tourists are faced with a decent-sized shopping area, prominently featuring 'Port & Wines' and the slogan 'your journey starts here', a final invitation to buy mementos of the place (and of their experience) to take home with them. Before taking off, the airport lounges and corridors offer the tourist one last glimpse of all the attractions that he or she had the opportunity to see; if not visited, these places and landscapes beckon for future visits.

Rural wine routes

Portugal has a well established tradition of wine consumption, and the wine sector is of great importance to the national economy (Costa & Dolgner, 2003). In terms of production, it is the fifth largest wine producer in the European Union and the production/export ratio is one of the highest in the world (a production of more than six million hectolitres, of which about 2.4 million are for export). In terms of vine area, Portugal is ranked among the top 10 countries worldwide. This long, narrow country, roughly 600 kilometres long by 200 kilometres wide, has over 240,000 hectares of vine area divided into 14 wine regions and 31 Denominations of Origin. According to Novais and Antunes (2009), as a result of the vitality of the wine sector, there has been a substantial growth in the articulation of the vineyards and their wine with other tourism-related activities.

As a type of tourism generally located outside of metropolitan areas, wine tourism has had an important role in regional development and is an important tool for the development and promotion of new tourism products. The most visible aspect of the practice of wine tourism in Portugal is the 11 wine routes that associate the wine sector with the surrounding regions, constituting a cultural product which engages tourists in a sequence of visits

Figure 13.4 Douro: The river and the valley

to key places and historical moments. These routes include tours associated with the wines of the Lisbon region, with the Alentejo and Setúbal regions (south of Lisbon), and with the Dão and Bairrada wines of central Portugal.

> In this way, the cultural itineraries or routes are a system that brings together resources and/or products that provide cultural content to the places visited, granting distinction, that is, a marker of social prestige for the visitors who travel, as well as the acquisition of knowledge and economic redistribution. (Santana *et al.*, 2005: 271, our translation)

Portugal's wine routes have been established since 1996 and are the result of the joining up of the vineyards and the wine with the natural landscape (Figure 13.4), the estates, the historical, architectural and cultural heritage and gastronomy of particular districts. They support the development and promotion of new tourist products by including a series of planned activities, such as walks in the vineyards, boat trips, guided tours and tastings of wines at local vineyards. Each wine route is based upon a number of thematic motifs which suggest key stops at places of interest, such as museums and regional craft shops. The Port Wine Route, for example, presents the thematic route *Douro Superior*, which associates the natural landscape with the beauty of the estates. These cultural itineraries contribute to the identity and the economy of the region and the country.

Wine routes are for the most part located inland. Port wine is an exception because it is produced exclusively in the demarcated Douro region and aged down-river in the urban cellars. So, up-river, the Port Wine Route is limited to the production area in the upper Douro, whereas, down-river, an urban wine route has recently been created in Oporto, which includes, but is not limited to, places and buildings related to the history, storage and shipping of port wine.

The Urban Wine Route

Urban tourism has emerged in many parts of Europe as a response to growing deindustrialisation, job losses, deterioration of living conditions, and other socioeconomic problems. In addition, as Ferreira argues, social changes, including the increase in mass travel, low-cost flights and short city breaks have contributed to changing patterns of tourism and an increased demand for tourism activities and products in urban areas:

> The great transformations of the economy and society have created conditions for tourism development in the urban environment. On a cultural level, the growing interest in heritage and cultural activities carried out by the development of new consumption patterns and tastes led to a phenomenon of development and promotion of tourism in urban spaces. (Ferreira, 2011: 37, our translation)

Urban tourism has many dimensions, including infrastructure development, environmental concerns, image building and community membership, and can contribute to the economic and social regeneration of the more fragile parts of the urban fabric and to the development and renovation of a city's monuments and heritage. As with many historic city centre renewals, the type of tourism developed in the cities of Oporto and Gaia combines a concern with the present with the desire for recognition of the past:

> It is in the city, a humanised space *par excellence*, that we find a sharper and more contrasting time gap between past and present. And it is through the present that the many 'marks' of the past acquire meaning and can be valued from a heritage perspective that favours a revival of the collective memory, creates an identification of the locals with their surroundings and, ultimately, enables the use of the area for urban tourism and leisure. (Falcão, 2000: 63, our translation)

The importance and usefulness of urban routes lie in their capacity to transform cultural heritage into readily consumable tourist products, attracting inward investment and supporting conservation and renewal.

The Urban Wine Route in Oporto, established in 2011, the first of its kind in Portugal, enables the visitor to explore the city in a new way, drawing attention to its monuments and its personality. Similarly to other wine routes located inland or in rural areas, the Urban Wine Route allows us to understand the importance of the wine to the history of the city, how it has helped to define its character. When presenting the Urban Wine Route to the public, Rui Rio, the Mayor of Porto at the time, said that it

> draws attention to the monuments and sites of Oporto, to our history, to the people who lived in the town. And, above all, to the great importance that the wine had to what Oporto is today, its identity and its character – which is what tourists most like to feel in their visits. (Câmara Municipal do Porto, 2011, our translation)

The Urban Wine Route reveals the relationship between tourism and culture by linking the specificities of the city with wine tourism and the wine regions associated with it (the upper Douro valley and vinho verde regions), fitting them into the urban system. Visitors are invited to explore the 'marks' the wine left in the urban landscape, its architecture, commerce and trade, society and internationalisation. The Urban Wine Route takes in 23 key sites and historic buildings, symbolic places in the relationship between the city and the wine, in particular with regard to the importance and contribution of port wine to the international development of the region:

> The Urban Wine Route will allow tourists to understand how the money generated by trade, taxes and levies on wine could influence and help to develop the defensive structures of the city, the water supply system, the construction of new roads, as well as the definition of its identity and way of life of its inhabitants. (Wines of Portugal, 2011, our translation)

When following the Urban Wine Route, tourists visit key venues which are directly related to port wine production and marketing. One such stop is the Port and Douro Wines Institute, the body responsible for certifying and supervising all Porto origin wines, where tourists are invited into a neoclassical building dating from 1843. They can take a guided tour or taste the tradition and history elegantly poured in a glass of port. The route takes the tourists to the inevitable shop, where they can buy another piece of history to take home. Another key stop is the Feitoria Inglesa, a building in neo-Palladian style, built between 1785 and 1790 to serve as a venue for English businessmen living in Porto. Finally, the route takes them over the city's iconic bridge to the Ribeira, in nearby Vila Nova de Gaia, where the main port wine warehouses are located.

A Meeting Point … of People and Places with Port

Tourism and all the activities it involves generate culture through moments of intercultural interaction. It can thus be understood as a social and relational phenomenon, a cultural practice which provides and encourages the encounter between different cultures, and intercultural contact between people, places, smells and flavours. Motivated by the search for multiple and varied emotions and experiences, which provide them with a significant contrast with everyday life at home, tourists often seek and find essential versions of other cultures, packaged and sold for their benefit. As Boissevain (1996: 3) writes: 'it is clear that all tourists, whatever their individual motives, seek some form of contrast with their everyday existence, a break, however short, with their familiar surroundings and routines'.

Pérez states that tourism is an encounter between cultures, or even a mechanism of communication between cultures, 'a vehicle for intercultural exchange between people and human groups, between *us* and *others*' (Pérez, 2009: 10). In this case, the main meeting point for different cultures, for the tourists' encounter with difference, is the Ribeira and the port wine cellars, one of the leading tourist destinations in the country, and a key area for the generation of Portugal as a holiday destination (part of a successful triumvirate with the greater Lisbon area and the Algarve). If, on the one hand, port (the wine) is a symbol of Portugal, on the other hand, the wine cellars and the Ribeira are spaces that bring people together from all over the world. The wine cellars are a point of contact and exchange that every year welcome large numbers of tourists, representative of different sociocultural groups and nationalities, who come to Oporto looking for the port wine experience, the tastes and smells, the sounds and languages, the people and places which make this experience unique.

The story of port wine has been retold and repackaged to appeal to the tastes and desires of the contemporary tourist (who is less interested in the scientific, technical or historical details than in the immediate experience of Port/Oporto/Portugal). The tourist who experiences the upper Douro feels immersed in the culture of the region. The tour he or she follows includes a glass of port wine, on a route that markets the silence of the Douro, the flavours of the wine and the colours of the landscape. This route is a potted and sleek version of what, historically, was a hard and exploitative reality for the people who tamed the rock to grow the vines, and tamed the river to transport the wine to Oporto.

For the contemporary tourist, port wine has been packaged in the city and the city has been packaged through the wine. When the wine is sold to tourists or exported, it is not just the drink which is being sold, it is Oporto, it is the dramatic landscapes of the Douro valley, it is the buildings where the wine made the fortunes of its makers. It is the social history of the port families on their estates, the animation of the Ribeira streets, the dark, dank wine caves, the taste and flavours of the wine, the relaxation and sunshine of being on holiday, the chatter in foreign tongues. Mansilha (2002) wrote that 'The Douro can only be known when experienced, visited, observed' (our translation). And, believe us, a glass of port wine is not the same after one has felt the colours and the smells of the Douro. Wherever it is subsequently drunk, the taste will never be the same.

References

Boissevain, J. (1996) *Coping with Tourists*. Providence, RI: Berghahn Books.

Borges, A.J. (2006) Douro: Quadro de suor, sinfonia humana, ópera da natureza. *Douro – Estudos & Documentos* (no. 21). Porto: Faculdade de Letras da Universidade do Porto.

Câmara Municipal do Porto (2011) Rota urbana do vinho – Um 'instrumento' a ser desenvolvido e explorado pelos agentes turísticos. At http://www.cm-porto.pt/gen.pl?p=print&op=view&fokey=cmp.stories/16955&sid=cmp.sections/3 (accessed 20 April 2012).

Castelo, N. (2002) A visão que o Douro me transmite. *Douro – Estudos & Documentos* (no. 14). Porto: Faculdade de Letras da Universidade do Porto.

Costa, A. and Dolgner, M. (2003) *Enquadramento Legal do Enoturismo*. Guarda: Escola Superior de Tecnologia e Gestão, Instituto Politécnico da Guarda.

Crouch, D. and Lübbren, N. (2003) *Visual Culture and Tourism*. Oxford: Berg.

Falcão, M. (2000) O Porto, os planos municipais e o turismo. *Revista da Faculdade de Letras – Geografia* (I série) 15/16, 63–68.

Ferreira, E.L. (2000) Apontamentos sobre o lazer e o património urbano edificado no centro histórico de Vila Nova de Gaia. *Revista da Faculdade de Letras – Geografia* (I série), 15/16, 117–129.

Ferreira, F.D. (2011) *Percursos, Territórios e Património: O Caso de Vila Nova de Gaia – Dissertação de Mestrado*. Porto: FLUP – Departamento de Geografia.

GoOporto – Europe's Vintage Port City (2013) The soul of Porto. At http://www.gooporto.com/porto-sights/ribeira.html (accessed 9 May 2013).

Jack, G. and Phipps, A. (2005) *Tourism and Intercultural Exchange: Why Tourism Matters*. Clevedon: Channel View Publications.

Mansilha, A. (2002) *Alto Douro Vinhateiro: Património Mundial*. Peso da Régua: Notícias do Douro.

Mayson, R. (2013) *Port and the Douro*. Oxford: Infinite Ideas Limited.

Novais, C.B. and Antunes, J. (2009) O contributo de Enoturismo para o desenvolvimento regional: O Caso das Rotas dos Vinhos. *XV Congresso APDR (Cabo Verde)*, 1253–1280.

Pérez, X.P. (2009) *Turismo Cultural: Uma Visão Antropológica*. Tenerife: Pasos.

Santana, M.O. *et al.* (2005) Propostas para um itinerário cultural no Douro. *Douro – Estudos & Documentos* (no. 19). Porto: Faculdade de Letras da Universidade do Porto.

Wines of Portugal (2011) Porto cria Rota Urbana do Vinho. At http://winesofportugal.info/pagina.php?codNode=118682 (accessed 17 October 2011).

14 Cultural Interfaces and Perceptions of Space: A Polish–Portuguese Comparative Study

Danuta Gabryś-Barker

International tourism implies contact and interaction in a domain where sociocultural aspects are central to appropriate functioning in an unfamiliar and foreign language and context. A significant category for this sociocultural component of interaction is the construct of *space*, which constitutes an important factor in successful communication between people. It varies 'according to their relationship with and attitude to other people, and according to norms and contexts' (Banyard & Hayes, 1994: 128). It may be safely assumed that those norms and contexts are culturally grounded. Also, artefacts that surround us in our daily life demonstrate space perceptions characteristic of a given country. In this chapter, the focus is on the similarities and differences between the perceptions of space held by Polish and Portuguese informants. The data collected come from automatic association tests in response to a stimulus word, SPACE, where no further instruction was provided. It is believed that 'associative responses to a stimulus word should largely reflect elements and aspects of schemas and categories in an individual's conceptual system' (Sharifian, 2004: 77). I would go further and claim that associations are not only idiosyncratic but primarily culture-grounded, something my study intends to demonstrate. Misalignment of space perceptions has implications for the way information is exchanged in multicultural contexts, like that of foreign travel and tourism.

The Construct of Space

Defining space

The most consulted but also most synoptic definition of 'space' in our time, one imagines, is that of Wikipedia:

the boundless, three-dimensional extent in which objects and events occur and have relative position and direction. Physical space is often conceived in three linear dimensions, although modern physicists usually consider it, with time, to be part of a boundless four-dimensional continuum known as spacetime.... The concept of space is considered to be of fundamental importance to an understanding of the physical universe although disagreement continues between philosophers over whether it is itself an entity, a relationship between entities, or part of a conceptual framework. (http://en.wikipedia.org/wiki/Space, accessed 9 July 2013)

The debate over the nature of space goes back to ancient times, to the arguments and philosophical expositions of Socrates, Plato and Aristotle. Over the centuries and with the development of sciences and philosophy, space became a central issue in the thinking of Isaac Newton, Gottfried Leibniz, George Berkeley, Immanuel Kant and Albert Einstein. More recently, space has become one of the central topics in linguistic and psycho-linguistic research, for example, in looking at the way language reflects spatial relationships and how terms for these relationships are acquired in first (L1) and then second (L2) languages (Coventry *et al.*, 2011).

According to Clark (1992), time and space are two basic anthropological categories marking the identity of a man, whereas the history of man's development is a longitudinal process of freeing oneself from the constraints that time and space impose. The experience of extended space starts with the inception of sailing and trade in prehistoric times, to continue through territorial expansion from ancient times in Egypt till modern times and modern man's dream of walking on the moon and journeying through space. Over the centuries, man moved from a tribal space, a limited existence within the first fences separating off members of the community from external danger, to creating more expansive territorial power through the political organisation of separate districts, regions and nations, guarding one's frontiers to protect one's assets and one's identity, and often fighting long and destructive wars in so doing. Geographical voyages of discovery and the development of trading brought about contacts between peoples from all over the world and so promoted the first mixings of distant cultures. The development of the human race is very strongly marked by the widening of horizons due to the development of scientific thinking and technology, resulting in expanded perceptions of space – not just experiential space here on earth, but also mental modelling of space out there in the universe.

Different dimensions of space

It is important to address this complex construct of space in both its physical and mental aspects. In relation to the latter, psychological studies have reflected upon its various dimensions, especially those of a personal nature, betokening altruism and aggression. They have also dealt with interactive aspects, such as acting in the presence of an audience, social facilitation, personal space and territoriality. Psychology has affirmed the importance of personal space, defined as 'the physical distance which people like to maintain between themselves and others; this varies according to their relationship with and attitude to other people, and according to norms and contexts' (Banyard & Hayes, 1994: 128). Personal space can shape the type of interaction between people and thus it can be seen 'a mechanism for regulating social interaction' (Banyard & Hayes, 1994: 469). It is closely related to the concept of territoriality, understood as

> almost any place or spatial zone that might be occupied by a human being [which brings about] a set of behaviours which involve establishing and maintaining access to a particular area, while refusing the same to potential competitors of one's own species. (Banyard & Hayes, 1994: 475)

The domains of human territoriality are classified as three types, primary, secondary and public territory (Table 14.1), each with their own specific style of territorial behaviour (Altman, 1975, quoted in Baynard & Hayes, 1994: 469).

Table 14.1 The domains of human territoriality

Territory	Example	Sense of ownership	Personalisation defence
Primary	Home	High – perceived to be owned in a relatively permanent manner	Extensively personalised; unwelcome entry to the space is a serious issue
Secondary	Office or classroom	Moderate – the occupant is perceived as one of a number of qualified or licensed users of the space	Could be personalised during occupancy; some chance of defence when the person has the right to be there
Public	Area on a beach, parking space or a table in a restaurant	Low – control is difficult to assert and the occupant is perceived as just one of many possible users	May be personalised in a temporary way; very little likelihood of defending the space

Space as culture

Young (1994) extends the idea of space to 'cultural space' by saying 'the most capacious space within which we think about ourselves is called culture', which can be characterised as being learnt within certain frameworks characteristic of a community and not biologically determined. It is not necessarily consciously perceived but it nonetheless structures both thinking and the perception of oneself and the world around one.

Another anthropologist, Edward Hall, discusses space as a 'hidden dimension' (Hall, 1966) of culture and assumes that everything we do is associated with our experience of space, which constitutes a system of communication, though it is often not consciously perceived as such. Space is described as organised differently in different cultures and numerous examples illustrate this, among them the many uses of personal, social, architectural and urban spaces. In the modern world, a person expands his or her space not only territorially but by acquiring or building on his or her 'extensions' such as the computer (a brain extension), the telephone (a voice extension) or the motorised wheel (a leg/feet extension). Hall even goes so far as to suggest that these extensions have to some extent taken over and are rapidly replacing naturally occurring capacities. It would be difficult not to concede the appropriateness of this observation.

According to Hall, proxemics (meaning systems of spatial regulation) can be studied at three levels:

- intra-cultural and related to the past in terms of territoriality, spacing and population control;
- pre-cultural and related to the senses, thus physiologically based;
- micro-cultural and related to cross-cultural differences in relation to fixed, semi-fixed and informal distances.

The micro-cultural level embraces three dimensions of space, expressed as:

- fixed (buildings, the layout of towns and interiors of houses);
- semi-fixed, expressing sociofugal spaces (i.e. asocial, that is, keeping people apart, for example at the railway station) and sociopetal spaces (that is, prosocial, bringing people together, for example the arrangement of tables and chairs in a café);
- informal, demonstrated as the personal and social distances kept in interactions (intimate, personal, social and public) and expressing how people feel towards each other.

Hall (1966) believes that comparisons of proxemic patterns may shed light on our awareness of how space perception affects our behaviour, but it will also lead to better cross-cultural understanding and should allow us to share and function better in common spaces (towns, buildings, offices, homes). Hall quotes numerous examples of possible daily misunderstandings relating to wrong or divergent interpretations of behaviours when representatives of different nations or cultures are thrown into coexistence. Examples quoted by Hall include the following:

- Shut doors in America mean the need for privacy, but in England they can remain open without the occupant perceiving their privacy to be violated.
- The layout of American offices often indicates the employee's position within a hierarchy (for example, the central desk is the boss's place).
- The Mediterranean habit of packing people closely in restaurants and cafés may be quite disturbing for a northern European.
- The size of a flat (or a house) and the way furniture is arranged in it (centred in Japan versus de-centred in America) can lead to a feeling of being uncomfortable, from not knowing the prevailing cultural norm.
- Standing close by during an act of communication may be perceived by some nations as signifying the existence of or desire for intimacy.

Such differences are also observed in two major European ways of structuring space, as in the example of traditional towns and cities. A 'radiating star' represents a sociopetal pattern conducive to public involvement and with all lines leading to the centre (e.g. a Spanish plaza), whereas a 'grid', in contrast, represents an old Middle Eastern and Roman pattern imposed on places in northern Europe; it represents a sociofugal pattern, which is not conducive to social contact and public gatherings.

Hall (1966) also connects time perception and space by suggesting that people who perceive time monochromatically (in a linear way) demonstrate less involvement and more compartmentalisation in life, whereas 'polychromatic people', who favour doing several things at the same time, are more active and involved in what they do. This is reflected in the design of towns. For example, the former is demonstrated in the English high street, the latter by the Spanish plaza. Hall goes even further by suggesting that ignorance of these hidden proxemic dimensions of culture is responsible for ethnic conflict and for America's inability to become a true 'melting pot'. It is responsible for flash-points in crowded urban places and for national minorities functioning in space patterns which are often alien to them.

These few selected examples show how important the study of space perceptions is and how becoming aware of the issues connected with these perceptions may help us function better not only on an individual level but primarily on the societal level.

Study on Perceptions of Space from a Cross-cultural Perspective: Polish Versus Portuguese

The present study is a continuation of my research on similarities and differences in perceptions of culture-grounded constructs, such as paying compliments and taking offence (Gabryś-Barker, 2008), time (Gabryś-Barker, 2011) or naming habits (Gabryś-Barker, 2012). The construct of space seems to be one of the more significant variables one has to cope with when functioning in different contexts, both physically (the obvious literal or physical meaning of the term) and mentally (metaphorically). One context where proxemic expectations clearly come into play is in the activities associated with tourism and travel.

In this study the focus is on the similarities and differences between the perceptions of space held by Polish and Portuguese informants. It is postulated that the way we see the world derives from what we really want from it, consciously, with our thinking and reasoning, but also subconsciously, with our intuitions and emotions. Thinking is a conscious process of conceptualisation but it also involves deeply ingrained preconceptions of the world that we hold in our subconscious mind. For example, studies show that objects that are meaningful and desirable to us seem closer than ones less significant to us, and distances seem shorter if we really need to reach the target; at the same time, however, the more effort that is involved, the further off the target seems (Woods et al., 2009). How can we get through to these subconscious perceptions? Certainly the words we store and recall give evidence of the learnt, the acquired and the accommodated. So studying the ways in which we store language(s) and recall linguistic items (words, phrases, sayings) automatically (through associations, slips of tongue, code switches, etc.), without careful speculation, thinking or reasoning, allows us to see the way we perceive the world. It also shows us how we categorise and schematise the world and our experience of it, how idiosyncratic our perceptions can be but also how framed by our cultural grounding they are. The automatic recall of words is based on associative processes of 'sorting out meaningful – and that is, logical and syntactic relations among words – contrast and grouping' (Deese, 1965, cited in Söderman, 1993). Linguistic manifestations of thinking can give evidence of the world representations we hold. As such, word association tests can be used as research tools in linguistic studies as well as culture-focused ones.

In the present study a simple association task of the S–R (stimulus–response) type was used to elicit responses to the stimulus word *space* in a timed task in the subjects' L1, Polish for the Polish group and Portuguese for the Portuguese one. The 56 subjects (both Polish and Portuguese) were students at either the University of Silesia in Sosnowiec, Poland, or the University of Aveiro in Portugal. Additionally, at the initial stage of the project, the Polish subjects were asked to write a narrative on 'Perceptions of space as a cultural construct', in which they were encouraged to reflect upon the different aspects of space as mirroring the culture of a given nation.

The findings are based on an analysis of two corpuses of data (narratives and associations as well as observation comments). The first are opinions elicited from my Polish sample about space as an expression of culture in the form of the narratives they provided; the analysis of narratives presented here is followed by some structured observations of my own about Polish/ Portuguese culture in respect of space. The second corpus of data concerns association tests administered to both Polish and Portuguese subjects using the idea of space as a cue (or stimulus).

Dimensions of space as a cultural construct (narrative data)

Perceptions of space (narratives)

The following selection of quotations comes from the students' narratives and expresses their understanding of space as a cultural construct in all its various aspects (errors of expression have not been corrected):

Perception of space [is expressed] in relation to organising space in cities, in people's homes and between people in personal contacts. [In people's houses] again we can observe that people used to fill all the free space (some elderly still do this) … now there is a tendency to have spacious homes with limited furniture and decoration, lots of glass elements increasing the feeling of having more space … personal space between people.

Years ago people used to express their openness and friendship … by having more direct contact, e.g. standing very close to each other, kissing on the cheek or hugging. But again, it slightly changed – it is not good manners to stand too close to each other, not to interfere with the personal space, and not to offend someone.

In Scandinavian countries, they are keeping the distance, modern buildings: spacious, elements of glass. Whereas in Southern countries: people are very open, when they stand in a group they don't mind standing close to each other, their cities and houses reflect that. Narrow streets, cute houses with cosy interiors.

Personal space has connotations with freedom and expansiveness of a given culture.

Perceptions of personal space across cultures [are expressed by] physical distance maintained between people in social contacts and directness in communication with others ... misunderstandings may occur based on the concept of personal space.

... space is very much connected with freedom in the USA. It is not only the huge, empty areas of land ... but also the freedom of voicing one's opinions and living in one's own way so much accentuated in American culture.

[In Britain] people in accordance with the popular proverb 'My home is my castle' are very protective towards their privacy and homes as personal living space..... [In Polish culture] we even allow strangers to enter our private living space inviting people to meet rather at home than in a restaurant.

The notion of space, be it in the social distance in communication or personal living space and freedom, is different in different cultures. Invading one's space without acknowledging the differences may be embarrassing or even abusive, therefore, the notion of space should be taken into account in contacts between cultures.

[Space perception is demonstrated by] the way particular places are arranged: home – open space versus stuffed, parks, gardens, markets and train and bus stations. These manifestations of space reflect the nations' views on such things as practicality and beauty of their surroundings.

Space is a distance between people in terms of their relationship and as a physical distance. It has a role in the way people live. In the past: meetings to talk, exchange views, family meetings. Now: mobile, internet, Skype 'You can even drink a beer with your friends while chatting on Skype.' IT shortened space personally but not emotionally. Anonymity exists even in a family (phone contacts only). In the countryside, bounds are more tight, more personal talk.

A close distance may exert a negative influence on the person and increase communication apprehension. Distance also depends on per-sonalities (extraverted vs introverted). Spanish are open and gestural,

Poles distrustful and defending their privacy. Politically oppressed nations are more cautious to whom they reveal their opinions.

It is connected with our sense of belonging.... The concept of space and how we perceive it implies what kind of people we are and determines our openness. Poles are believed to be friendly and open which can stem from the way we see and define space. On the contrary, Japanese people always keep distance and are rarely direct....

... going abroad, meeting new people, learning new cultures may shed a different light on what space means and how I personally perceive it ... every journey teaches us something new, for instance how to respect other nations and their borders, cultural and personal.

There are two things that come to my mind immediately when I hear the word space. Limit someone's space and that someone needs space.... I imagine that cultures which got accustomed to living in open spaces, like African tribes, would never feel good in closed spaces, in big developed cities where natural space is very limited. Space in such a case is associated with oxygen, the less people have, the less oxygen they have to breathe and to live.

[The concept of freedom] Limiting one's space is like limiting someone's freedom.

I agree that space from a cultural point of view is significant and it may reflect the character of a given nation, its features, attitude towards life and other people and their way of living. It may be treated literally as our comfort zone, or more like a metaphor, for example when space is related to time (more time, more space) to freedom, or to our lifestyle and relationships.

These comments on the different dimensions of space can be classified as either literal or metaphoric. The literal perceptions of space relate to: travelling (distances in kilometres), architectural (design of cities), housing (flats and their size, interior decorations and furniture), physical space in public places (surgeries, waiting rooms, restaurants, bars) and physical distance in verbal and social interactions (physical closeness, kissing, hugging). On the other hand, the metaphoric understanding of space is expressed in the associations relating to freedom, security and privacy.

Polish and Portuguese tourist contexts

I believe that these various attitudes to space, as suggested by the data, are reflected and have meaningful consequences in tourist contexts. Their culture-specific understandings will be most visible in the ability of tourists to successfully function and interact in the following contexts, among many others:

- getting information on places and distances (e.g. obtaining and inter-preting directions or road signs);
- travelling by public or private transport (involving driving and parking habits, seating behaviour, etc.);
- contacts with strangers (or recently met people), where greetings and light conversation are required;
- in public places most commonly frequented by tourists (places of re-laxation, for example beaches, and places of eating, like restaurants and cafes).

How do Poles and Portuguese people typically behave in these contexts? What does it tell us about their approach to territoriality? Here we might propose a specific focus on public territory in tourist contexts, an example of which is the popular British perception of (or prejudice towards) Germans as efficiently reserving their places by the poolside with towels. What does this tell us about different levels of micro-cultural proxemics (fixed, semi-fixed and informal)?

Such areas of contact between natives and non-natives (and between different non-natives) can bring about misunderstandings through different perceptions and needs concerning space. The comments that follow are based on my personal observations of my own Polish context (an *emic* per-spective) and of the Portuguese context, based on nearly 20 years of visiting the country (an *etic* perspective).

Getting information on places and distances: The example of road signs

(1) In Poland, great precision is attached to road signs, even in the centres of town. One may wonder, for example, why we need to know that KFC in my hometown is 1.7 km from a certain point and not just an approximate 1.5 km or 2 km away.

(2) When travelling across Portugal, if you are not local, you may easily get lost. Many villages do not feature on any maps, however detailed. Streets often have names but not street signs. You may need to know the place quite well to find your desired destination unaided; you will almost certainly do what nearly all Portuguese visitors do and stop to ask.

Conclusion. The Portuguese seem to exhibit a high sense of rootedness, where knowledge of the locality or specific information is obtainable by direct/intimate contact, not made impersonally available. A certain closed territoriality is implicit in this, as opposed to a low Polish sense of territorial ownership or investment in territoriality (when perceived as public space). Information provision is therefore neutral, impersonal. Whether this is reflective of communist dispossession of territorial private ownership in recent history, or a longer history of spatial invasion and occupation, with ownership of many districts of the homeland contested by various nations and peoples, is a moot point.

Travelling by public or private transport: The example of driving and parking habits

(1) The Polish driver, though maybe not the most disciplined in the world, generally sticks to the regulations when on the road, not always because of conviction but because of serious apprehension of traffic police and heavy fines and penalty points for bad driving. What is most abusive about Polish driving is disrespect towards pedestrians, who seem scared to cross the road (even at appointed crossings) and when they do, you often see people scuttling across the road to avoid injury or being run over. Road rage and impatience are common reactions to bad road behaviour in Poland. A Polish driver is fairly disciplined as far as parking habits are concerned and uses the places assigned for this purpose or at least those not visibly prohibited. Also, walking from a parked car to a destination is natural, so parking far away is not at all unusual.

(2) Portuguese drivers seem much more relaxed about following the rules of the road, as over-regulation is not to the taste of the Portuguese and, furthermore, the police have not been in the past as diligent as in Poland in tracking and stopping drivers who commit infractions (though in this time of economic crisis, traffic fines have been discovered to be a very useful revenue stream for a cash-strapped government – fines generated 40% more revenue in 2012 than 2011). What is most striking for me as a foreign visitor is the parking habits of Portuguese drivers. Parking on corners? Parking on pedestrian crossings? Parking across people's garage entries and exits? Double parking when one is just having a quick cup of morning coffee in the main *Avenida*. As the generalised ownership and use of motor vehicles is a relatively recent phenomenon and walking is still associated with a certain kind of social disadvantage, the Portuguese driver usually tries to drive up to and park near a destination. On the other hand, what can be observed in Portugal (and not in Poland) is patience and courtesy with pedestrians, even those jaywalking in the street or crossing in a leisurely manner. Nor can much road rage be

observed, even in cases of the most flagrant violations of traffic rules (at least as judged by Polish standards).

Conclusion. On one hand, we may observe that the Portuguese express a sociopetal attitude to space (a lack of clear boundaries, a preference for commodiousness over order) versus the Polish affirmation of one's right to space as expressed formally or safeguarded legally. On the other hand, one could argue that it works the other way round. The Portuguese attitude is sociofugal as it shows lack of respect for others, mostly caring for one's comfort, versus a Polish prosocial (sociopetal) attitude in respecting the rules. Behaviour is complex and potentially contradictory, governed by other, not strictly spatial considerations, like the rule of law.

Contacts with strangers (or recently met people): The example of greetings

(1) In Portugal when meeting a new person, the situation is fluid but it is certainly an occasion where a kiss (or two) on a cheek as a form of introduction and friendly greeting of a new acquaintance (in the case of woman to woman and woman to man) would not be out of place.

(2) In Poland on such an occasion, a physical distance is kept. Shaking hands is natural between both sexes and verbal exchanges are controlled and pretty formal (as in the English phrase 'Nice to meet you'). The hand-kissing habit may be seen as the closest to approved Portuguese forms of greeting, but it is a habit disappearing from daily encounters and nowadays it is seen as highly old-fashioned.

Conclusion. Close proximics in the case of the Portuguese may seem almost a forced intimacy to a Pole, when compared with the Polish habit of keeping a physical distance with a stranger or a newly acquainted person, and of generally valuing the neutral space between unacquainted social groups. The Portuguese, on the other hand, might view a Polish greeting as frosty or over-formal.

In public places commonly frequented by tourists: The example of beaches

(1) Portuguese beaches are generally not crowded (unless you go to the Algarve in summer, with its picturesque smaller beaches, or the coastal parts of seaside towns), yet in many respects they can seem crowded, as Portuguese families (often unknown to each other) like to stay next to each other on the beach. Your comfort (or protective) zone or person-alised space, generated by a windbreak or tent or umbrella, will provide you with only marginal separation.

(2) Good Polish beaches are in shorter supply and are usually crowded. This is the product of a larger population and less prime beach space. Never-theless, for a Pole arriving on a beach, it is natural to try to get away

from others as much as possible and Poles will build windbreaks and put up sand walls around their settled areas as far as possible, to define it against other beach users.

Conclusion. Here Portuguese sociopetal attitudes in the form of social herding are most visible and express the importance and security of the group, whereas a Polish person reveals the need to defend his or her privacy, which points to the importance of individuality and clear boundaries.

In public places commonly frequented by tourists: The example of restaurants

(1) In Portuguese restaurants, it seems to be a rule that tables are arranged quite close to each other and, what is more, they are often shared by complete strangers (e.g. a waiter can move a table 10–20 cm away to make it seem like a separate eating space). This adds to the spirit of community of eaters and the enjoyment of extended company (or no privacy if this spirit is disagreeable to you). Many folk festivals involve the setting up of communal trestle tables in a tented space, where it often difficult to move around and strangers are obliged to mix and socialise.

(2) In Poland, the Portuguese way of serving and eating food would seem strange and the restaurants would be considered crammed, as, for a Pole, a restaurant needs to offer enough space not only on the table for the food to be served but also around the table to be able to move freely and maintain one's own comfort zone and to be spared the conversations of others (social privacy). A Polish restaurant on the other hand might seem to a Portuguese person to be a failing business. The Portuguese see full restaurants as markers of quality cooking or good value for money.

Conclusion. The Portuguese communal habit of eating is reflected in the space patterns and arrangements of an eatery and are contrary to Polish perceived needs to be left alone to digest and to enjoy company, but only the company of one's own choosing.

Conceptualising space (association tasks data)

The students were given a timed association task, in which they were asked 'What automatic responses does the term "space" bring to you?' Their responses can be categorised into the following groups (Table 14.2):

- literal (physical) associations – place, nature, astronomy;
- abstract (metaphoric) associations – emotions and feelings, expressions of freedom;
- syntagmatic (adjective + noun) associations qualifying space.

In addition, word formation was evident in the data, and an additional category, of abstract associations.

Although there was an almost complete overlap between the types of responses of the two groups of subjects, Polish and Portuguese, their contents were often quite different.

Place
(1) Polish: *mój dom* (my home/house), *mój pokój* (my room), *uczelnia* (university), *własny kąt* (one's own place).
(2) Portuguese: *area desportivo* (sports area), *espaço desportivo* (sports area), *espaço recreativo* (recreation room), *quarto* (bedroom space), *casa* (home).

Nature
(1) Polish: *zieleń* (greenery), *wiatr* (wind), *pola* (fields), *łąka* (meadow), *lasy* (woods), *ocean* (ocean), *park* (park), *słóáce* (the sun), *krajobraz* (landscape).
(2) Portuguese: *campo aberto* (open field), *cães* (dogs), *gatos* (cats).

Astronomy
(1) Polish: *słońce* (the sun), *galaktyka* (galaxy).
(2) Portuguese: *lua* (moon), *planetas* (planets), *estrelas* (stars), *nave especial* (spaceship), *universo* (universe), *buracos negros* (black holes), *asteroides* (asteroids), *astronautas* (spacemen), *astronomia* (astronomy), *sol* (sun), *sistema solar* (solar system), *Venús* (Venus), *céu* (sky), *Star Wars*.

Emotions, feelings
(1) Polish: *przyjaźń* (friendship), *miłość* (love), *spokój* (calmness), *ulga* (relief), *radość* (joy), *odpowiedzialność* (responsibility), *nieskrępowanie* (being unrestricted/uninhibited), *odprężenie* (relaxation).
(2) Portuguese: *estou na lua* (over the moon), *preciso de espaço* (need space), *comodidade* (convenience), *criatividade* (creativity), *espiritualidade* (spirituality), *mente aberta* (open mind).

Freedom
(1) Polish: *wolność* (freedom), *niezależność* (independence), *samodzielność* (autonomy).
(2) Portuguese: *liberdade* (liberty).

Syntagmatic
(1) Polish: *prywatna* (private), *artystyczna* (artistic), *kulturalna* (cultural), *zamknięta* (closed), *pusta* (empty), *ograniczona* (limited), *do życia* (for life), *zbyt mała* (too small).

(2) Portuguese: *público* (public), *grande* (large), *infinita* (infinite), *limpeza, espaço em branco* (white space), *vago, pessoal* (personal), *privado* (private), *reservado* (reserved), *especial* (special), *temprario* (temporary), *eterno* (eternal), *reflexivo* (reflexive), *imaginário* (imaginary), *cheio* (closed), *infinito* (infinite), *finito* (finite), *pequeno* (small), *vasto* (vast), *calmo* (calm), *informatiovo* (informative), *luminoso* (bright).

Word formation
(1) Polish: *przestrzenny* (spacious).
(2) Portuguese: *espaçado* (spaced out), *espaçamento* (spacing), *espaçoso* (spacious), *espacial* (spatial), *especial* (special), *espacejar* (to separate, space out), *espacinho* (little space).

Abstract
(1) Polish: *czas* (time), *czasoprzestrzeń* (spacetime).
(2) Portuguese: *tempo* (time).

The following observations based on the association responses can be proposed:

- Private/personal responses are found in the Polish data versus socially oriented ones in the Portuguese responses. Defensiveness is expressed by the Polish versus sharing expressed by the Portuguese.
- The presence of nature is marked by responses relating to the immediate context of here and now in the Polish data versus astronomical associations of 'out there' in the responses of the Portuguese.
- The Polish associations articulate feelings of relaxation, freedom and well-being versus stimulation and spirituality in the Portuguese ones. In other words, the Polish responses were more grounded in the everyday, as opposed to the imagined and the unattainable in the Portuguese.

To summarise, on the micro-cultural level of proxemics, which relates to cross-cultural differences (Hall, 1966), Polish and Portuguese subjects demonstrate significant differences in their space perception and their functioning within it. The Portuguese show more prosocial instincts of being together and sharing common space (sociopetal space perception), whereas the Polish informants seem to be more concerned about their own privacy and thus set spatial defences around themselves (sociofugal space perception). Also, in the context of interaction, the informal distance kept by the Portuguese most often seems personal, if not intimate to Polish people, whose informal distance, in contrast, is more social, if not public (more formal). In their associative responses, the Portuguese subjects seemed not to acknowledge the role of space as a daily functional category but rather as something abstract, 'out there in space', whereas the Polish subjects' associations were directly pointing to their immediate surroundings and interactions with others, emphasising the importance of personal space as a comfort zone necessary for one's well-being.

Conclusions

The perception of space is an important dimension of our functioning as individuals, as 'Our sense of space is complemented by our sense of ourselves as both part of and as separate from the world' (Hirst & Cooper, 2008: 444). However, we function in a group and as a part of a society, and 'Social reality is not just coincidentally spatial existing "in" space.... There is no unspatialised asocial reality. There are no aspatial social processes' (Soja, 1996: 46). In this chapter I have discussed some cases where it seems to me that Polish and Portuguese people behave differently due to their different perceptions of space. Obviously, with further analysis, it would be possible to come up with many more instances to illustrate these differences beyond those discussed in this chapter.

Travelling allows us to experience and through this experience to reflect on how deeply ingrained our attitudes to space are and how we react both positively (with pleasure) and negatively (with discomfort) to a different sense of spatial functioning and organisation in the contexts we encounter. This reflective process seems to be a significant part of intercultural communicative competence, understood as

> the ability of a person to behave adequately in a flexible manner when confronted with actions, attitudes and expectations of representatives of foreign cultures (capacity) to stabilise one's self-identity in the process of cross-cultural mediation, and of helping other people to stabilise their self-identity. (Meyer, 1991: 137)

Of course, the perception of space constitutes only one of the many dimensions of intercultural competence, which manifest the differences between social groupings and nations where, for example

> the attitude to work is different, that there is a different feeling for time and space, there are other role perceptions, other rules of communication, a different view of the importance of group versus the individual, different ways of dealing with hierarchy, other forms, superstitions, taboos as well as other value systems. (Engelbert, 2004: 204)

To conclude, I strongly believe that our awareness of our own as well as others' perceptions of space is conducive to functioning successfully in both the national and the international contexts of travel and tourism. Professionals in these fields need to be aware of these differences, and organisers of holiday and leisure events should certainly take them into account when planning homogeneous and heterogeneous social happenings.

References

Altman, I. (1975) *The Environment and Social Behavior.* Monterey, CA: Brooks/Cole.

Banyard, P. and Hayes, N. (1994) *Psychology: Theory and Application.* London: Chapman & Hall.

Clark, G. (1992) *Space, Time and Man: A Prehistorian's View.* Cambridge: Cambridge University Press.

Coventry, K.R., Guijarro-Fuentes, P. and Valdés, B. (2011) Spatial language and second language acquisition. In V. Cook and B. Bassetti (eds) *Language and Bilingual Cognition* (pp. 263–286). New York: Psychology Press.

Deese, J.E. (1965) *The Structure of Associations in Language and Thought.* Baltimore, MD: Johns Hopkins University Press.

Engelbert, S. (2004) Intercultural training in exchange situations for experts and management: Critical reflection. *Intercultural Education* 15 (2), 195–208.

Gabryś-Barker, D. (2008) White people in fur coats versus dark-haired and exotic: A Polish–Portuguese study of offence and flattery. In A. Barker (ed.) *Giving and Taking Offence* (pp. 123–138). Aveiro: Universidade de Aveiro.

Gabryś-Barker, D. (2011) Time as a cultural construct: Some preliminary remarks on the conceptualizations of time in L1 and L2. In J. Arabski and A. Wojtaszek (eds) *Aspects of Culture in Second Language Acquisition and Foreign Language Learning* (pp. 151–165). Heidelberg: Springer.

Gabryś-Barker, D. (2012) What's in a name? Naming habits in Polish and Portuguese food culture. A paper delivered at the 24th International Conference on Second/Foreign Language Acquisition, Szczyrk, 17–19 May.

Hall, E. (1966) *The Hidden Dimension.* New York: Doubleday. [Consulted in the Polish 2005 translation, *Ukryty wymiar.* T. Hołówka (trans.). Warsaw: Warszawskie Wydawnictwo Literackie MUZA SA.]

Hirst, E. and Cooper, M. (2008) Keeping them in line: Choreographing classroom spaces. *Teachers and Teaching: Theory and Practice* 14 (5–6), 431–445.

Meyer, M. (1991) Developing transcultural competence: Case studies of advanced foreign language learners. In D. Buttjes and M. Byram (eds) *Mediating Languages and Cultures* (pp. 136–158). Clevedon: Multilingual Matters.

Sharifian, F. (2004) Cultural conceptualisations in English words: A study of Aboriginal children in Perth. *Language and Education* 19 (1), 74–88.

Söderman, T. (1993) Word associations of foreign language learners and native speakers. In H. Ringbom (ed.) *Near-Native Proficiency in English* (pp. 33–52). Turku: Abö Akademy.

Soja, E.W. (1996) *Third Place: Journeys of Los Angeles and Other Real-and-Imagined Places.* Cambridge, MA: Blackwell.

Woods, A.J., Philbeck, J.W. and Danoff, J.V. (2009) The various perceptions of distance: An alternative view of how effort affects distance judgements. *Journal of Experimental Psychology: Human Perception and Performance* 35 (4), 1104–1117.

Young, R.M. (1994) *Mental Space.* London: Process Press.

15 Eating Portugal: Translating Food

Susan Howcroft

Introduction

When travelling, food becomes a major focus of attention and what and where we eat can be a vital part of planning any journey or indeed the whole point of the journey itself. If we do not know the language of the country we are visiting, it becomes imperative that the translations on the menus that we are given not only provide us with information about the dish but that this is put in such a way as to make the food appealing. In Portugal, the resorts that receive a large number of tourists, such as the Algarve in summer, often have menu descriptions of traditional dishes, such as those made with *bacalhau* (rehydrated salted cod), translated in such a way as to make them indecipherable, even to me, despite the fact that, having lived in Portugal for many years, I know most of them and have made many of them myself. In addition, there is also a tendency for the food to be less Portuguese and more international, which may be because of tourists' conservative tendency to order dishes they recognise and would eat in their own countries.

Menu translations can add to the reluctance of tourists to even try the food on offer in some restaurants. The worst case of mistranslation I have ever encountered was at a restaurant in central Portugal which had an imposing, large, leather-bound menu printed in four languages, one of which was English. As we were about to entertain an important English visitor for a formal dinner with a number of other important people, we had decided to choose the food prior to the dinner in question in order to avoid delays later. The English menu proved very strange reading and we speculated on what our important visitor would think if we presented him with the following items taken from that menu: as a starter, 'Salted mountaineer with a large melon', followed by 'Badly cooked food'! Neither of these items was in fact as startling as these descriptions suggest; no cannibalism was involved at all, as the former referred to 'Melon with Parma ham', except that the ham came from the Portuguese mountains, or *serra*, which had led to the very unfortunate mistranslation of 'mountaineer'.

Having taught for many years, there are a number of false friends that I would expect to find in novice translators' work; nevertheless the dish described as 'Badly cooked food to Penacovense' was impossible to understand without recourse to the original Portuguese, where we discovered that it actually referred to a method of slow cooking or casseroling, usually overnight in a wood-fired oven in a traditional black earthenware pot, to make the main ingredient (generally lamb or mutton) extremely tender. The dish, known as *chanfana*, is hotly contested by a number of places in central Portugal, such as Penacova, as 'their' speciality dish.

We became more and more like solvers of *The Times* crossword puzzle as we perused the menu further and found 'Grill Kentledge to Maître d'Hotel', which was the next conundrum. If I explain that this was found in the fish section, then perhaps the puzzle begins to become clearer. Kent is of course the county within which we find Dover and the fish that likes to live on the shelf just off the white cliffs is sole. This gives us the solution: this dish was in fact grilled (Dover) sole. The translation for chicken on this menu was invariably 'cock', which is of limited use as a culinary term in English, most notably used in cock-a-leekie soup. This dubious translation, providing as it does a taboo term in English, which could be found offensive by many people, led to some very strange dishes indeed, especially when coupled with the name of the restaurant (the Castle), which provided us with dishes such as 'Old Cock Rice / Young Cock at Castel' when trying to describe chicken cooked to their special recipe.

Needless to say, we avoided showing this menu to our distinguished guests and I am afraid that the restaurant closed down some time after that visit, so I am unable to provide you with the chance to try some of the dishes but I did keep a copy of the translation as a warning to my own students of what problems such food translations can bring. I should add that these translation problems were found long before people began to use automatic translation software such as Google translate and other such translation-mangling devices, so that the culprit can be surmised to be the use of bilingual dictionaries by inexperienced translators!

Food History and Portugal

Portugal prides itself on being the nation that brought a number of exotic foods and spices to Europe, with Lisbon being classified as the most important market for this trade in the 16th century (Castro, 1983b: 621). This early globalisation in food still stands in sharp contrast with the observation that one of the distinguishing features between cultures is claimed to be their culinary habits and eating choices. Indeed, there are many scholarly publications, such as the Berg Publisher's *Food, Culture and Society: An International Journal of Multidisciplinary Research*, which studies the connections between cultures and food.

How Portugal portrays its food and unique culinary traditions through translations into English on its tourist websites demonstrates the problems of trying to make another culture's food sound appetising to a visitor and the pitfalls that may occur, which are unhappily often and not always amusing. Anthony Bourdain visited the Azores in season 5 (2009) of his television programme *No Reservations* and, apart from finding the smell of the geysers unpleasant, notably chided one of his guides about the language he chose to describe the dish they were about to eat. Although the food was good, according to Bourdain, the culinary guide needed to introduce it in a more enticing manner, rather than describing it as stewed intestines or some such unappetising description. Some bloggers, commenting on an earlier broadcast by Bourdain on Portugal and its culinary traditions which involved the slaughter of a pig, complained that this kind of information showed the Portuguese in a bad light, as rather backward and primitive, and ignored the modern, more sophisticated cuisine that can be found in Portugal nowadays. Bourdain claimed that by visiting Portugal and trying the local food he had gained an understanding of the immigrant roots of a number of American restaurants and their home-cooked food, which he loved.

On the website dedicated to advertising Portugal, and Portuguese food in particular, to foreign tourists, 'Taste Portugal: Portugal, a gastronomic destination' we find a lament which may be explained by some of the translation problems described above. It asks,

> How it is possible that Portugal still isn't viewed as a first-class gastronomic destination, notwithstanding the gratitude owed to us for the key historic role we have played in the development of European and world gastronomy, and the fine quality of our products, recipes and Chefs? (http://www.taste-portugal.com/sobre-o-programa/about-program)

The historic importance of Portugal in bringing spices to Europe is well known but has not, as the quotation above shows, led to a clear understanding by tourists of Portugal as a gastronomic destination. It is estimated that in the 16th century almost half of Portugal's state revenues came from the pepper and spice trade (Castro, 1983a: 249). It must also be said that the Portuguese were thought to be responsible for causing the price of pepper to fall to less than one-fifth of the price on the Venetian market by bringing such large quantities of it to Europe. Given the present economic crisis, it would be advantageous for Portugal to improve its gastronomic image for tourists and thereby earn more revenue from this particular market.

That the Portuguese dominance in spices had any connection with the Spanish overrunning Portugal in the 16th century is debatable (Maria de Fátima Coelho, 1983: 589) but the Spanish role in introducing new food-stuffs into Europe was definitely built on Portuguese success with trade in spices. However, the Spanish attempt to encroach on the spice trade led to some linguistic confusions that persist today, with Columbus naming the American natives 'Indians' and chillies being called 'red' peppers.

The Spanish are, however, credited with introducing tomatoes into Europe. Unfortunately, at the time these were often perceived to be poisonous and were therefore used only for table decoration in England; only later, in the 18th century, did they become a popular foodstuff. This proves the point that people can be particularly squeamish about trying any different or new foods. If Portugal wants to attract foreign visitors for a unique but pleasant gastronomic experience, the translator must describe Portuguese food in a more appetising way to overcome the natural resistance people have for the strange or different. There are always exceptions and this is the case with the television programme *Bizarre Foods*, which appeals to a small segment of the population who wish to be horrified by journalist Andrew Zimmern devouring all manner of 'delicacies' that many people would find disgusting or ghoulish. *Bizarre Foods*, which is shown on the Travel Channel, is described in the following way in the show summary on tv.com:

> Andrew Zimmern wanders the globe searching for strange and unusual delicacies. In each destination, Andrew samples the native culinary delights. However, he doesn't go in for the normal foods that tourists would be drawn to. Instead, he goes after the strangest foods that the location has to offer. He explains the taste, texture and history of all the foods he tastes. (http://www.tv.com/shows/bizarre-foods-with-andrew-zimmern/)

The juxtaposition of 'native' foods and the 'normal foods' tourists would like begs the question of what exactly the difference between these is; nevertheless, it should alert the unwary translator to the fact that there are foods considered strange in different parts of the world and that these foods could well be shunned by tourists.

In the 16th century spices were not only used to add to food to make it more palatable but were also believed to cure illness. Scientific discussions about these were carried on at the time, such as the disagreement about pepper between a Mozambican pharmacist and Garcia de Orta, a physician and naturalist who published his book *Colóquio dos Simples e Drogas e Coisas Medicinais da Índia* ('Colloquies on Drugs and Medicinal Things from India') in Goa in 1563 (Castro, 1983c: 631). The fact that cures were involved led to spices being extremely lucrative, literally 'worth their weight in gold'. The modern equivalent of this could be the so-called 'Mediterranean diet', which is believed to be a very important healthy alternative to many people's eating habits and which is based largely on traditional Greek food. Despite Greece's economic problems, this diet has undoubtedly changed the use of olive oil, wine, cheese and dried pulses and stimulated exports from not only Greece, but also other southern European countries like Italy, Spain and Portugal, all countries that need to try to find some alternative ways out of the present economic crisis. It was because spices were also linked to health that the trade was so very lucrative, as cures for both the plague and venereal disease were much sought after in the 16th century. Keeping slim and staying healthy are predominant concerns of people today and constitute a segment of the economy that is extremely robust. This can also be seen as providing an opportunity for Portugal to advertise itself as a destination for tourists looking for healthy cuisine, to claim a part of this lucrative market segment and reclaim some of its former reputation for excellence. In order to achieve this, it is vitally important to present Portuguese food to visitors so that they will want to try it.

The word 'spice' itself has its origins in Latin, coming from *species*, which originally meant 'kind or sort of something' and only became the verb meaning to season with spices in the early 14th century. The trade in nutmeg was first captured by the Portuguese, once again beating the Spanish to the port of Malacca in 1511, and today nutmeg is still one of the 'secret' ingredients in Coca-Cola, a product whose marketing straddles the globe and tries hard to keep its recipe a secret in order to maintain that dominance.

There is still some confusion about what a spice is and what herbs are. The *Encyclopaedia Britannica* gives the following definitions: 'Spice seeds are the tiny aromatic fruits and oil-bearing seeds of herbaceous plants'; 'Herbs are the fresh or dried aromatic leaves of ... plants'. But it then goes on to say, 'Spices, spice seeds, and herbs are employed as adjuncts to impart flavour and aroma or piquancy to foods', without explaining the difference between spices and spice seeds (http://www.britannica.com/EBchecked/topic/559769/spice-and-herb#ref141183).

Early pharmacists recognised four 'types' of spices: saffron, cloves, cinnamon and nutmeg. Black (1993: 107), talking about British food, says 'medieval people wanted more than just salt, pepper and mustard as condiments' and describes how some of the spices used then, such as 'galingale, grains of paradise and cubebs', are no longer in use today.

Even within English-speaking cultures different terms and categorisations of herbs and spices can be found and prove stumbling blocks for translators. What is clear, however, is that the spice trade has had a very strong influence on Portugal and its history. This in itself, as mentioned above, is no guarantee that Portuguese food is held in high regard or that this early influence has been maintained in the food offered in restaurants.

Food Globalisation

Although it can be argued that globalisation in food has already taken place and indeed dates back to those early Portuguese traders, and that this situation is what makes it possible for *The Economist* to use the price of hamburgers, specifically the McDonald's version or Big Mac, to measure how the exchange rate is working in different countries (http://www.economist.com/blogs/graphicdetail/2012/01/daily-chart-3). This, together with pizzarias being found in every major city, does not preclude every culture regarding its culinary traditions as unique and part of what defines the difference between peoples in the world. If we take the 'traditional' English breakfast as an example, we can find many examples of globalised food: bacon from Denmark; marmalade, a word borrowed from Portuguese, where it refers to quince jelly, and adapted to refer to a jam made from bitter (Seville) oranges in the 17th century; and notably tea, the 'national drink', which of course mostly comes from India, Sri Lanka or China. It is interesting that the Portuguese word for tea, *cha*, can also be found in English, often written as 'char' in 'a cup of char', dating from the 16th century. The more modern and fashionable drink of the 20th century, 'chai', still retains some of this historical connection but has managed to appeal to a more sophisticated clientele. What we and most tourists regard as very traditional in Britain is then in fact a mixture of foods drawn from other near and distant cultures or an entrenched version of food globalisation caused in part by those hardy Portuguese mariners trading between the East and the West. As the European Union (EU) has come to play a dominant role in organising and regulating our lives, we find that the word 'marmalade' is now protected by European law and can be used only for jams made from oranges, lemons and grapefruit. The *Etymological Dictionary* gives the following entry for 'marmalade':

late 15c., from M.Fr. *marmelade*, from Port. *marmelada* 'quince jelly, marmalade,' from *marmelo* 'quince,' by dissimilation from L. *melimelum* 'sweet apple,' originally 'fruit of an apple tree grafted onto quince,' from Gk. *melimelon*, from *meli* 'honey' (see *Melissa*) + *melon* 'apple.' Extended 17c. to 'preserve made from citrus fruit.' (http://www.etymonline.com)

Thus the original Portuguese quince jelly, *marmelada*, has been usurped by the British citrus fruit 'marmalade' in Europe. With the changes taking place in the written language and the spelling of words through agreement between Portuguese-speaking nations (the Acordo Ortografico, 2009), there is even more likelihood that the roots of words will become even more obscure and other derivations will be lost, producing even more difficulties for translators.

Idioms often prove obstacles for novice translators, especially if they have been encouraged to translate into the foreign language (L2) and not into their dominant language. A student working as a translator for the local tourist board for a few months as a trainee came across the Portuguese expression *cair como sopa no mel* in the texts he was translating about regional food specialities. This expression requires considerable knowledge about the etymology of the word *sopa* in this context. An inexperienced translator will render this as 'soup', which makes the expression seem extremely strange and unappetising, as we are associating soup and honey (*mel*), literally letting the soup fall into the honey. However, recognising that the word *sopa* can have a different meaning, especially today, used mainly in the plural *sopas*, we then realise that we are talking about small pieces of bread that are used to *ensopar*, that is, to soak or mop up any tasty sauce. The expression thus gradually begins to take on the meaning of having the necessary ingredients together at the right moment (both the bread and the honey, which go well together) or of the right thing happening at the right time, which is what the idiom is used to mean. The ease with which bread and honey combine is a much more appealing prospect than that of soup (accidentally?) falling into honey, which, if translated literally, would make the reader believe that the Portuguese combine some very strange tastes. That a student could render the expression 'falling like soup into honey' without recognising how strange this sounds is also because we are used to hearing idiomatic expressions which appear to bear no relationship to what they literally denote. To 'kick the bucket' is an example that most students will have come across in learning English and thus it is not surprising that they may accept strange-sounding expressions uncritically, although they themselves would be unlikely to find the concept of soup and honey together appetising. What would the idiomatic expression actually be then in English? It could be something as different as 'to hit the spot', with its meaning of being exactly the right thing at that moment and being associated with food and drink. To find this alternative expression would be asking a lot of a student working under time constraints associated with deadlines to be met and would be challenging even for translators translating into their dominant language.

Kastberg (2007: 108), examining the presence of a cultural component in technical genres, concludes with the idea that cultural knowledge together with general language competence, and competence in language for special purposes (LSP; that is, knowledge of the relevant domain) and LSP translation are all equally important. Kastberg believes that competent translations can be produced only if the translator is aware of the cultural differences that are found in any text, even technical ones. The question then becomes how to ensure that translators take cultural differences into account when translating. Websites produced for tourists, such as the Taste Portugal website cited above, demonstrates some of the difficulties translators encounter in this domain.

Taste Portugal

The website (http://www.taste-portugal.com) dedicated to informing tourists in English about Portuguese food and regional specialities is a combination of very professional resources, with film and animation together with captions on the opening screen, alongside more amateurish features, with sections containing poor translations, such as that entitled 'Portugal's Good Tasting', which suggests that parts of the site were less well funded than others, or at least that the editing of those parts was less scrupulous. As part of the 'Documentation' on this site, there is what is described as a flyer, which presents the better part of the site, with such entries as the following, discussing Portuguese olive oil:

> Our pure olive oil, in the words of the great 19th century novelist Eça de Queiroz 'is worthy of Plato's lips'.
>
> Given its highly favourable Mediterranean climatic conditions and perfect soil for planting olive groves, Portugal's olive oil has conquered worldwide fame and prestigious awards.
>
> With its distinctive personality, based on traditional olives, Portugal's fragrant, opalescent olive oil is extremely healthy and a pillar of modern cuisine.

However, together with these more lyrical and successful translations, we find many less successful sections. The Taste Portugal website is run by

Turismo de Portugal, the official tourist bureau. According to the site itself, it is intended for the following 'recipients':

> At an international level, the promotion of gastronomy is directed both to the tourists of our main target markets and to international opinion leaders.
> At a national level, the actions are designed for the national tourists but also to all professionals who contribute to the qualification of the gastronomic offer.

For competent English-speakers, this text contains some unidiomatic usages, terms which sound strange because they are normally used in English in rather different contexts. For example, the British National Corpus (BNC; at http://www.natcorp.ox.ac.uk) shows that the word 'recipients' is not very common but is used often in connection with those who receive something, often some kind of aid, as in the following example:

> Welfare is seen as a drug of addiction but studies of long-term welfare recipients have found that only one in five daughters of dependent mothers themselves become dependent.

Also used in an unusual way is the word 'qualification', which in the BNC is generally employed to describe academic qualifications or football qualification in international competitions.

Further investigation of the Taste Portugal site leads to the discovery of 'qualified products'; examination of the descriptions of these products shows that what in fact is being referred to is the certification of products in terms of either the region they come from, Protected Designation of Origin (PDO), or the region where they are produced, Protected Geographical Indication (PGI), or because of the way they are traditionally made or produced, Traditional Speciality Guaranteed (TSG). These designations are a product of European integration and are used throughout the EU. The editing of the Taste Portugal site can be called into question, as there is another part of the site which uses the term correctly, since it refers to the hotel and tourism schools that are found around the country which provide the industry with 'qualified' people.

The use of 'actions' in the description of the 'recipients' given above is a direct translation from Portuguese, which should be 'activities' in English. However this term has taken on a life of its own within Europe, where 'actions' are often to be found in projects rather than specific activities or actions to be taken. The term 'actions' can then be seen to be a part of

European jargon which most member countries have come to accept as suitable English expressions and which have indeed developed into such because of the frequency with which they are now used. Mossop (2007: 6) describes this as 'the French-influenced Euro-English of the European Commission'. Presumably in this sentence 'actions' is referring to the various activities which are being undertaken to promote Portuguese cuisine and foodstuffs.

Similarly, although 'gastronomic' can be found in relation to the food of a particular country, it is never found together with 'offer' in the BNC. As we know from Sinclair's work (1991), the fact that we do not find an item in a large corpus does not automatically mean that the item cannot occur or is in some way taboo, but when it does appear in a translation for tourists, we can suggest that a more natural sounding expression should be used.

'Offer' is often used by students as a false friend when they mean 'give', as in 'I offered her a present' rather than 'I gave her a present', but in this case the meaning of 'certified foodstuffs on offer' can be seen to mean the range of products that are available.

Other problems in the second sentence that lead to a lack of agreement across the sentence and the text include the prepositions 'at', 'for' and 'to', the use of the definite article before 'national tourists' and the conjunction 'but'. The sentence then might better be rendered:

> In Portugal activities are designed not only for internal tourism but also for all those professional people who work to get foodstuffs certified.

Also on the Taste Portugal website we find another example of the use of 'offer' and further examples of the kind of problems that translators face when translating from Portuguese into English. One such appears in the section on partners:

> The Program intends to be able to mobilize all agents who are, either direct or indirectly, associated to the offer of Gastronomy and Wines, so that we have the ability to pass on to those who visit us, in a harmonized way, the cultural values associated to these two areas and the enrichment that it can provide to the experience of a stay in Portugal.

Despite being a difficult sentence to digest, in this case we can see that the 'offer' is the provision of food and wine but we can also observe how the Portuguese language can tag together a series of clauses one after the other which in English would be much more characteristic of speech than writing. This fact often means that the translator has to decide at what point to stop and start a new sentence to make it more comprehensible in English. Novice translators often lack the necessary confidence to chop up the source text in this way and opt for much more literal translations, which make them feel safe. The result is, however, difficult to understand and would not help tourists. If websites do not give visitors what they are looking for quickly, the site is usually left. Visitors will not stay to work out what sites are trying to say with such confusing language.

Training Translators

Nida (2001: 53) points out that translators are usually so concerned about the meaning of a text that they seldom give much thought to grammatical structures in the source or target text, which leads to translations that 'frequently seem unnatural, awkward, or even misleading' and that 'Such difficulties often result from misleading grammatical terminology and from grammatical systems that are largely unrelated to meaningful relations between words'. Online dictionaries are seen to be a valuable aid for the translator to provide fast, flexible access to data (Peters & Picchi, 1997: 249); however, as Howcroft (2004, 2005) has shown, information that is vitally important for the translator is not always available through this resource, as dictionaries invariably work at the word level and ignore the relationships between words, their usual co-selection, collocation and semantic prosody. Moreover, Sinclair (2004: 122) points out that this presumption, that it is the word that carries meaning, turns 'a blind eye to the hundreds of common words which can hardly be said to denote anything'.

In contexts that are specific this becomes even more pronounced, although online resources have been expanding and becoming ever more inclusive, which is one of the advantages of the increasing capacity to store information now available. Nevertheless, they will never manage to provide the specific information the translator requires and which can only be developed over time through the translator's selection of specific parallel texts which can answer the questions posed in any translation. Online dictionaries do have one advantage over terminology banks, in that they are constantly being revised, whereas the terminology bank may contain out-of-date data. Indeed, the European Terminology Database (EURODICAUTOM), although it dates only from 1995, has now been replaced by the InterActive Terminology for Europe (IATE) database, because it was felt to be out of date. IATE is an EU inter-institutional terminology database that has been used in EU institutions and agencies since summer 2004. However, through the use of computer corpora, students can be alerted to the most natural constructions in the target language through the use of concordancing software, which pays attention not only to terminology but also to the grammatical relations and style in a specialised text. Making and verifying hypotheses on the basis of the analysis of actual data are necessary skills for the translator. Helping students to gain experience analysing corpora is possible in the university but it is only with extensive translation work that the translator will be able to produce, keep and consult his or her own corpora of texts in both L1 and L2, which can lead to much better translations.

Mossop (2007: 20) describes why revision is so necessary in translation: because of errors which are peculiar to written translations, which are 'mistranslations, omissions, and the strange unidiomatic language which is so hard to avoid when translating (odd word combinations or sentence structures calqued from the source text)'. This odd language, called 'translationese', is regarded as unavoidable when translators are translating into their L2 (see Baker, 1992: 54; Baker, 1993: 243–245; Baker, 2004: 28–38; Gellerstam, 1996; Hartmann, 1995; Laviosa, 1997: 315; McEnery & Wilson, 2001: 71–72; Teubert, 1996: 247). For this reason, corpora which contain translated texts are seen as unreliable for use as examples of L1 and therefore for contrastive studies. Corpora which include the target language in the appropriate context are seen to be an aid to translators once they have decided on the translation of a term, as they can then see examples of appropriate usages of that term and see the common patterns associated with it. Using computer corpora as investigative tools to analyse the specialised language of translation in both the target and source texts can help the translator to overcome some of these problems. Hatim and Munday (2004: 36) point out how important it is for students of translation to be able to disambiguate between terms that have a number of translational possibilities, especially when the translated term covers a wider semantic field in the target language than in the source language.

Over the last few decades computer corpora have developed exponentially and they have begun to be used in many areas. However, according to Snell-Hornby (2006: 115), empiricism came into translation studies only in the 1990s and the 'call for … empirical investigations was overdue'. Corpora can show a wealth of information concerning meaning and usage which is simply not available through any other means, which makes corpus use invaluable for students. Despite the fact that we are accustomed to thinking of our students as much more technologically adept than we were at their age, with the bewildering range of corpus and corpus-type material now available it is essential for students to learn about the main kinds of corpora, their uses and abuses, and to be aware of some of the pitfalls that can spoil their work. This means that higher education has a role to play in introducing reflection on the corpora used for translational purposes, based on a clear understanding of what is appropriate and trustworthy. The analyses and results of that work can then be applied to improve the target text produced. Students who are less familiar with investigating concordance data taken from corpora will need many more examples of concordance output to analyse before they become confident enough to deal with their own data and eventually build up their own corpora based on the translations that they do.

In the introduction to the Taste Portugal programme we also find:

> The Taste Portugal program intends to establish Portugal as a gastronomic destination country, creating both a national and international awareness of our gastronomy's many qualities, sustained by genuine products of great quality and by professionals which reinvent our wines and cuisine every single day. (http://www.taste-portugal.com/sobre-o-programa/about-program)

This is not an ideal invitation for tourists to try Portuguese food and wine and leads to confusion with the suggestion that these are in constant flux, not to mention the derogatory use of 'which' to refer to the people involved in this process.

Examples abound of translations which are inappropriate for their context when translated by inexperienced translators. In Portugal it is customary to find a complete menu on offer in restaurants that is a fixed and often more economical choice than the individual items ordered separately. This more economic menu usually contains the 'dish of the day', which is often unwittingly literally translated as 'plate'. For example, in one of our own university's cafés we find 'The menu includes bread, soup, plate, desert, coffee, and one drink'. A more experienced translator might use an expression such as 'today's special' for the food for that day but this could be misunderstood as the restaurant's speciality dish because of the way this appears on Portuguese menus (*especialidades da casa*). The spelling error in 'dessert' on this sign is also to be expected, as the doubling of letters in English is a common stumbling block for Portuguese students.

Although this case can be attributed to students, non-native speakers translating the items on a menu in Portugal, menus can also cause problems for inexperienced native speakers. Many years ago in a restaurant in Takapuna, New Zealand, I asked the waitress what the 'soup du jour' (which appeared on the menu) was, to which she innocently replied 'That means soup of the day!' It was with some difficulty that I got her to realise that I had understood the French expression but that what I actually wanted to know was what kind of soup it was that day. When realisation dawned, she told me that she did not know and that she would have to go to the kitchen to find out!

We overlook the fact that translators, when they are young, as was the case with this waitress and is the case with our students, have not had much worldly experience. Traineeships are very valuable experiences for students but there is a good argument to be made for getting translators to spend at least a part of their studies in the country(ies) of the language(s) they hope to specialise in, so that cultural differences can be observed first-hand and students can begin to question many of their firmly held ideas about what is 'normal' or acceptable in different societies. It is essential that this questioning takes place so that students recognise the limits of their knowledge and can therefore seek help from other sources, rather than taking it for granted that the whole world sees life, and in this case food, in exactly the same way. The sensitivity necessary to avoid offending or perplexing people with the translations produced is difficult to teach on translation courses but some awareness of this needs to be fostered, as the ramifications of insensitivity can have important economic effects.

Conclusion

Finally, therefore, in order to train future translators a number of aspects need to be borne in mind. These things include the age and experience of the student, the level of expertise in the languages translated from and into, cultural awareness and travel to or staying in the culture in question, world knowledge and understanding of attitudes, and ultimately technological resources and the benefits and dangers of these. Universities can try to deal with some of these aspects but others will be mastered only over time, provided that the students have the curiosity and insight to explore different cultures and cuisines, together with the dedication and determination to explore the language resources that they can find and develop using computer technology. Just as in the past with the explorers, Portuguese translators need to go beyond the limits of the classroom to find rich sources of information and knowledge which they can then bring back to make their translations more effective.

References

Baker, M. (1992) *In Other Words: A Coursebook on Translation*. London: Routledge.
Baker, M. (1993) Corpus linguistics and translation studies: Implications and applications. In M. Baker, G. Francis and G. Tognini-Bonelli (eds) *Text and Technology: In Honour of John Sinclair* (pp. 233–352). Amsterdam: John Benjamins.

Baker, M. (2004) The treatment of variation in corpus-based translation studies. *Language Matters* 35 (1), 28–38.

Black, M. (1993) Medieval Britain. In P. Brears, M. Black, G. Corbishley, J. Renfrew and J. Stead (eds) *A Taste of History: 10,000 Years of Food in Britain* (pp. 95–136). London: English Heritage, British Museum Press.

Castro, A. de (1983a) Actividade comercial e financeira. In J.H. Saraiva (ed.) *Historia de Portugal 1245–1640* (pp. 243–256). Lisbon: Publicações Alfa SARL.

Castro, A. de (1983b) A transição para a formação económico-social portuguesa moderna. In J.H. Saraiva (ed.) *Historia de Portugal 1245–1640* (pp. 619–628). Lisbon: Publicações Alfa SARL.

Castro, A. de (1983c) A economia da expansão ultramarine. In J.H. Saraiva (ed.) *Historia de Portugal 1245–1640* (pp. 629–658). Lisbon: Publicações Alfa SARL.

Coelho, M. de F. (1983) A evolução social entre 1481 e 1640. In J.H. Saraiva (ed.) *Historia de Portugal 1245–1640* (pp. 579–618). Lisbon: Publicações Alfa SARL.

Gellerstam, M. (1996) Translations as a source for cross-linguistic studies. In K.Aijmer, B. Altenberg and M. Johansson (eds) *Language in Contrast: Papers from a Symposium on Text-Based Cross-linguistic Studies, Lund, March 1994* (pp. 53–62). Lund: Lund University Press.

Hartmann, R. (1995) Contrastive textology. *Language and Communication* 5, 25–37.

Hatim, B. & Munday, J. (2004) *Translation: An Advanced Resource Book.* London: Routledge.

Howcroft, S. (2004) Bad teachers, mad scientists and corrupt politicians: a linguistic view of stereotypes. In A.D. Barker (ed.) *O Poder e a Persistência dos Estereótipos* (pp. 185–192). Aveiro: Universidade de Aveiro.

Howcroft, S. (2005) The regrowth of ESP. In G. Moreira and S. Howcroft (eds) *Línguas e Mercado* (pp. 245–254). Aveiro: Universidade de Aveiro.

Kastberg, P. (2007) Cultural issues facing the technical translator. *Journal of Specialised Translation* 8, 104–108.

Laviosa, S. (1997) How comparable can 'comparable corpora' be? *Target* 9, 289–319.

McEnery, A. and Wilson, A. (2001) *Corpus Linguistics* (1st edn 1996). Edinburgh: Edinburgh University Press.

Mossop, B. (2007) *Revising and Editing for Translators.* Manchester: St Jerome Publishing.

Nida, E.A. (2001) *Contexts in Translating.* Amsterdam: John Benjamins.

Peters, C. and Picchi, E. (1997) Reference corpora and lexicons for translators and translational studies. In A. Trosborg (ed.) *Text Typology and Translation* (pp. 247–274). Amsterdam: John Benjamins.

Sinclair, J. (1991) *Corpus, Concordance, Collocation.* Oxford: University Press.

Sinclair, J. (2004) *Trust the Text. Language, corpus and discourse*, London: Routledge.

Snell-Hornby, M. (2006) *The Turns of Translation Studies,* Amsterdam: John Benjamins.

Teubert, W. (1996) Comparable or parallel corpora? *International Journal of Lexicography* 9 (3), 238–64.